World Military Guide
Germany

Compiled by
Kermit Brantley

Scribbles

Year of Publication 2018

ISBN : 9789352979073

Book Published by

Scribbles

(An Imprint of Alpha Editions)

email - alphaedis@gmail.com

Produced by: PediaPress GmbH
Limburg an der Lahn
Germany
http://pediapress.com/

The content within this book was generated collaboratively by volunteers. Please be advised that nothing found here has necessarily been reviewed by people with the expertise required to provide you with complete, accurate or reliable information. Some information in this book may be misleading or simply wrong. Alpha Editions and PediaPress does not guarantee the validity of the information found here. If you need specific advice (for example, medical, legal, financial, or risk management) please seek a professional who is licensed or knowledgeable in that area.

Sources, licenses and contributors of the articles and images are listed in the section entitled "References". Parts of the books may be licensed under the GNU Free Documentation License. A copy of this license is included in the section entitled "GNU Free Documentation License"

The views and characters expressed in the book are those of the contributors and his/her imagination and do not represent the views of the Publisher.

Contents

Articles   **1**

Introduction   **1**
    Bundeswehr 1

History   **27**
    Military history of Germany 27
    History of Germany during World War I 53

Command Structure   **73**
    Command and obedience in the Bundeswehr 73

German Army   **81**
    German Army 81
    List of modern equipment of the German Army 99

German Navy   **109**
    German Navy 109
    List of active German Navy ships 122

German Air Force   **127**
    German Air Force 127

Special Forces   **157**
    German special forces 157

Appendix 161

References 161

Article Sources and Contributors 167

Image Sources, Licenses and Contributors 168

Article Licenses 175

Index 177

Introduction

Bundeswehr

	Federal Defence Forces of Germany
	*Bundeswehr*
	Insignia of the Bundeswehr (the Iron Cross)
Founded	12 November 1955
Current form	3 October 1990
Service branches	German Army **Heer** German Navy **Marine** German Air Force **Luftwaffe** Joint Support Service Joint Medical Service Cyber and Information Space Command
Headquarters	Berlin, Bonn, and Potsdam
Website	www<wbr/>.bundeswehr<wbr/>.de[1]
	**Leadership**

Supreme Command	During normal peacetime: the Minister of Defence After declaration of state of defence: the Federal Chancellor
Federal Chancellor	Angela Merkel
Minister of Defence	Ursula von der Leyen
Inspector General	General Eberhard Zorn (Heer)
Manpower	
Military age	17
Conscription	Yes, suspended
Active personnel	179,753 (28 February 2018)
Reserve personnel	27,900 (2017)
Deployed personnel	3,791 (26 March 2018)
Expenditures	
Budget	€38.93 billion (FY18)
Industry	
Domestic suppliers	Airbus Heckler & Koch Rheinmetall Krauss-Maffei Wegmann Howaldtswerke-Deutsche Werft Walther arms ThyssenKrupp
Foreign suppliers	European Union member nations; United States
Annual imports	Volume of about $1 billion (2009 est.)
Annual exports	Volume of about €6.88 billion (2016)

The ***Bundeswehr*** (German: [ˈbʊndəsˌveːɐ̯] (listen), *Federal Defence*) is the unified armed forces of Germany and their civil administration and procurement authorities. The States of Germany are not allowed to maintain armed forces of their own, since the German Constitution states that matters of defense fall into the sole responsibility of the federal government.

The *Bundeswehr* is divided into a military part (armed forces or *Streitkräfte*) and a civil part with the armed forces administration (*Wehrverwaltung*). The military part of the federal defense force consists of the German Army, the

German Navy, the German Air Force, the Joint Support Service, the Joint Medical Service, and the Cyber and Information Space Command.

As of 28 February 2018[2], the *Bundeswehr* has a strength of 179,753 active soldiers, placing it among the 30 largest military forces in the world and making it the second largest in the European Union behind France in terms of personnel. In addition the Bundeswehr has approximately 27,900 reserve personnel (2017). With German military expenditures at €38.93 billion, the Bundeswehr is among the top ten best-funded forces in the world, even if in terms of share of German GDP, military expenditures remain average at 1.13% and below the NATO target of 2%. Germany aims to expand the Bundeswehr to around 198,000 soldiers by 2024 to better cope with increasing responsibilities.

History

Founding principles

The name *Bundeswehr* was first proposed by the former Wehrmacht general and Liberal politician Hasso von Manteuffel. The Iron Cross *(Eisernes Kreuz)* is its official emblem. It is a symbol that has a long association with the military of Germany. The *Schwarzes Kreuz* is derived from the black cross insignia of the medieval Teutonic knights; since 1813 the symbol has been used to denote a military decoration for all ranks.

When the *Bundeswehr* was established in 1955, its founding principles were based on developing a completely new military force for the defence of West Germany. In this respect the *Bundeswehr* did not consider itself to be a successor to either the *Reichswehr* (1921–1935) of the Weimar Republic or Hitler's *Wehrmacht* (1935–1946). Neither does it adhere to the traditions of any former German military organization. Its official ethos is based on three major themes:

- the aims of the military reformers at the beginning of the 19th century such as Scharnhorst, Gneisenau, and Clausewitz
- the conduct displayed by members of the military resistance against Adolf Hitler, especially the attempt of Claus von Stauffenberg and Henning von Tresckow to assassinate him.
- its own tradition since 1955.

One of the most visible traditions of the modern Bundeswehr is the *Großer Zapfenstreich*; this is a form of military tattoo that has its origins in the landsknecht era. The FRG reinstated this formal military ceremony in 1952, three years before the foundation of the *Bundeswehr*. Today it is performed by a military band with 4 fanfare trumpeters and timpani, a corps of drums, up

Figure 1: *A Großer Zapfenstreich at Ramstein Air Base in 2002.*

to two escort companies of the *Bundeswehr*'s Wachbataillon (or another deputized unit) and Torchbearers. The *Zapfenstreich* is only performed during national celebrations or solemn public commemorations. It can honour distinguished persons present such as the German federal president or provide the conclusion to large military exercises.

Another important tradition in the modern German armed forces is the *Gelöbnis*; the solemn oath made by conscripts (until 2011) now recruits during basic training and serving professional soldiers. There are two kinds of oath: for conscripts/recruits it is a pledge but it's a solemn vow for full-time personnel.

The pledge is made annually on 20 July, the date on which a group of *Wehrmacht* officers attempted to assassinate Adolf Hitler in 1944. Recruits from the *Bundeswehr*'s *Wachbataillon* make their vow (*Gelöbnis*) at the Bendlerblock in Berlin. This was the headquarters of the resistance but also where the officers were summarily executed following its failure. National commemorations are held nearby within the grounds of the Reichstag. Similar events also take place across the German Republic. Since 2011 (when conscription was placed in abeyance within the *Bundesrepublik Deutschland*), the wording of the ceremonial vow for full-time recruits and volunteer personnel is:

> *"Ich gelobe, der Bundesrepublik Deutschland treu zu dienen und das Recht und die Freiheit des deutschen Volkes tapfer zu verteidigen."*

Figure 2: *The Federal Republic of Germany joined NATO in 1955.*

> *"I pledge to serve the Federal Republic of Germany loyally and to defend the right and the freedom of the German people bravely."*

Serving *Bundeswehr* personnel replace *"Ich gelobe, ..."* with *"Ich schwöre, ..."* ("I vow to...").

Cold War 1955–1990

After World War II the responsibility for the security of Germany as a whole rested with the four Allied Powers: the United States, the United Kingdom, France and the Soviet Union. Germany had been without armed forces since the *Wehrmacht* was dissolved following World War II. When the Federal Republic of Germany was founded in 1949, it was without a military. Germany remained completely demilitarized and any plans for a German military were forbidden by Allied regulations. Only some naval mine-sweeping units continued to exist, but they remained unarmed and under Allied control and did not serve as a national defence force. Even the Federal Border Protection Force, a mobile, lightly armed police force of 10,000 men, was only formed in 1951. A proposal to integrate West German troops with soldiers of France, Belgium, the Netherlands, Luxembourg and Italy in a European Defence Community was proposed but never implemented.

There was a discussion among the United States, the United Kingdom and France over the issue of a revived (West) German military. In particular,

Figure 3: *Leopard 2 tanks*

France was reluctant to allow Germany to rearm in light of recent history (Germany had invaded France twice in living memory, in World War I and World War II, and also defeated France in the Franco-German War of 1870/71; (see also French–German enmity)). However, after the project for a European Defence Community failed in the French National Assembly in 1954, France agreed to West German accession to NATO and rearmament.

With growing tensions between the Soviet Union and the West, especially after the Korean War, this policy was to be revised. While the German Democratic Republic (East Germany) was already secretly rearming, the seeds of a new West German force started in 1950 when former high-ranking German officers were tasked by Chancellor Konrad Adenauer to discuss the options for West German rearmament. The results of a meeting in the monastery of Himmerod formed the conceptual base to build the new armed forces in West Germany. The *Amt Blank* (Blank Agency, named after its director Theodor Blank), the predecessor of the later Federal Ministry of Defence, was formed the same year to prepare the establishment of the future forces. Hasso von Manteuffel, a former general of the *Wehrmacht* and liberal politician, submitted the name *Bundeswehr* for the new forces. This name was later confirmed by the West German *Bundestag*.

The *Bundeswehr* was officially established on the 200th birthday of Scharnhorst on 12 November 1955. In personnel and education terms, the most important initial feature of the new German armed forces was to be their orien-

Figure 4: *The Bundeswehr was the first NATO member to use the Soviet-built MiG 29 jet, taken over from the former East German Air Force after reunification.*

tation as citizen defenders of a democratic state, fully subordinate to the political leadership of the country.[3] A personnel screening committee was created to make sure that the future colonels and generals of the armed forces were those whose political attitude and experience would be acceptable to the new democratic state.[4] There were a few key reformers, such as General Ulrich de Maiziere, General Graf von Kielmansegg, and Graf von Baudissin,[5] who reemphasised some of the more democratic parts of Germany's armed forces history in order to establish a solid civil-military basis to build upon.

After an amendment of the Basic Law in 1955, West Germany became a member of NATO. The first public military review took place at Andernach, in January 1956.[6] A US Military Assistance Advisory Group (MAAG) helped with the introduction of the Bundeswehr's initial equipment and war material, predominantly of American origin.Wikipedia:Citation needed In 1956, conscription for all men between the ages of 18 and 45 was reintroduced, later augmented by a civil alternative with longer duration (see Conscription in Germany). In response, East Germany formed its own military force, the *Nationale Volksarmee* (NVA), in 1956, with conscription being established only in 1962. The *Nationale Volksarmee* was eventually dissolved with the reunification of Germany in 1990. Compulsory conscription was suspended – but not completely abolished as an alternative – in January 2011.

During the Cold War the *Bundeswehr* was the backbone of NATO's conventional defence in Central Europe. It had a strength of 495,000 military and 170,000 civilian personnel. Although Germany had smaller armed forces than France and the United States, Cold War Historian John Lewis Gaddis assesses the Bundeswehr as "perhaps world's best army".[7] The Army consisted of three corps with 12 divisions, most of them heavily armed with tanks and APCs. The Luftwaffe owned significant numbers of tactical combat aircraft and took part in NATO's integrated air defence (NATINAD). The Navy was tasked and equipped to defend the Baltic Approaches, to provide escort reinforcement and resupply shipping in the North Sea and to contain the Soviet Baltic Fleet.

During this time the Bundeswehr did not take part in combat operations. However, there were a number of large-scale training and operational casualties. The first such incident was in June 1957, when 15 paratroop recruits were drowned in the Iller river, Bavaria.[8]

German Reunification 1990

At the time of reunification, the German military boasted a manpower of some 585,000 soldiers. As part of the German reunification process, under the Treaty on the Final Settlement with Respect to Germany (Two-Plus Four Treaty), which paved the way for reunification, the Bundeswehr was to be reduced to 370,000 personnel, of whom no more than 345,000 were to be in the Army and Air Force. This would be Germany's contribution to the Treaty on Conventional Armed Forces in Europe, and the restrictions would enter into force at the time the CFE treaty would. As a result, the Bundeswehr was significantly reduced, and the former East German *Nationale Volksarmee* (NVA) was disbanded, with a portion of its personnel and material being absorbed into the Bundeswehr.

About 50,000 *Volksarmee* personnel were integrated into the *Bundeswehr* on 2 October 1990. This figure was rapidly reduced as conscripts and short-term volunteers completed their service. A number of senior officers (but no generals or admirals) received limited contracts for up to two years to continue daily operations. Personnel remaining in the *Bundeswehr* were awarded new contracts and new ranks, dependent on their individual qualification and experience. Many were granted and accepted a lower rank than previously held in the *Volksarmee*.

In general, the unification process of the two militaries – under the slogan "*Armee der Einheit*" (or "Army of Unity") – has been seen publicly as a major success and an example for other parts of the society.

With the reduction, a large amount of the military hardware of the *Bundeswehr*, as well as of the *Volksarmee*, had to be disposed of. Most of the armoured vehicles and fighter jet aircraft (the Bundesluftwaffe – due to reunification – was the only air force in the world that flew both Phantoms and MIGs) were dismantled under international disarmament procedures. Many

Figure 5: *Bundeskader - Sportfördergruppe der Bundeswehr - Girls tracksuit*

ships were scrapped or sold, often to the Baltic states or Indonesia (the latter received 39 former *Volksmarine* vessels of various types).

With reunification, all restrictions on the manufacture and possession of conventional arms that had been imposed on the Bundeswehr as a condition for West German rearmament were lifted.[9]

Since 1996, Germany also has its own Special Forces, the Kommando Spezialkräfte (Special Forces Command). It was formed after German citizens had to be rescued in Rwanda by Belgian Para-Commandos as the Special Commands of the Federal Police were not capable of operating in a war zone.

Reorientation

A major event for the German military was the suspension of the compulsory conscription for men in 2011. In 2011/12, a major reform of the Bundeswehr was announced, further limiting the number of military bases and soldiers. The last reform set a required strength of 185,000 soldiers.[10] As of 31 December 2017[2], the number of active military personnel in the Bundeswehr was down to 179,753, corresponding to a ratio of 2.2 active soldiers per 1,000 inhabitants. Military expenditure in Germany was at €37 billion in 2017, corresponding to 1.2% of GDP.

German military expenditures are lower than comparable countries of the European Union such as France and the United Kingdom, especially when taking into account Germany's larger population and economy. This discrepancy is often criticized by Germany's military allies, especially the United States.

In September 2014, the Bundeswehr acknowledged chronic equipment problems that rendered its armed forces "unable to deliver its defensive NATO promises". Among the problems cited were dysfunctional weapons systems, armored vehicles, aircraft, and naval vessels unfit for immediate service due to a neglect of maintenance, and serious equipment and spare parts shortages. The situation was so dire that it was acknowledged that most of Germany's fighter aircraft and combat helicopters were not in deployable condition.

In 2015, as a result of serious NATO-Russian tensions in Europe, Germany announced a major increase in defense spending. In May 2015, the German government approved an increase in defense spending, at the time 1.3% of GDP, by 6.2% over the following five years, allowing the Ministry of Defense to fully modernize the army. Plans were also announced to significantly expand the tank fleet to a potential number of 328, order 131 more Boxer armored personnel carriers, increase the submarine fleet, and to develop a new fighter jet to replace the Tornado. Germany considered increasing the size of the army, and in May 2016 it announced it would spend €130 billion on new equipment by 2030 and add nearly 7,000 soldiers by 2023 in the first German military expansion since the end of the Cold War. In February 2017, the German government announced another expansion, which would increase the number of its professional soldiers by 20,000 by 2024.

Coordination with European Partners

The Bundeswehr is to play a greater role as "anchor army" for smaller NATO states, by improving coordination between its divisions and smaller members' Brigades . A further proposal, by Minister of Defence von der Leyen, to allow non-German EU nationals to join the Bundeswehr, has been met by strong opposition, even from her own party.

As a consequence of improved Dutch-German cooperation, 2 of 3 Royal Netherlands Army Brigades are now under German Command. In 2014, the 11th Airmobile Brigade was integrated into the German Division of fast forces (DSK). The Dutch 43rd Mechanized Brigade will be assigned to the 1st Panzer Division (Bundeswehr) of the German army, with the integration starting at the beginning of 2016, and the unit becoming operational at the end of 2019. Also, the Seebatallion of the German Navy will start operating under Royal Dutch Navy command until 2018. The Dutch-German military cooperation is seen as an example for setting up a European defense union.

Bundeswehr

Figure 6: *Civil Emblem of the Bundeswehr*

Figure 7: *Minister of Defense, Ursula von der Leyen*

Also the Czech Republic's 4th Rapid Deployment Brigade, and Romania's 81st Mechanized Brigade, will be integrated into Germany's 10 Armoured Division and Rapid Response Forces Division.

Command organisation

With the growing number of missions abroad it was recognized that the *Bundeswehr* required a new command structure. A reform commission under the

Figure 8: *A German Navy Frigate*

chairmanship of the former President Richard von Weizsäcker presented its recommendations in spring 2000.

In October 2000 the Joint Support Service, the Streitkräftebasis, was established to concentrate logistics and other supporting functions such as military police, supply and communications under one command. Medical support was reorganised with the establishment of the Joint Medical Service. In 2016, the Bundeswehr created its youngest branch the Cyber and Information Space Command.

The combat forces of the Army are organised into three combat divisions and participate in multi-national command structures at the corps level. The Air Force maintains three divisions and the Navy is structured into two flotillas. The Joint Support Service and the Joint Medical Service are both organized in four regional commands of identical structure. All of these services also have general commands for training, procurement, and other general issues.

The minister of defence or the chancellor is supported by the Chief of Defense (CHOD, *Generalinspekteur*) and the service chiefs (*Inspekteure*: Inspector of the Army, Inspector of the Air Force, Inspector of the Navy) and their respective staffs in his or her function as commander-in-chief. The CHOD and the service chiefs form the Military Command Council (*Militärischer Führungsrat*) with functions similar to those of the Joint Chiefs of Staff in

Figure 9: *German Army soldiers in Afghanistan (2009) in front of Dingo infantry mobility vehicles*

the United States. Subordinate to the CHOD is the Armed Forces Operational Command (*Einsatzführungskommando*). For smaller missions one of the service HQs (e.g. the Fleet Command) may exercise command and control of forces in missions abroad. The *Bundestag* must approve any foreign deployment by a simple majority. This has led to some discontent with Germany's allies about troop deployments e.g. in Afghanistan since parliamentary consent over such issues is relatively hard to achieve in Germany.

Mission

The role of the *Bundeswehr* is described in the Constitution of Germany (Art. 87a) as absolutely defensive only. Its only active role before 1990 was the *Katastropheneinsatz* (disaster control). Within the *Bundeswehr*, it helped after natural disasters both in Germany and abroad. After 1990, the international situation changed from East-West confrontation to one of general uncertainty and instability.

Today, after a ruling of the Federal Constitutional Court in 1994 the term "defence" has been defined to not only include protection of the borders of Germany, but also crisis reaction and conflict prevention, or more broadly as guarding the security of Germany anywhere in the world. According to the definition given by former Defence Minister Struck, it may be necessary to defend Germany even at the Hindu Kush. This requires the Bundeswehr to take part in operations outside of the borders of Germany, as part of NATO or the European Union and mandated by the UN.

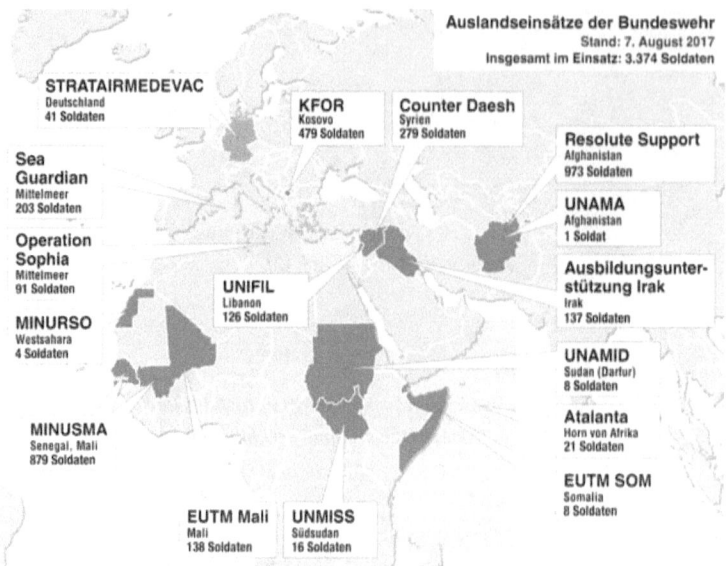

Figure 10: *Bundeswehr current international operations*

Operations

Since the early 1990s the *Bundeswehr* has become more and more engaged in international operations in and around the former Yugoslavia, and also in other parts of the world like Cambodia or Somalia. After the 11 September 2001 attacks, German forces were employed in most related theaters except Iraq.

Currently (26 March 2018) there are *Bundeswehr* forces in:

- Afghanistan
  - Resolute Support Mission
    - 1,133 personnel
    - (mandate limit: 1,300)
- Kosovo
  - KFOR
    - 411 personnel
    - (mandate limit: 800)
- South Sudan
  - UNMISS
    - 15 personnel
    - (mandate limit: 50)
- Sudan
  - UNAMID

Figure 11: *Frigate Karlsruhe of the German Navy rescuing shipwrecked people off the coast of Somalia where it is patrolling*

- 4 personnel
- (mandate limit: 50)
- ⊤ Lebanon
  - UNIFIL
    - 130 personnel
    - (mandate limit: 300)
- Mali
  - EUTM Mali
    - 148 personnel
    - (mandate limit: 300)
- Mali / Senegal
  - MINUSMA
    - 998 personnel
    - (mandate limit: 1,000)
- Horn of Africa / Indian Ocean
  - Operation Atalanta
    - 73 personnel
    - (mandate limit: 600)
- Somalia
  - EUTM Somalia

- 4 personnel
  - (mandate limit: 20)
- Mediterranean Sea
  - Operation Sea Guardian
    - 193 personnel
    - (mandate limit: 650)
- Mediterranean Sea
  - Operation Sophia
    - 194 personnel
    - (mandate limit: 950)
- (Middle East)
  - (Operation Counter Daesh)
    - 306 personnel
    - (mandate limit: 800)
- ≡ Iraq
  - Peshmerga training in northern Iraq
    - 135 personnel
    - (mandate limit: 150)
- Western Sahara
  - Minurso
    - 3 personnel
    - (mandate limit: 20)

In addition to the numbers above, 42 soldiers are on permanent stand-by for medical evacuation operations around the world in assistance of ongoing German or coalition operations (STRATAIRMEDEVAC).

In support of Allied stabilization efforts in Iraq, the *Bundeswehr* is also training the new Iraqi forces in locations outside Iraq, such as the United Arab Emirates and Germany.

Since 1994, the *Bundeswehr* has lost about 100 troops in foreign deployments. *See also: German Armed Forces casualties in Afghanistan.*

Equipment

According to the new threat scenario facing Germany and its NATO allies, the *Bundeswehr* is currently reorganising itself. To realise growth in mobility and the enlargement of the air force's capabilities, the *Bundeswehr* is going to buy 53 Airbus A400M transports as well as 140 Eurofighter Typhoon fighters and also several unmanned aerial vehicle models. 57 Eurocopter Tiger, 100 NH90 (18 of them in the naval version) and 15 special forces helicopters are being delivered. For the ground forces it plans to produce 350 Puma infantry fighting vehicle, at least 400 Boxer MRAV, started to introduce a novel land soldier system and a new generation of transportation vehicles and light vehicles, such as the Fennek, and KMW Grizzly. Further, the German Navy is going to build 4 new F125 class frigates, 6 new multi-role combat ships (dubbed MKS 180) and 6 Type 212 submarines.

Figure 12: *NH90 helicopter*

Figure 13: *Boxer MRAV*

Figure 15: *German Army signallers in service uniforms.*

Figure 14: *Airbus A400M*

Appearance

Uniforms

The service uniform is theoretically the standard type of Bundeswehr uniform for general duty and off-post activity, but is most associated, however, with ceremonial occasions. The army's service uniform consists of a light gray,

Figure 16: *A German infantryman stands at the ready with his Heckler & Koch G36 during a practice exercise in 2004. US troops watch in the background. All rifles in the photo are equipped with blank firing adapters.*

single-breasted coat and darker grey trousers, worn with a light blue shirt, black tie, and black shoes. The peaked, visored cap has been replaced by the beret as the most common form of headgear. Dress uniforms featuring dinner jackets or double-breasted coats are worn by officers for various social occasions. The battle and work uniform consists of Flecktarn camouflage fatigues, which are also worn on field duty. In practice, they are also used for general duty and off-post at least at barracks where there is also field duty even by others, and for the way home or to the post, and generally regarded as *the* Heer uniform.[11] In all three services, light sand-coloured uniforms are available for duty in warmer climates. In 2016 a new *Multitarn* pattern was launched, similar to the MultiCam uniforms of the British Army or US Army.[12]

A different, traditional variety of the service uniform is worn by the *Gebirgsjäger* (mountain infantry), consisting of ski jacket, stretch trousers, and ski boots. Instead of the beret, they wear the grey "mountain cap". (see here for details.) The field uniform is the same, except for the (optional) metal Edelweiss worn on the forage cap.

The traditional arm-of-service colours appear as lapel facings and as piping on shoulder straps. Generals wear an inner piping of gold braid; other officers wear silver piping. Lapel facings and piping are maroon for general staff, green for infantry, red for artillery, pink for armour, black for engineers, yellow for communications, dark yellow for reconnaissance and various other colors for the remaining branches. Combat troops wear green (infantry), black (armour), or maroon (airborne) berets. Logistics troops and combat support troops, such as artillery or engineers, wear red berets. A gold or silver badge on the beret denotes the individual branch of service.

The naval forces wear the traditional navy blue, double-breasted coat and trousers; enlisted personnel wear either a white shirt or a navy blue shirt with the traditional navy collar. White uniforms provide an alternative for summer. The officer's dress cap is mounted with a gold anchor surrounded by a wreath. The visor of the admiral's cap bears a double row of oak leaves.

The air force service uniform consists of a blue jacket and trousers with a light blue shirt, dark blue tie, and black shoes. Olive battle dress similar to the army fatigue uniform is worn in basic training and during other field duty. Flying personnel wear wings on their right breast. Other air force personnel wear a modified wing device with a symbol in its centre denoting service specialisation. These *Tätigkeitsabzeichen* come in bronze, silver, or gold, depending on one's length of service in the specialty. Wings, superimposed over a wreath, in gold, silver, or bronze, depending on rank, are also worn on the service or field cap.

Ranks

In general, officer ranks are those used in the Prussian and pre-1945 German armies. Officer rank insignia are worn on shoulder straps or shoulder boards. Army (*Heer*) and air force (*Luftwaffe*) junior officers' insignia are four pointed silver stars while field grade officers wear silver (black or white on camouflage uniforms) stars and an oak wreath around the lowest star. The stars and wreath are gold for general officers. In the case of naval (*Marine*) officers, rank is indicated by gold stripes on the lower sleeve of the blue service jacket and on shoulder boards of the white uniform.

Soldier and NCO ranks are similar to those of the Prussian and pre-1945 German armies. In the army and air force, a Gefreiter corresponds to the NATO rank OR-2 and Hauptgefreiter to OR-3. An Unteroffizier is the lowest-ranking sergeant (OR-5), followed by Stabsunteroffizier (OR-6), Feldwebel and Oberfeldwebel (OR-7), Hauptfeldwebel (OR-8), Stabsfeldwebel (OR-9) and Oberstabsfeldwebel. Ranks of army and air force enlisted personnel are designated by stripes, chevrons, and "sword knots" worn on rank slides. Naval enlisted rank designations are worn on the upper (OR 1–5) or lower (OR-6 and above) sleeve along with a symbol based on an anchor for the service specialization (rating). Army and air force officer candidates hold the separate ranks of Fahnenjunker, Fähnrich and Oberfähnrich, and wear the appropriate rank insignia

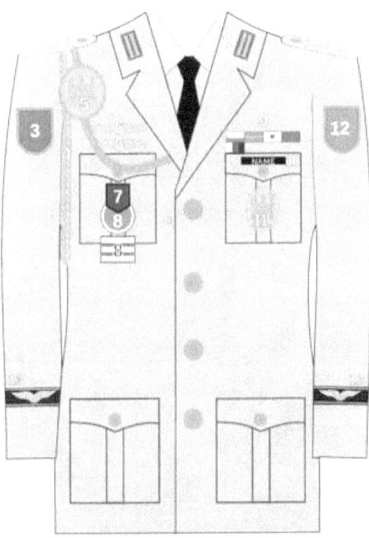

Figure 17: *Service Uniform Army (Heer)*

plus a silver cord bound around it. Officers candidates in the navy Seekadett (*sea cadet*; equivalent to OR-4) and Fähnrich zur See (*midshipman second class*; OR-5) wear the rank insignia of the respective enlisted ranks but with a gold star instead of the rating symbol, while an Oberfähnrich zur See (*midshipman first class*; OR-7) wears an officer type thin rank stripe.

Medical personnel of all three services wear a version of the traditional caduceus (staff with entwined serpents) on their shoulder straps or sleeve. The officers' ranks have own designations differing from the line officers, the rank insignias however are basically the same.

Women

Women have served in the medical service since 1975. From 1993 they were also allowed to serve as enlisted personnel and non-commissioned officers in the medical service and the army bands. In 2000, in a lawsuit brought up by Tanja Kreil, the European Court of Justice issued a ruling allowing women to serve in more roles than previously allowed. Since 2001 they can serve in all functions of service without restriction, but they are not subject to conscription. There are presently around 19,064 women on active duty and a number of female reservists who take part in all duties including peacekeeping missions and other operations. In 1994, Verena von Weymarn became Generalarzt der

Figure 18: *Ulrike Flender, the first female combat pilot in the unified German military*

Luftwaffe ("Surgeon General of the Air Force"), the first woman ever to reach the rank of general in the armed forces of Germany.

For women, lower physical performance requirements are required in the basic fitness test, which must be completed at the time of recruitment and later on annually. The sex surcharge for the sprint test and the 1,000m run is 15%, for chin-up 40%.

Rank structure

Army and Air Force

Enlisted

- **Schütze/Flieger** or equivalent rank – Private/Airman Basic/Aircraftman or equivalent rank
- **Gefreiter** – Private/Airman E2
- **Gefreiter-UA** – Private/Airman E2 – NCO Candidate (Sergeants/Staff Sergeants)
- **Gefreiter-FA** – Private/Airman E2 – NCO Candidate (Staff Sergeant/Flight Sgts.)
- **Gefreiter-OA** – Private/Airman E2 – Officer Candidate

Figure 19: *General Wolfgang Schneiderhan*

- **Obergefreiter** – Private First Class / Airman First Class
- **Hauptgefreiter** – Lance Corporal / Senior Airman
- **Stabsgefreiter** – Corporal
- **Oberstabsgefreiter** – Specialist / Master Corporal

Non-commissioned officers

- **Unteroffizier** – Lance sergeant
- **Unteroffizier-FA** – Lance-Sergeant – Candidate Staff Sergeant
- **Stabsunteroffizier** – Sergeant
- **Feldwebel** – Staff Sergeant / Flight Sergeant
- **Oberfeldwebel** – Technical or Tech Sergeant / Flight Sergeant
- **Hauptfeldwebel** – Master Sergeant / Sergeant First Class
- **Stabsfeldwebel** – Senior Master Sergeant / Quartermaster Sergeant
- **Oberstabsfeldwebel** – Chief Master Sergeant / Sergeant Major

Officer Cadets

- **Fahnenjunker** – Cadet / Officer Candidate (with the rank of Lance Sergeant)
- **Fähnrich** – Ensign (with the rank of Staff Sergeant)
- **Oberfähnrich** – Senior Ensign (with the rank of Sergeant First Class)

Officers

- **Leutnant** – 2nd Lieutenant
- **Oberleutnant** – 1st Lieutenant/Lieutenant
- **Hauptmann** – Captain (OF-2)
- **Stabshauptmann** – Senior Captain
- **Major**
- **Oberstleutnant** – Lieutenant Colonel
- **Oberst** – Colonel
- **Brigadegeneral** – Brigadier General/Brigadier
- **Generalmajor** – Major General
- **Generalleutnant** – Lieutenant General
- **General**

Navy

Enlisted

- **Matrose** – Seaman Recruit
- **Gefreiter** – Seaman Apprentice E2
- **Gefreiter-MA** – Seaman Apprentice E2 – Petty Officer Candidate
- **Gefreiter-BA** – Seaman Apprentice E2 – Chief Petty Officer Candidate
- **Gefreiter-OA** – Seaman Apprentice E2 – Officer Candidate
- **Obergefreiter** – Seaman
- **Hauptgefreiter** – Able Seaman
- **Stabsgefreiter** – Leading Seaman
- **Oberstabsgefreiter** – Master Seaman

Non-commissioned officers

- **Maat** – Petty Officer 3rd Class
- **Maat-BA** – Petty Officer 3rd Class – Probationary Petty Officer 1st Class
- **Obermaat** – Petty Officer 2nd Class
- **Bootsmann** – Petty Officer 1st Class
- **Oberbootsmann** – Chief petty officer
- **Hauptbootsmann** – Senior Chief Petty Officer
- **Stabsbootsmann** – Master Chief Petty Officer
- **Oberstabsbootsmann** – Master Chief Petty Officer, Fleet/Force Master Chief Petty Officer

Officer cadets

- **Seekadett** – Sea Cadet in the rank of Petty Officer 3rd Class
- **Fähnrich zur See** – Midshipman 2nd class in the rank of Petty Officer 1st Class
- **Oberfähnrich zur See** – Midshipman 1st class in the rank of Senior Chief Petty Officer

Officers

- **Leutnant zur See** – Ensign
- **Oberleutnant zur See** – Lieutenant (junior grade) / Sublieutenant
- **Kapitänleutnant** – Lieutenant/Captain Lieutenant
- **Stabskapitänleutnant** – Senior Lieutenant/Senior Captain Lieutenant
- **Korvettenkapitän** – Lieutenant Commander
- **Fregattenkapitän** – Commander
- **Kapitän zur See** – Captain/Captain at Sea
- **Flottillenadmiral** – Flotilla Admiral
- **Konteradmiral** – Counter Admiral, Rear Admiral
- **Vizeadmiral** – Vice Admiral
- **Admiral**

Awards

- Badge of Honour of the Bundeswehr
- Combat Action Medal of the Bundeswehr
- German Armed Forces Badge of Marksmanship
- German Armed Forces Badge for Military Proficiency
- German Armed Forces Service Medal
- German Flood Service Medal (2002)
- German Flood Service Medal (2013)
- German Parachutist Badge

References

- This article incorporates public domain material from the Library of Congress document: Jean R. Tartte. "Germany: A country study"[13]. Federal Research Division. Uniforms, Ranks, and Insignia.

Further reading

- Searle, Alaric (2003). *Wehrmacht Generals, West German Society, and the Debate on Rearmament, 1949–1959*. Westport, CT: Praeger Publishers. ISBN 978-0-275-97968-3.

External links

 Wikimedia Commons has media related to *Bundeswehr*.

- *Bundeswehr*[14] – Official site (in German)
- Federal Ministry of Defence[15] official site (in German, English and French)
- Bundesamt für Wehrtechnik und Beschaffung[16] official site (in German)
- Bundesamt für Informationsmanagement und Informationstechnik der Bundeswehr[17] official site (in German)
- Territoriale Wehrverwaltung[18] official site (in German)
- Y – Magazine of the Federal Defence Forces (in German)[19]
- Zeitschrift für Innere Führung (in German)[20]
- Reader Sicherheitspolitik (in German)[21]

History

Military history of Germany

Part of a series on the
History of Germany
Topics
• Chronology • Historiography • Military history • Economic history • Women's history • Territorial evolution • List of German monarchs
Early history
• Germanic peoples • Migration Period • Frankish Empire
Middle Ages
• East Francia • Kingdom of Germany • Holy Roman Empire • Eastward settlement
Early Modern period
• Sectionalism • 18th century • Kingdom of Prussia

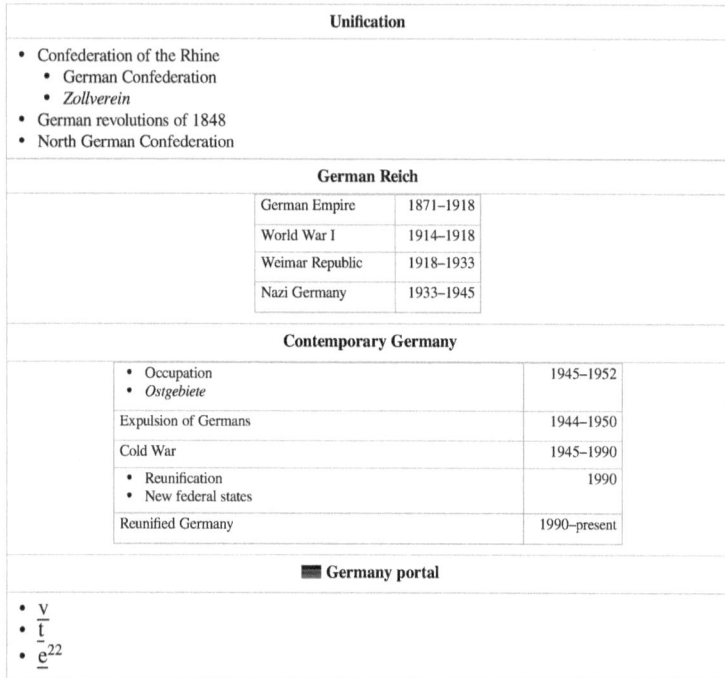

While German-speaking people have a long history, **Germany** as a nation state dates only from 1871. Earlier periods are subject to definition debates. The Franks, for instance, were a union of Germanic tribes; nevertheless, some of the Franks later identified themselves as Dutch, Flemish, French and again others as Germans. The capital of medieval ruler Charlemagne's empire was the city of Aachen, now part of Germany, yet he was a Frank. France was named after the Franks and the Dutch and Flemish people are the only ones to speak a language that descends from Frankish (the language of the Franks). Hence nearly all continental Western European historians can claim his victories as their heritage. The Holy Roman Empire he founded was largely but far from entirely German speaking. The Kingdom of Prussia, which unified Germany in the 19th century, had significant territory in what is now Poland. In the early 19th century, the philosopher Schlegel referred to Germany as a *Kulturnation*, a nation of shared culture and political disunity, analogous to ancient Greece. Until the unification of 1871, Austria was considered a part of Germany even though much of its empire was not in the Holy Roman Empire and was non-German.

Germany is regarded as one of the most powerful militaries in the world due to its successful long history of military warfare.Wikipedia:Citation needed

Figure 20: *Roman limes and modern boundaries.*

Ancient times

During the ancient and early medieval periods the Germanic tribes had no written language. What we know about their early military history comes from accounts written in Latin and from archaeology. This leaves important gaps. Germanic wars against the Romans are fairly well documented from the Roman perspective, such as the infamous Battle of the Teutoburg Forest. Germanic wars against the early Celts remain mysterious because neither side recorded the events.

Germanic tribes are thought to have originated during the Nordic Bronze Age in northern Germany and southern Scandinavia. The tribes spread south, possibly motivated by the deteriorating climate of that area. They crossed the River Elbe, probably overrunning the territories of the Celtic Volcae in the Weser Basin. The Romans recorded one of these early migrations when the Cimbri and the Teutons tribes threatened the Republic itself around the late 2nd century BC. In the East, other tribes, such as Goths, Rugii and Vandals, settled along the shores of the Baltic Sea pushing southward and eventually settling as far away as Ukraine. The Angles and Saxons migrated to England. The Germanic peoples often had a fraught relationship with their neighbours, leading to a period of over two millennia of military conflict over various territorial, religious, ideological and economic concerns.

Figure 21: *"Death of Frederick of Germany" by Gustav Dore*

Middle Ages

The Holy Roman Empire of the German Nation (also referred as the First German Empire) emerged from the eastern part of the Carolingian Empire after its division in the Treaty of Verdun of 843, and lasted almost a millennium until its dissolution in 1806. It was never a unitary state; from the beginning it was made up of many ethnicities and languages and would at its height comprise territories ranging from eastern France to northern Italy. Its unifying characteristic was its Carolingian heritage and strong religious connotations, its claim to "German-ness" the ethnicity of most of its subjects and rulers.[23]

From 919-36, the Germanic peoples (Franks, Saxons, Swaben and Bavarians) were united under Henry the Fowler, then Duke of Saxony, who took the title of King. For the first time, the term Kingdom of the Germans ("Regnum Teutonicorum") was applied to the Frankish kingdom.

In 955, the Hungarians (Magyars) were decisively defeated at Lechfeld by his son Otto the Great, ending the threat from the Eurasian steppes for four centuries. In 962, partly on the strength of this victory, Otto went to Rome and was crowned the first Emperor of the Holy Roman Empire by the pope.

Third Crusade

By 1155, the German states had descended into disorder. Emperor Frederick I Barbarossa managed to restore peace through diplomacy and skillfully arranged marriages. He claimed direct imperial control over Italy and made several incursions into northern Italy, but was ultimately defeated by the Lombard League at Legano in 1176. In 1189, Frederick embarked on the Third Crusade. After a few initial successes against the Turks, notably at the Battle of Iconium, Frederick died when trying to cross a river. Leaderless, panicked and attacked on all sides, only a tiny fraction of the original forces continued onward.

Teutonic Knights

In 1226 Konrad I of Masovia appealed to the Teutonic Knights, a German crusading military order, to defend his borders and subdue the pagan Baltic Prussians.[24] The conquest and Christianisation of Prussia was accomplished after more than 50 years, after which the Order ruled it as a sovereign Teutonic Order state. Their conflict of interests with the Polish-Lithuanian state lead in 1410 to Battle of Grunwald (Tannenberg) where a Polish-Lithuanian army inflicted a decisive defeat and broke its military power, although the Order withstood the following Siege of Marienburg and managed to retain most of its territories.[25]

Hussite wars

The Hussite Wars, fought between 1419 and 1434 in Bohemia, had their origins in a conflict between Catholics and the followers of a religious sect founded by Jan Hus. The inciting action of the war was the First Defenestration of Prague, in which the mayor and the town council members of Prague were thrown from the windows of the town building. Emperor Sigismund, a firm adherent of the Roman Catholic Church, obtained the support of Pope Martin V who issued a papal bull in 1420 proclaiming a crusade. In all, four crusades were launched against the heretics, all resulting in defeat for the Catholic troops. The Hussites, capably led by Jan Žižka, employed novel tactics to defeat their numerically superior enemies, decisively at Aussig. Whenever a crusade would end, the Hussite armies go on "Beautiful Rides" and would invade the lands where the crusaders were from. One such place was Saxony. After Žižka's death in 1424, the Hussite armies were led by Prokop the Great to another victory at the Battle of Tachov in 1427. The Hussites repeatedly invaded central German lands, though they made no attempt at permanent occupation, and at one point made it all of the way to the Baltic Sea. The Hussite movement was ended in 1434, however, at the Battle of Lipany.[26]

Reformation

During the German Peasants' War, spanning from 1524 to 1525 in the Holy Roman Empire, the peasants rebelled against the nobility. The rebellion ultimately failed in the end and Emperor Charles V became much harsher.[27]

Thirty Years War

From 1618 to 1648 the Thirty Years' War ravaged Germany, when it became the main theatre of war in the conflict between France and the Habsburgs for predominance in Europe. Besides being at war with Catholic France, Germany was attacked by the Lutheran King Gustavus Adolphus of Sweden, who won many victories until he was killed at Lützen. The war resulted in large areas of Germany being laid waste, causing general impoverishment and a loss of around a third of its population; it took generations to recover. It ended with the Peace of Westphalia, which stabilized the nation states of Europe.[28]

The imperial general Prince Eugene of Savoy faced the Ottoman Turks on the battlefield, first coming to prominence during the last major Turkish offensive against the Austrian capital of Vienna in 1683. By the closing years of the 17th century, he was already famous for securing Hungary from the Turks, and soon rose to the role of principal Austrian commander during the War of the Spanish Succession.

18th century

From 1701-1714 the War of the Spanish Succession, Germany fought with the English and the Dutch against the French. During the early part of the war, the French were successful until Camille de Tallard was victorious in the Palatinate. Later, in 1706, the Germans took back their land with the help of the Dutch and the English. The Austrians pushed the French back in North Italy and the coalition scored several successes in the low countries. At that time, half of the Dutch or the British armies were composed of German mercenaries. The German states that participated in the war were Austria (which contributed the most), Prussia and Hanover.

During the reign of Frederick William I (1713–40), the military power of Prussia was significantly improved. He organized the government around the needs of his army, and produced an efficient, highly disciplined instrument of war. The Prussian Army was expanded to 80,000 men, about 4% of the total population. Peasants were drafted into the military and trained for duty, but were sent home for ten months out of each year.

Frederick the Great

Frederick the Great, king of Prussia from 1740-86, modernized the Prussian army, introduced new tactical and strategical concepts, fought mostly successful wars and doubled the size of Prussia. Frederick had a rationale based on Enlightenment thought: he launched total wars for limited objectives. The goal was to convince rival kings that it was better to negotiate and make peace than to fight him.[29]

In the War of Austrian Succession (1740-48) Empress Maria Theresa of Austria fought successfully for recognition of her succession to the throne. However, during the subsequent Silesian Wars and the Seven Years' War, King Frederick the Great (Frederick II) occupied Silesia and forced Austria to formally cede control in the Treaty of Hubertusburg of 1763. Prussia had survived the combined force of its neighbours, each larger than itself, and gained enormously in influence at the cost of the Holy Roman Empire. It became recognised as a great European power, starting a rivalry with Austria for the leadership of the German-speaking lands.[30]

During the Seven Years' War, Prussia fought on the side of Britain against Russia, Sweden, Austria, France, and Saxony. Frederick II of Prussia first invaded Saxony and defeated a Saxon army at Lobositz. Frederick would then invade Bohemia, the Prussians besieged Prague, but they were defeated at Kolin. Since Prussia looked vulnerable, the Austrians and French invaded Prussian lands. However, the French were defeated at Rossbach and the Austrians at Leuthen. In 1758, Frederick the Great tried to invade Austria, but he failed. Now, the Russians tried to defeat the Prussians, but the Prussians earned a pyrrhic victory at the Zorndorf. The Swedes, however, fought the Prussians to a draw at Tornow. However, Austria gained a victory against the Prussian main army at Hochkirch. In 1759, the Prussians lost at Kunersdorf to the combined Russians and Austrians. Berlin itself was taken for a few days in 1762, but its army could not be destroyed. However, the great alliance against Prussia broke up when Elizabeth of Russia died. It was from her death that a pro-Prussian ruler, Peter III would sue for peace. It was thanks to this "miracle of the House of Brandenburg" and to the unshakable will of Frederick that Prussia survived.[31]

Napoleonic Wars (1805-15)

The Napoleonic era ended the Holy Roman Empire and created new German-speaking states that would eventually form modern Germany. Napoleon I of France reorganized many of the smaller German-speaking states into the Confederation of the Rhine following the battle of Austerlitz in 1805.[32] Essentially this enlarged the more powerful states of the region by absorbing the smaller

Figure 22: *Napoleon at the battle of Austerlitz, by François Pascal Simon, Baron Gérard*

ones, creating a set of buffer states for France and a source of army conscripts. Neither of the two largest German-speaking states were part of this confederation: the Kingdom of Prussia and the Austrian Empire remained outside it.[33]

King Frederick William III of Prussia viewed the Confederation of the Rhine as a threat to Prussian interests and allied against Napoleon. At this time the reputation of the Prussian army remained high from the period of the Seven Years' War. Unfortunately they retained the tactics of that period and still relied heavily on foreign mercenaries. The lack of military reforms would prove disastrous. Prussian defeats at Jena and Auerstedt led to a humiliating settlement that reduced the size of the country by half.

The Electorate of Hanover, up till the Convention of Artlenburg ruled in personal union by the English King George III, was incorporated into Prussia. The King's German Legion formed in Britain from officers and soldiers of the dissolved Hanoverian army, was the only army of a German state that was continually fighting the Napoleonic army.

A demoralised Prussia brought its distinguished old general Gebhard von Blücher out of retirement and reorganized the army. The reforms of the Prussian military were led by Scharnhorst and Gneisenau, and converted the professional army into one based on national service. They brought in younger leaders, increased the rate of mobilisation and improved their skirmishing and unit tactics. They also organized a centralized general staff and a professional officer corps.[34]

Following Napoleon's defeat in Russia, Prussia, Austria and a few other German states saw their chance and joined the anti-French forces in the Sixth

Figure 23: *the original Iron Cross military medal from 1813*

Coalition, which won a decisive victory over France at Leipzig in 1813 and forced the abdication of Napoleon. Although declared an outlaw by the Congress of Vienna, Napoleon returned and met a final defeat at the hands of Blücher and Wellington at Waterloo in 1815.[35]

Uniting Germany (1815–71)

By 1815 there were 39 separate German-speaking states, loosely joined (for free trade purposes) in the German Confederation, under the leadership of Prussia and Austria. Under the leadership of Chancellor Otto von Bismarck, Prussia united the German states and defeated both Austria and France, 1866 to 1871, allowing the formation of a powerful German Empire, which lasted until 1918. Bismarck after 1871 dominated European diplomacy, and set up a complex system of balances that kept the peace. He was replaced in 1890 by the young Kaiser Wilhelm II, who built up a powerful Navy to challenge the British, and engaged in reckless diplomacy.

Figure 24: *Otto von Bismarck became Chancellor of a united Germany after defeating France in 1871*

Clausewitz

Carl von Clausewitz (1780–1831) was the most important German military theorist; he stressed the moral and political aspects of war. Clausewitz espoused a romantic or Hegelian conception of warfare, stressing the dialectic of how opposite factors interact, and noting how unexpected new developments unfolding under the "fog of war" called for rapid decisions by alert commanders. Clausewitz saw history as a complex check on abstractions that did not accord with experience. In opposition to his great rival Antoine-Henri Jomini he argued war could not be quantified or graphed or reduced to mapwork and graphs. Clausewitz had many aphorisms, of which the most famous is, "War is not merely a political act, but also a political instrument, a continuation of political relations, a carrying out of the same by other means," a working definition of war which has won wide acceptance.[36]

Wars of Unification

After a period of constitutional deadlock between crown and parliament in Prussia, a crisis arose in 1863 over the duchies of Schleswig and Holstein, disputed between Denmark and the German Confederation. After the Danish annexation of Schleswig, Otto von Bismarck, the new prime Minister of

Figure 25: *The Prussian 7th Cuirassiers charge the French guns at the Battle of Mars-La-Tour, August 16, 1870*

Prussia, made the smaller states of the German Confederation join Prussia and Austria in the war with Denmark. The Second Schleswig War ended with the defeat of the Danes at Dybbøl, and an agreement between Austria and Prussia to jointly administer Schleswig and Holstein.

Bismarck then set about making Prussia the undisputed master of northern Germany, weakening Austria and the German Confederation. This eventually led to a German civil war, the Austro-Prussian War, in which in the Battle of Langensalza (the last battle between Germanic states on German soil) Hanover won a victory, but was so weakened by it, that it could offer no resistance to the occupation by Prussia and ceased to be an independent state. The victory of Prussia and its allies at Königgrätz in July 1866, against Austria and its allies sealed this. The result was the dissolution of the German Confederation, and the creation of the North German Confederation one year later.[37]

Bismarck wanted a war with France to unify the German peoples, and French Emperor Napoleon III, unaware of his military weakness, provided the Franco-Prussian War of 1870–71, expecting support from Prussia's recent enemies. Unlike in the war only a few years ago, the Germans turned not against each other, with the first emergence of a strong German national sentiment in the background. Instead, the southern German monarchs of Bavaria, Württemberg, and Baden honoured their secretly negotiated treaties of mutual defence with Berlin, while Austria remained neutral.

The Germans, led by King William I of Prussia and Moltke the Elder, mobilized a mass conscript army of 1.2 million men (300,000 regulars and 900,000 reserves and Landwehr) which faced 492,585 experienced regular French soldiers and *420,000 Garde Mobile* under Napoleon III of France. Within the first month of war the German army encircled big French armies, at Gravelotte, Metz, and Sedan and destroyed them. The war culminated with the defeat of the French army during the Siege of Paris, and was followed by the proclamation of the German Empire in 1871.[38]

Naval race

The results of these wars was the emergence of a powerful German nation-state and a major shift in the balance of power on the European continent. The Imperial German Army now was the most powerful military in Europe. Although Germany now had a parliament, it did not control the military, which was under the direct command of the Kaiser (Emperor). The German economy was rapidly growing, as was German pride and intense nationalism.

After 1890, Germany made a major effort to build up its navy, leading to a naval arms race with Britain. Germany also sought coaling stations because the coal-burning warships had to be refueled frequently, and Britain had a large worldwide network. Efforts to gain coaling stations in the Caribbean or west Indies failed. By 1900, the possibility of a conflict between Germany and Britain loomed larger, as Germany built up its own (much smaller) colonial empire, and started a naval race to try and catch up with Britain, the world's dominant naval power.[39,40]

First World War (1914–18)

The German Schlieffen plan to deal with the Franco-Russian alliance involved delivering a knock-out blow to the French and then turning to deal with the more slowly mobilised Russian army. At the start of the First World War, Germany attacked France through Belgium to avoid French defenses on the French-German border. They were beaten back at the First Battle of the Marne. Three years of stalemated trench warfare on the Western Front produced millions of casualties (with one-third killed). New tactics in 1918 opened up the war, but a series of massive German offensives failed in spring 1918, and Germany went on the defensive as fresh American soldiers arrived at the rate of 10,000 a day. Militarily defeated, stripped of allies, and exhausted on the homefront, Germany signed an armistice in November 1918 that amounted to a surrender.[41]

In the East, however, the war was not confined to trenches. The Russian initial plans for war had called for simultaneous invasions of Austrian Galicia

Figure 26: *German soldiers on the front in the First World War*

Figure 27: *German artillery shown on a 1914 postcard*

and German East Prussia. Although Russia's initial advance into Galicia was largely successful, it was driven back from East Prussia by the victories of the German generals Hindenburg and Ludendorff at Tannenberg and the Masurian Lakes in August and September 1914. Russia's less-developed economic and military organisation soon proved unequal to the combined might of the German and Austro-Hungarian Empires. In the spring of 1915 the Russians were driven back in Galicia, and in May the Central Powers achieved a remarkable breakthrough on Poland's southern fringes, capturing Warsaw on 5 August and forcing the Russians to withdraw from all of Poland, known as the "Great Retreat".

The German Fleet spent most of the war bottled up in port; the great Battle of Jutland in 1916 showed superior German tactics could not overwhelm the more powerful British fleet. Submarines – the U-boats- were used by the Imperial German Navy to sink merchant ships bringing supplies to England. This strategy alienated the United States, which declared war in April 1917. Shipments of food and munitions to Britain and France were increased, as the convoy system largely neutralized the U-boats.[42]

By 1917 the German army had begun employing new infiltration tactics in an effort to break the trench warfare deadlock.[43] Units of stormtroopers, were trained and equipped for the new tactics, and were used with devastating effect along the Russian front at Riga then at the Battle of Caporetto in Italy. These formations were then deployed to the Western front to counter the British tank attack at the Battle of Cambrai.[44]

In March 1918 the German army Spring Offensive began an impressive advance creating a salient in the allied line. The offensive stalled as the British and French fell back and then counterattacked. The Germans did not have the airpower or tanks to secure their battlefield gains.[45] The Allies, invigorated by American manpower, money, and food, counterattacked in late summer and rolled over the depleted German lines, as the German navy rebelled and support for the war on the homefront evaporated.

Weimar Republic and the Third Reich (1918–39)

The treaty of Versailles imposed severe restrictions on Germany's military strength. The army was limited to one hundred thousand men with an additional fifteen thousand in the navy. The fleet was to consist of at most six battleships, six cruisers, and twelve destroyers, and the Washington Naval Treaty established severe tonnage restrictions for German warships. Tanks and heavy artillery were forbidden and the air force was dissolved. A new post-war military (Reichswehr) was established in March 1921. General conscription was not allowed. The new Weimar Republic had to follow these restrictions, which worsened its already low public esteem.[46]

General Hans von Seeckt the Army Commander, used the lessons of the First World War and the latest technology to develop advanced tactical doctrines, more efficient organizational structures, and better training that kept the small army ready for expansion. The government secretly trained soldiers in the Soviet Union, but otherwise generally followed the Versailles restrictions while retaining a strong cadre of officers and senior non-coms.[47]

The Nazis came to power in 1933 and began remilitarisation. Heavy military spending quickly restored the depression-ravaged economy, making Adolf Hitler popular with the people and the military. German armed forces were named the Wehrmacht from 1935 to 1945. The Army (Heer) was encouraged to experiment with tanks and motorised infantry, using the ideas of Heinz Guderian. The Kriegsmarine restarted naval construction and Hitler established the Luftwaffe, an independent air force.

Threats to use military force were a staple in Nazi foreign policy. They were not actually used except as German involvement in the Spanish Civil War (1936–39), where the Luftwaffe gained important combat experience.

Second World War (1939–45)

Farrell argues that the historiography of the army in World War Two has been "extremely difficult" because of the stark dichotomy between its superb combat performance and the horrors of its destruction and crimes against civilians and prisoners.[48]

At first Germany's military moves were brilliantly successful, as in the "blitzkrieg" invasions of Poland (1939), Norway and Denmark (1940), the Low Countries (1940), and above all the stunningly successful invasion and quick conquest of France in 1940. Hitler probably wanted peace with Britain in late 1940, but Winston Churchill, standing alone, was dogged in his defiance. Churchill had major financial, military, and diplomatic help from President Franklin D. Roosevelt in the U.S., another implacable foe of Hitler. Rising tensions with the Soviet Union eventually led Germany to launch a full-scale invasion of its former ally in June 1941. Hitler's insistence on maintaining high living standards postponed the full mobilization of the national economy until 1942, years after the great rivals Britain, Russia, and the U.S. had fully mobilized.

In September 1939, Germany invaded Poland using new tactics that combining the use of tanks, motorised infantry, and air support – known as Blitzkrieg – caused Polish resistance to collapse within weeks. From the beginning of the campaign German forces committed war crimes. Britain and France declared war but over the winter of 1939–40 there was very little combat in what was called the Phoney War.

In April 1940, in Operation Weserübung, German combined air, land and sea forces invaded and occupied neutral Denmark with little fighting. Then they fought a successful Norwegian Campaign against the British and Norwegian forces to conquer Norway and to secure access to the North Sea and to Swedish iron ore. Sweden remained neutral throughout the war, but Finland fought two wars against the Soviets and became a German ally.[49]

France

The French plans were largely based on a static defense behind the Maginot Line – a series of formidable defensive forts along the French-German border.[50] German General Erich von Manstein thought on an idea which led eventually to the approval of a *Sichelschnitt* ('Sickle Cut') plan to the conquest of France. On 10 May 1940 the Germans bypassed the Maginot Line by launching another *Blitzkrieg* through neutral Belgium, Luxemburg and the Netherlands, drawing the Allied forces out. The main thrust of the Battle of France attack however was through the Ardennes which were to that time believed impenetrable to tanks. The British Expeditionary Force and other allied units were driven back to the coast at Dunkirk, but managed to escape with most of their troops when Germany made a mistaken decision not to attack with tanks. In June 1940, with French troops encircled and cut off in the north, France asked for an armistice that allowed Germany to control most of the French coast and left Vichy France under German domination.[51]

Battle of Britain

Hitler at least wanted to threaten an invasion of Britain, perhaps to force a peace, so an armada of small boats and a large combat force was assembled in northern France. The Battle of Britain was of basic strategic significance, for Berlin believed that it could defeat Britain only by physical invasion by the Army, codenamed Operation Sea Lion. The British Army had rescued its soldiers at Dunkirk but lost most of its equipment and weapons, and was no match for the fully equipped German army. The invasion could succeed only if the Luftwaffe could guarantee the Royal Navy would not be able to attack the landing force. To do so, the Royal Air Force had to be defeated.

The Battle took place August to September 1940. The Luftwaffe used 1300 medium bombers guarded by 900 fighters; they made 1500 sorties a day from bases in France, Belgium and Norway. The Royal Air Force (RAF) had 650 fighters, with more coming out of the factories every day. Thanks to its new radar system, the British knew where the Germans were, and could concentrate their counterattacks.[52] The Germans used their strategic bombing doctrine to focus on RAF airfields and radar stations. After the RAF bomber forces (quite separate from the fighter forces) attacked Berlin and other cities, Hitler swore revenge and diverted the Luftwaffe to attacks on London. The success the Luftwaffe was having in rapidly wearing down the RAF was squandered, as the civilians being hit were far less critical than the airfields and radar stations that were now ignored.[53] The last German daylight raid was September 30; the Luftwaffe was taking unacceptable losses and broke off the attack; occasional blitz raids hit London and other cities from time to time before May 1941, killing some 43,000 civilians. The Luftwaffe lost 1733 planes, the British, 915. The British showed more determination, better radar, and better ground control, while the Germans violated their own doctrine with wasted attacks on London.[54]

The British surprised the Germans with their high quality airplanes; flying close to home bases where they could refuel, and using radar as part of an integrated air defense system, they had a significant advantage over German planes operating at long range. The Hawker Hurricane fighter plane played a vital role for the RAF in winning the Battle of Britain in the summer of 1940. A fast, heavily armed monoplane that went into service in 1937, the Hurricane was effective against both German fighters and bombers and accounted for 70-75% of German losses during the battle. The Germans immediately pulled out their Stukas, which were so slow they were child's play for the Hurricanes and Spitfires. The Battle of Britain showed the world that Hitler's vaunted war machine could be defeated.

Barley (2004) identifies numerous failures by the German high command. Hitler was indecisive, failing to identify a political goal that would define the military mission. Luftwaffe planning was muddled, and overlooked the important lessons learned in Spain. The operation was poorly supported by German intelligence. Germany failed to adhere to two key principles of war: know your enemy and yourself, and select and maintain your aim.[55]

Balkans

To support their weakened Italian allies who had started several invasions, in early 1941 Germany deployed troops in Greece, Yugoslavia and North Africa. In the Balkans it was a matter of guerrilla war which was extremely violent on all sides.[56] These deployments disrupted Berlin's timetable, and delayed the invasion of the Soviet Union.

Operation Barbarossa

Hitler made the fateful decision to invade Russia in early 1941, but was delayed by the need to take control of the Balkans. Europe was not big enough for both Hitler and Stalin, and Hitler realized the sooner he moved the less risk of American involvement. Stalin thought he had a long-term partnership and rejected information coming from all directions that Germany was about to invade in June 1941. As a result, the Russians were poorly prepared and suffered huge losses, being pushed back to Moscow by December before holding the line. Hitler imagined that the Soviet Union was a hollow shell that would easily collapse, like France. He therefore had not prepared for a long war, and did not have sufficient winter clothing and gear for his soldiers.[57,58] Weinberg (1994) argues that decisions concerning the invasion of the Soviet Union in June 1941 must be understood in the broader context of Hitler's ideological motivations and long-term goals. Although Hitler had decided to invade the Soviet Union as early as 1940, German resources never reflected this; armaments production, tank and aircraft construction, and logistical preparations focused on the West. Diplomatic activity was similarly skewed; Hitler granted Stalin any territory he wanted (such as Lithuania), knowing they would soon be at war and Germany would reclaim it anyway. Hitler, blinded by his racist prejudices against Slavs, believed the Eastern campaign would be quick and easy. His real strategic concern was Great Britain and the United States, and his planning consistently demonstrated this.[59]

The Balkan operation had caused a delay, and about six weeks later than planned, on 22 June 1941, Germany reneged on its non-aggression pact with the Soviet Union and launched Operation Barbarossa. The German army and its allies made enormous territorial gains in the first months of the war, reaching the outskirts of Moscow when winter set in. Expecting another *Blitzkrieg* victory, the Germans had not properly prepared for warfare in winter and over long distances.[60]

High Point and Collapse

The years 1941/1942 saw the high point for the German army which controlled an area from France deep into Russia, and from Norway to western Egypt. Consequently, it also proved to be the turning point. The harsh Russian winters and long supply lines worked in Russia's favour and German armies were decisively defeated in early 1943 at Stalingrad and later in the gigantic tank battle at Kursk.[61] British and American forces cut off reinforcements to North Africa, defeated Field Marshal Erwin Rommel, and captured the German and Italian forces there.[62]

Figure 28: *The Axis-controlled territory in Europe at the time of its maximal expansion (1941–42).*

Hitler was technologically oriented and promoted a series of new secret weapons, such as the jet plane, the jet-powered missile (V-1), the rocket-powered missile (V-2), and vastly improved submarines. However he failed to support development of nuclear weapons or proximity fuses, and trailed the Allies in radar. He failed to take advantage of the German lead in jet planes.[63]

In early 1943 the Soviet victory at Stalingrad marked the beginning of the end, as Germany was unable to cope with the superior manpower and industrial resources of the Allies. North Africa, Sicily, and southern Italy fell in 1943. Hitler rescued Mussolini from prison. Mussolini set up a new "Salo Republic" but he was a mere puppet, as German forces blocked the Allies from the industrial northern third of Italy. The Russians pushed forward relentlessly in the East, while the Allies in the west launched a major bombing campaign in 1944-45 that destroyed all major and many smaller German cities, ruined transportation, and signaled to Germans how hopeless was their cause.

The Allies invaded France in June 1944 as the Russians launched another attack on the east. Both attacks were successful and by the end of 1944, the end was in sight. Hitler did launch a surprise attack at the Bulge in December 1944; it was his last major initiative and it failed, as Allied armor rolled into Germany. Disregarding his generals, Hitler rejected withdrawals and retreats,

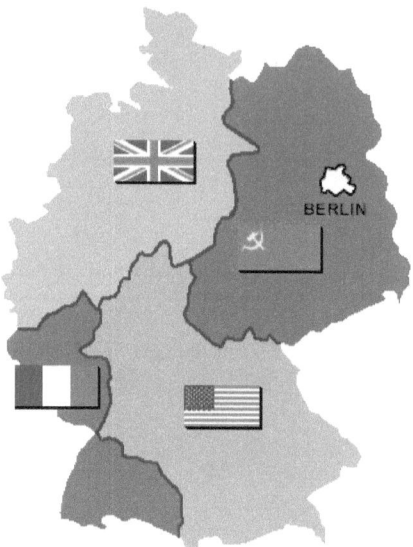

Figure 29: *Occupation zones of Germany in 1945.*

counting more and more on nonexistent armies. He committed suicide in his underground bunker in Berlin as his last soldiers were overwhelmed by Soviet armies in intensely bloody battles overhead.[64]

Cold War (1945–89)

Among the legacies of the Nazi era were the Nuremberg Trials of 1945-1949. These established the concept of war crimes in international law and created the precedent for trying future war criminals.

West Germany

In 1949, West Germany (Federal Republic of Germany) was formed from the French, British and American zones, while the Soviet zone formed East Germany (German Democratic Republic). The western territory of Germany fell under the protection of the NATO alliance in the west, while the eastern state joined the Warsaw Pact. Each state possessed its own military force, with eastern Germany formed along the Soviet model and federal Germany adopting a more 'western' organisation. The allied zones of Berlin became de facto part of the Federal Republic of Germany despite the city's location deep in the German Democratic Republic. That resulted in a special situation for Berlin,

Figure 30: *Corps sectors of military responsibility in NATO's central region in the 1980s.*

i.e. the draft was not in effect in West Berlin. This condition continued until 1990 when the two states were reunited.

The Bundeswehr was established in 1955 in West Germany. In 1956, conscription for all men between 18 and 45 in years was introduced after heavy discussions about re-militarising Germany. A significant exception came from the conscientious objector clause in the West German constitution: West Germany was the first country to grant alternative service to all men who objected to military service on ethical grounds, regardless of religious affiliation. This was named "Zivildienst" roughly translated as "civil services".

Cold War analysts considered Germany the most likely location for the outbreak of a possible third world war. Tensions ran high during 1948 when the Soviet Union and "Sowjetische Besatzungszone" (Soviet Occupied Territories) closed all roads bringing supplies to West Berlin. The Berlin Airlift sustained the population and avoided a new war. Construction of the Berlin Wall in 1961.

During the Cold War the Bundeswehr had a strength of 495,000 military and 170,000 civilian personnel. The army consisted of three corps with 12 divisions, most of them armed with tanks and APCs. The air force owned major numbers of tactical combat aircraft and took part in NATO's integrated air defence (NATINADS). The navy was tasked to defend the "Baltic Approaches" and to contain the Soviet Baltic Fleet.

The United States played a dominant role in NATO, and had its own forces stationed in Germany as well. Cooperation between the two militaries was extensive and cordial. Joint exercises and close collaboration allowed the German and American armies to learn from each other regarding strategy, tactics and technology.[65] However, there were failures when it came to a joint venture in tank design in the 1960s, and the lack of cooperation in developing infantry fighting vehicles.[66]

East Germany

In East Germany, the Nationale Volksarmee (National People's Army) or NVA was founded on 1 March 1956. It grew steadily by gradual stages from the police force in the Soviet occupation zone in 1945 until the consolidation in the defense establishment in the 1970s. It was a professional volunteer army until 1962, when conscription was introduced. In 1987 at the peak of its power, the NVA numbered 175,300 troops. Approximately 50% of this number were career soldiers, while the remaining half were short-term conscripts. The armed forces were controlled by the National Defense Council, except that the mobile forces were under the Warsaw Pact Unified Command. Political control of the armed forces was through close integration with the SED (Communist Party), which vetted all the officers. Popular support for the military establishment was bolstered by military training provided by the school system and through the growing militarization of society. From a Leninist perspective, the NVA stood as a symbol of Soviet-East German solidarity and became the model Communist institution—ideological, hierarchical, and disciplined.[67] The NVA synthesized Communist and Germanic symbolism, naming its officers' academy after Marx's coauthor Friedrich Engels, and its highest medal after Prussian General Gerhard von Scharnhorst.[68]

At the critical moment in its history in November 1989, the NVA rallied to its Germanic heritage and rejected Communism, refusing to battle the demonstrators protesting the Communist regime. Mikhail Gorbachev refused to let Soviet troops become engaged, and so not just the leadership but the entire Communist system in East Germany collapsed, and the country was soon absorbed by West Germany.[69]

Bundeswehr

Post-Cold War to present-day

German reunification

In the Treaty on the Final Settlement with Respect to Germany (1990), Germany agreed to reduce the strength of its combined armed forces to no more than 370,000 men. After reunification, the Bundeswehr absorbed parts of the Nationale Volksarmee of the GDR, which was being dissolved. In 1999, the NATO war on Yugoslavia in Kosovo was the first offensive conflict in which the German military actively took part since the Second World War. In 2000, the European Court of Justice opened up the previously all-male (besides medical divisions and the music corps) Bundeswehr to women. Since the early 1990s, the Bundeswehr became more engaged in international peacekeeping missions in and around the former Yugoslavia, Cambodia, Somalia, Djibouti, Georgia, and Sudan.

War on Terrorism

As part of Operation Enduring Freedom as a response to those attacks, Germany deployed approximately 2,250 troops including KSK special forces, naval vessels and NBC cleanup teams to Afghanistan. German forces have contributed to ISAF, the NATO force in Afghanistan, and a Provincial Reconstruction Team.[70] German army CH-53 helicopters have deployed to Afghanistan, one crashed in December 2002 in Kabul, killing seven German soldiers. Eleven other German soldiers have been killed: four in two different ordnance-defusing accidents, one in a vehicle accident, five in two separate suicide bombings, and one in landmine explosion. German forces were in the more secure north of the country and Germany, along with some other larger European countries (with the exception of the UK, Estonia, the Netherlands and Norway), and were criticised for not taking part in the more intensive combat operations in southern Afghanistan in 2006.[71]

Reorientation of the Bundeswehr

A major event for the German military was the suspension of the compulsory conscription for men in 2011. In 2011/12, a major reform of the Bundeswehr was announced, further limiting the number of military bases and soldiers. As of December 2012, the number of active military personnel in the Bundeswehr was down to 191,818, corresponding to a ratio of 2.3 active soldiers per 1,000 inhabitants. Military expenditure in Germany was at €31.55 billion in 2011, corresponding to 1.2% of GDP. Both the number of active soldiers and the military expenditure placed Germany below comparable countries of the European Union such as France and the United Kingdom. While this was already true in absolute terms, the difference was even more pronounced when taking into account Germany's larger population and economy. Thus, Germany appears less prepared to pay for the military and to attach less importance to defense than comparable countries. This stance often draws criticism from Germany's military allies, especially the United States.

In May 2016, the German government announced it would spend €130 billion on new equipment by 2030 and add nearly 7,000 soldiers by 2023 in the first German military expansion since the end of the Cold War. In February 2017, the German government announced another expansion, which would increase the number of its professional soldiers by 20,000 by 2024.

Reduction of foreign armed forces

Whereas Soviet/Russian soldiers fully withdrew from reunified Germany after the Cold War, the United States have only reduced their forces, maintaining a contingent of 47,761 troops as of 2012. The British Armed Forces will discontinue their deployment in Germany by 2020.Wikipedia:Citation needed French soldiers will continue to be deployed on German soil as a part of the Franco-German Brigade.Wikipedia:Citation needed

Naval history

Several naval forces have operated in Germany at different times. See

- Prussian Navy, 1701-1867
- Reichsflotte (Fleet of the Realm), 1848–52
- North German Federal Navy, 1867–71
- Imperial German Navy, 1871-1918
- Reichsmarine, 1919–35
- Kriegsmarine, 1935–45
- German Mine Sweeping Administration, 1945 to 1956
- Bundesmarine, 1956 to 1994

- Volksmarine, the navy of East Germany, 1956–90
- German Navy, since 1995

Further reading

- Barnett, Correlli, ed. *Hitler's Generals* (2003) essays by experts on 23 top generals
- Brose, Eric Dorn. *The Kaiser's Army: The Politics of Military Technology in Germany during the Machine Age, 1870-1918* (2004) excerpt and text search[72]
- Citino, Robert M. *The German Way of War: From the Thirty Years' War to the Third Reich* (2008) excerpt and text search[73]
- Craig, Gordon A. *The Politics of the Prussian Army: 1640-1945* (1964) excerpt and text search[74]
- Evans, Richard J. *The Third Reich at War: 1939-1945* (2009)
- Frevert, Ute. *A Nation in Barracks: Modern Germany, Military Conscription and Civil Society* (2004), history since 1800
- Hauptmann, Hermann. *The Rise and Fall of the Luftwaffe* (2012) excerpt and text search[75]
- Herwig, Holger H. *The First World War: Germany and Austria-Hungary 1914-1918* (2009)
- Hooton, Tim. *The Luftwaffe: A Complete History 1933-45* (2010)
- Kelly, Patrick J. *Tirpitz and the Imperial German Navy* (2011) excerpt and text search[76]
- Kitchen, Martin. *A Military History of Germany: From the Eighteenth Century to the Present Day* (1976)
- Krimmer, Elisabeth, and Patricia Anne Simpson, eds. *Enlightened War: German Theories and Cultures of Warfare from Frederick the Great to Clausewitz* (2011)
- Lider, Julian. *Origins and Development of West German Military Thought, Vol. I, 1949-1966*, (Gower, 1986)
- McNab, Chris. *Hitler's Armies: A history of the German War Machine 1939-45* (2011) excerpt and text search[77]
- Mosier, John. *Cross of Iron: The Rise and Fall of the German War Machine, 1918-1945* (2007) excerpt and text search[78]
- Murray, Williamson. *Strategy for Defeat: The Luftwaffe 1933–1945* (1983)
- Probert, H. A. *The Rise and Fall of the German Air Force 1933-1945* (1987), history by the British RAF
- Ripley, Tim. *The Wehrmacht: The German Army in World War II, 1939-1945* (2003)

- Ritter, Gerhard. *The Sword and the Scepter: The Prussian Tradition, 1740-1890* (1988); *The Sword and the Scepter: The Problem of Militarism in Germany: The European Powers and the Wilhelminian Empire, 1890-1914* (1972); *Sword and the Scepter: The Problem of Militarism in Germany-The Tragedy of Statesmanship : Bethmann Hollweg As War Chancellor, 1914-1917* (1972); *The Sword and the Scepter: The Reign of German Militarism and the Disaster of 1918* (1988)
- Stone, David J. *Fighting for the Fatherland: The Story of the German Soldier from 1648 to the Present Day* (2006)
- Thomas, Charles S. *The German Navy in the Nazi Era* (1990)

External links

 Wikimedia Commons has media related to *Military history of Germany*.

- Web Sources for Military History[79]
- West Point Atlas[80], especially for World Wars I and II
- Documents of German unification[81] (in English)
- Clausewitz Homepage[82]
- Primary documents from 18th and 19th century German history[83] (links and background in English, documents in German).
- Maps of nineteenth century German unification[84]
- Hussite Wars[85]

History of Germany during World War I

Part of **a series** on the
History of Germany

Topics

- Chronology
- Historiography
- Military history
- Economic history
- Women's history
- Territorial evolution
- List of German monarchs

Early history

- Germanic peoples
- Migration Period
- Frankish Empire

Middle Ages

- East Francia
- Kingdom of Germany
- Holy Roman Empire
- Eastward settlement

Early Modern period

- Sectionalism
- 18th century
- Kingdom of Prussia

Unification

- Confederation of the Rhine
  - German Confederation
  - *Zollverein*
- German revolutions of 1848
- North German Confederation

German Reich

German Empire	1871–1918
World War I	1914–1918
Weimar Republic	1918–1933
Nazi Germany	1933–1945

Contemporary Germany

• Occupation • *Ostgebiete*	1945–1952
Expulsion of Germans	1944–1950
Cold War	1945–1990
• Reunification • New federal states	1990
Reunified Germany	1990–present
■ Germany portal	

- v
- t
- e[86]

During World War I, the German Empire was one of the Central Powers that lost the war. It began participation in the conflict after the declaration of war against Serbia by its ally, Austria-Hungary. German forces fought the Allies on both the eastern and western fronts, although German territory itself remained relatively safe from widespread invasion for most of the war, except for a brief period in 1914 when East Prussia was invaded. A tight blockade imposed by the Royal Navy caused severe food shortages in the cities, especially in the winter of 1916–17, known as the Turnip Winter. At the end of the war, Germany's defeat and widespread popular discontent triggered the German Revolution of 1918–19 which overthrew the monarchy and established the Weimar Republic.

Overview

The German population responded to the outbreak of war in 1914 with a complex mix of emotions, in a similar way to the populations in other countries of Europe; notions of overt enthusiasm known as the Spirit of 1914 have been challenged by more recent scholarship.[87] The German government, dominated by the Junkers, thought of the war as a way to end Germany's disputes with rivals France, Russia and Britain. The beginning of war was presented in Germany as the chance for the nation to secure "our place under the sun," as the Foreign Minister Bernhard von Bülow had put it, which was readily supported by prevalent nationalism among the public. The Kaiser and the German establishment hoped the war would unite the public behind the monarchy, and lessen the threat posed by the dramatic growth of the Social Democratic Party of Germany, which had been the most vocal critic of the Kaiser in the Reichstag before the war. Despite its membership in the Second International, the Social Democratic Party of Germany ended its differences with the Imperial government and abandoned its principles of internationalism to support the war effort.

Figure 31: *World War I mobilization, 1 August 1914*

It soon became apparent that Germany was not prepared for a war lasting more than a few months. At first, little was done to regulate the economy for a wartime footing, and the German war economy would remain badly organized throughout the war. Germany depended on imports of food and raw materials, which were stopped by the British blockade of Germany. Food prices were first limited, then rationing was introduced. In 1915 five million pigs were massacred in the so-called Schweinemord to both make food and preserve grain. The winter of 1916/17 was called "turnip winter" because the potato harvest was poor and people ate animal feed including vile-tasting turnips. During the war from August 1914 to mid-1919, the excess deaths over peacetime caused by malnutrition and high rates of exhaustion and disease and despair came to about 474,000 civilians.[88]

1914–15

The German army opened the war on the Western Front with a modified version of the Schlieffen Plan, designed to quickly attack France through neutral Belgium before turning southwards to encircle the French army on the German border. The Belgians fought back, and sabotaged their rail system to delay the Germans. The Germans did not expect this and were delayed, and responded with systematic reprisals on civilians, killing nearly 6,000 Belgian

Figure 32: *German soldiers on the way to the front in 1914. A message on the freight car spells out "Trip to Paris"; early in the war, all sides expected the conflict to be a short one.*

noncombatants, including women and children, and burning 25,000 houses and buildings.[89] The plan called for the right flank of the German advance to converge on Paris and initially, the Germans were very successful, particularly in the Battle of the Frontiers (14–24 August). By 12 September, the French with assistance from the British forces halted the German advance east of Paris at the First Battle of the Marne (5–12 September). The last days of this battle signified the end of mobile warfare in the west. The French offensive into Germany launched on 7 August with the Battle of Mulhouse had limited success.[90]

In the east, only one Field Army defended East Prussia and when Russia attacked in this region it diverted German forces intended for the Western Front. Germany defeated Russia in a series of battles collectively known as the First Battle of Tannenberg (17 August – 2 September), but this diversion exacerbated problems of insufficient speed of advance from rail-heads not foreseen by the German General Staff. The Central Powers were thereby denied a quick victory and forced to fight a war on two fronts. The German army had fought its way into a good defensive position inside France and had permanently incapacitated 230,000 more French and British troops than it had lost itself.

Figure 33: *In this contemporary drawing by Heinrich Zille, the German soldiers bound westwards to France and those bound eastwards to Russia smilingly salute each other.*

Despite this, communications problems and questionable command decisions cost Germany the chance of obtaining an early victory.

1916

1916 was characterized by two great battles on the Western front, at Verdun and the Somme. They each lasted most of the year, achieved minimal gains, and drained away the best soldiers of both sides. Verdun became the iconic symbol of the murderous power of modern defensive weapons, with 280,000 German casualties, and 315,000 French. At the Somme, there were over 400,000 German casualties, against over 600,000 Allied casualties. At Verdun, the Germans attacked what they considered to be a weak French salient which nevertheless the French would defend for reasons of national pride. The Somme was part of a multinational plan of the Allies to attack on different fronts simultaneously. German woes were also compounded by Russia's grand "Brusilov offensive", where although Germany suffered less than their allies with $\sim$150,000 of the $\sim$770,000 Central powers casualties, were simultaneous to the Somme offensive and with German already committed to the Verdun offensive. German experts are divided in their interpretation of

Figure 34: *German soldiers digging trenches*

the Somme. Some say it was a standoff, but most see it as a British victory and argue it marked the point at which German morale began a permanent decline and the strategic initiative was lost, along with irreplaceable veterans and confidence.[91]

1917

In early 1917 the SPD leadership became concerned about the activity of its anti-war left-wing which had been organising as the *Sozialdemokratische Arbeitsgemeinschaft* (SAG, "Social Democratic Working Group"). On 17 January they expelled them, and on April 1917 the left-wing went on to form the *Independent Social Democratic Party of Germany* (German: *Unabhängige Sozialdemokratische Partei Deutschlands*). The remaining faction was then known as the *Majority Social Democratic Party of Germany*. This happened as the enthusiasm for war faded with the enormous numbers of casualties, the dwindling supply of manpower, the mounting difficulties on the homefront, and the never-ending flow of casualty reports. A grimmer and grimmer attitude began to prevail amongst the general population. The highlight only was the first use of mustard gas in warfare, in the Battle of Ypres.

After, morale was helped by victories against Serbia, Greece, Italy, and Russia which made great gains for the Central Powers. Morale was at its greatest since 1914 at the end of 1917 and beginning of 1918 with the defeat of Russia

Figure 35: *German soldiers operating a flamethrower in 1917*

following her rise into revolution, and the German people braced for what Ludendorff said would be the "Peace Offensive" in the west.[92,93]

1918

In spring 1918, Germany realized that time was running out. It prepared for the decisive strike with new armies and new tactics, hoping to win the war on the Western front before millions of American soldiers appeared in battle. General Erich Ludendorff and Field Marshal Paul von Hindenburg had full control of the army, they had a large supply of reinforcements moved from the Eastern front, and they trained storm troopers with new tactics to race through the trenches and attack the enemy's command and communications centers. The new tactics would indeed restore mobility to the Western front, but the German army was too optimistic.

During the winter of 1917-18 it was "quiet" on the Western Front—British casualties averaged "only" 3,000 a week. Serious attacks were impossible in the winter because of the deep caramel-thick mud. Quietly the Germans brought in their best soldiers from the eastern front, selected elite storm troops, and trained them all winter in the new tactics. With stopwatch timing, the German artillery would lay down a sudden, fearsome barrage just ahead of its advancing infantry. Moving in small units, firing light machine guns, the storm troopers would bypass enemy strongpoints, and head directly for critical bridges, command posts, supply dumps and, above all, artillery batteries. By cutting enemy communications they would paralyze response in the critical first half hour. By silencing the artillery they would break the enemy's firepower. Rigid schedules sent in two more waves of infantry to mop up the strong points that had been bypassed. The shock troops frightened and disoriented the first line of defenders, who would flee in panic. In one instance an easy-going Allied regiment broke and fled; reinforcements rushed in on bicycles. The panicky men seized the bikes and beat an even faster retreat. The stormtrooper tactics provided mobility, but not increased firepower. Eventually—in 1939 and 1940—the formula would be perfected with the aid of dive bombers and tanks, but in 1918 the Germans lacked both.[94]

Ludendorff erred by attacking the British first in 1918, instead of the French. He mistakenly thought the British to be too uninspired to respond rapidly to the new tactics. The exhausted, dispirited French perhaps might have folded. The German assaults on the British were ferocious—the largest of the entire war. At the Somme River in March, 63 divisions attacked in a blinding fog. No matter, the German lieutenants had memorized their maps and their orders. The British lost 270,000 men, fell back 40 miles, and then held. They quickly learned how to handle the new German tactics: fall back, abandon the trenches, let the attackers overextend themselves, and then counterattack. They gained an advantage in firepower from their artillery and from tanks used as mobile pillboxes that could retreat and counterattack at will. In April Ludendorff hit the British again, inflicting 305,000 casualties—but he lacked the reserves to follow up. Ludendorff launched five great attacks between March and July, inflicting a million British and French casualties. The Western Front now had opened up—the trenches were still there but the importance of mobility now reasserted itself. The Allies held. The Germans suffered as many casualties as they inflicted, including most of their precious stormtroopers. The new German replacements were under-aged youth or embittered middle-aged family men in poor condition. They were not inspired by the elan of 1914, nor thrilled with battle—they hated it, and some began talking of revolution. Ludendorff could not replace his losses, nor could he devise a new brainstorm that might somehow snatch victory from the jaws of defeat. The British likewise were bringing in boys and men aged 50, but since their home front was in good condition, and since they could see the Americans arriving steadily, their morale was higher. The great German spring offensive was a race against time, for everyone could see the Americans were training millions of fresh young men who would eventually arrive on the Western Front.[95,96]

The attrition warfare now caught up to both sides. Germany had used up all the best soldiers they had, and still had not conquered much territory. The British were out of fresh manpower, the French nearly so. Berlin had calculated it would take months for the Americans to ship all their men and supplies—but

Figure 36: *German troops in Kiev, March 1918*

the U.S. troops arrived much sooner, as they left their supplies behind, and relied on British and French artillery, tanks, airplanes, trucks and equipment. Berlin also assumed that Americans were fat, undisciplined and unaccustomed to hardship and severe fighting. They soon realized their mistake. The Germans reported that "The qualities of the [Americans] individually may be described as remarkable. They are physically well set up, their attitude is good... They lack at present only training and experience to make formidable adversaries. The men are in fine spirits and are filled with naive assurance."

By September 1918, the Central Powers were exhausted from fighting, and the American forces were pouring into France at a rate of 10,000 a day. The decisive Allied counteroffensive, known as the Hundred Days Offensive, began on 8 August 1918—what Ludendorff called the "Black Day of the German army." The Allied armies advanced steadily as German defenses faltered.

Although German armies were still on enemy soil as the war ended, the generals, the civilian leadership—and indeed the soldiers and the people—knew all was hopeless. They started looking for scapegoats. The hunger and popular dissatisfaction with the war precipitated revolution throughout Germany. By 11 November Germany had virtually surrendered, the Kaiser and all the royal families had abdicated, and the Empire had been replaced by the Weimar Republic.

Figure 37: *Military propaganda postcard: Wounded soldiers cheer to the German Emperor Wilhelm II, who is in a car.*

Home front

War fever

The "spirit of 1914" was the overwhelming, enthusiastic support of all elements of the population for war in 1914. In the Reichstag, the vote for credits was unanimous, with all the Socialists joining in. One professor testified to a "great single feeling of moral elevation of soaring of religious sentiment, in short, the ascent of a whole people to the heights."[97] At the same time, there was a level of anxiety; most commentators predicted the short victorious war – but that hope was dashed in a matter of weeks, as the invasion of Belgium bogged down and the French Army held in front of Paris. The Western Front became a killing machine, as neither army moved more than a few hundred yards at a time. Industry in late 1914 was in chaos, unemployment soared while it took months to reconvert to munitions productions. In 1916, the Hindenburg Program called for the mobilization of all economic resources to produce artillery, shells, and machine guns. Church bells and copper roofs were ripped out and melted down.[98]

Figure 38: *Collecting scrap metal for the war effort, 1916*

Economy

Germany had no plans for mobilizing its civilian economy for the war effort, and no stockpiles of food or critical supplies had been made. Germany had to improvise rapidly. All major political sectors initially supported the war, including the Socialists.

Early in the war industrialist Walter Rathenau held senior posts in the Raw Materials Department of the War Ministry, while becoming chairman of AEG upon his father's death in 1915. Rathenau played the key role in convincing the War Ministry to set up the War Raw Materials Department (Kriegsrohstoffabteilung - 'KRA'); he was in charge of it from August 1914 to March 1915 and established the basic policies and procedures. His senior staff were on loan from industry. KRA focused on raw materials threatened by the British blockade, as well as supplies from occupied Belgium and France. It set prices and regulated the distribution to vital war industries. It began the development of ersatz raw materials. KRA suffered many inefficiencies caused by the complexity and selfishness KRA encountered from commerce, industry, and the government.[99,100]

While the KRA handled critical raw materials, the crisis over food supplies grew worse. The mobilization of so many farmers and horses, and the shortages of fertilizer, steadily reduced the food supply. Prisoners of war were sent to work on farms, and many women and elderly men took on work roles. Supplies that had once come in from Russia and Austria were cut off.[101]

The concept of "total war" in World War I, meant that food supplies had to be redirected towards the armed forces and, with German commerce being stopped by the British blockade, German civilians were forced to live in increasingly meager conditions. Food prices were first controlled. Bread rationing was introduced in 1915 and worked well; the cost of bread fell. Allen says there were no signs of starvation and states, "the sense of domestic catastrophe one gains from most accounts of food rationing in Germany is exaggerated."[102] However Howard argues that hundreds of thousands of civilians died from malnutrition—usually from a typhus or a disease their weakened body could not resist. (Starvation itself rarely caused death.)[103] A 2014 study, derived from a recently discovered dataset on the heights and weights of German children between 1914-1924, found evidence that German children suffered from severe malnutrition during the blockade, with working-class children suffering the most. The study furthermore found that German children quickly recovered after the war due to a massive international food aid program.

Conditions deteriorated rapidly on the home front, with severe food shortages reported in all urban areas. The causes involved the transfer of so many farmers and food workers into the military, combined with the overburdened railroad system, shortages of coal, and the British blockade that cut off imports from abroad. The winter of 1916-1917 was known as the "turnip winter," because that hardly-edible vegetable, usually fed to livestock, was used by people as a substitute for potatoes and meat, which were increasingly scarce. Thousands of soup kitchens were opened to feed the hungry people, who grumbled that the farmers were keeping the food for themselves. Even the army had to cut the rations for soldiers.[104] Morale of both civilians and soldiers continued to sink.

The drafting of miners reduced the main energy source, coal. The textile factories produced Army uniforms, and warm clothing for civilians ran short. The device of using ersatz materials, such as paper and cardboard for cloth and leather proved unsatisfactory. Soap was in short supply, as was hot water. All the cities reduced tram services, cut back on street lighting, and close down theaters and cabarets.

The food supply increasingly focused on potatoes and bread, it was harder and harder to buy meat. The meat ration in late 1916 was only 31% of peacetime, and it fell to 12% in late 1918. The fish ration was 51% in 1916, and none at all by late 1917. The rations for cheese, butter, rice, cereals, eggs and lard were less than 20% of peacetime levels.[105] In 1917 the harvest was poor all across Europe, and the potato supply ran short, and Germans substituted almost inedible turnips; the "turnip winter" of 1916–17 was remembered with bitter

History of Germany during World War I 65

Figure 39: *Wartime ration stamps in Bavaria*

distaste for generations.[106] Early in the war introduced bread rationing, and the system worked fairly well, albeit with shortfalls during the Turnip Winter and summer of 1918. White bread used imported flour and became unavailable, but there was enough rye or rye-potato flour to provide a minimal diet for all civilians.[107]

German women were not employed in the Army, but large numbers took paid employment in industry and factories, and even larger numbers engaged in volunteer services. Housewives were taught how to cook without milk, eggs or fat; agencies helped widows find work. Banks, insurance companies and government offices for the first time hired women for clerical positions. Factories hired them for unskilled labor – by December 1917, half the workers in chemicals, metals, and machine tools were women. Laws protecting women in the workplace were relaxed, and factories set up canteens to provide food for their workers, lest their productivity fall off. The food situation in 1918 was better, because the harvest was better, but serious shortages continued, with high prices, and a complete lack of condiments and fresh fruit. Many migrants had flocked into cities to work in industry, which made for overcrowded housing. Reduced coal supplies left everyone in the cold. Daily life involved long working hours, poor health, and little or no recreation, an increasing fears for the safety of loved ones in the Army and in prisoner of war camp. The men

Figure 40: *Demobilization after World War I*

who returned from the front were those who had been permanently crippled; wounded soldiers who had recovered were sent back to the trenches.[108]

Defeat and revolt

Many Germans wanted an end to the war and increasing numbers of Germans began to associate with the political left, such as the Social Democratic Party and the more radical Independent Social Democratic Party which demanded an end to the war. The third reason was the entry of the United States into the war in April 1917, which changed the long-run balance of power in favor of the Allies. The end of October 1918, in Kiel, in northern Germany, saw the beginning of the German Revolution of 1918–19. Civilian dock workers led a revolt and convinced many sailors to join them; the revolt quickly spread to other cities. Meanwhile, Hindenburg and the senior generals lost confidence in the Kaiser and his government.

In November 1918, with internal revolution, a stalemated war, Bulgaria and the Ottoman Empire suing for peace, Austria-Hungary falling apart from multiple ethnic tensions, and pressure from the German high command, the Kaiser and all German ruling princes abdicated. On 9 November 1918, the Social Democrat Philipp Scheidemann proclaimed a Republic, in cooperation with the business and middle classes, not the revolting workers. The new government led by the German Social Democrats called for and received an armistice on 11 November 1918; in practice it was a surrender, and the Allies kept up the food blockade to guarantee an upper hand. The war was over; the history books closed on the German Empire. It was succeeded by the democratic, yet flawed, Weimar Republic.[109]

Seven million soldiers and sailors were quickly demobilized, and they became a conservative voice that drowned out the radical left in cities such as Kiel and Berlin. The radicals formed the Spartakusbund and later the Communist Party of Germany.

Germany lost the war because it was decisively defeated by a stronger military power; it was out of soldiers and ideas, and was losing ground every day by October 1918. Nevertheless, it was still in France when the war ended on Nov. 11 giving die-hard nationalists the chance to blame the civilians back home for betraying the army and surrendering. This was the false "Stab-in-the-back legend" that soured German politics in the 1920s and caused a distrust of democracy and the Weimar government.[110]

War deaths

Out of a population of 65 million, Germany suffered 1.7 million military deaths and 430,000 civilian deaths due to wartime causes (especially the food blockade), plus about 17,000 killed in Africa and the other overseas colonies.[111]

The Allied blockade continued until July 1919, causing severe additional hardships.[112]

Soldiers' experiences

Despite the often ruthless conduct of the German military machine, in the air and at sea as well as on land, individual German soldiers could view the enemy with respect and empathy and the war with contempt.[113] Some examples from letters home:

"A terrible picture presented itself to me. A French and a German soldier on their knees were leaning against each other. They had pierced each other with the bayonet and had dropped like this to the ground...Courage, heroism, does it really exist? I am about to doubt it, since I haven't seen anything else than fear, anxiety, and despair in every face during the battle. There was nothing at all like courage, bravery, or the like. In reality, there is nothing else than terrible discipline and coercion propelling the soldiers forward" Dominik Richert, 1914.[114]

"Our men have reached an agreement with the French to cease fire. They bring us bread, wine, sardines etc., we bring them schnapps. The masters

make war, they have a quarrel, and the workers, the little men...have to stand there fighting against each other. Is that not a great stupidity?...If this were to be decided according to the number of votes, we would have been long home by now" Hermann Baur, 1915.[115]

"I have no idea what we are still fighting for anyway, maybe because the newspapers portray everything about the war in a false light which has nothing to do with the reality.....There could be no greater misery in the enemy country and at home. The people who still support the war haven't got a clue about anything...If I stay alive, I will make these things public...We all want peace...What is the point of conquering half of the world, when we have to sacrifice all our strength?..You out there, just champion peace! ... We give away all our worldly possessions and even our freedom. Our only goal is to be with our wife and children again," Anonymous Bavarian soldier, 17 October 1914.[116]

Further reading

- Watson, Alexander. *Ring of Steel: Germany and Austria-Hungary in World War I* (2014), excerpt[117]

Military

- Cecil, Lamar (1996), *Wilhelm II: Emperor and Exile, 1900-1941*, **II**, Chapel Hill, North Carolina: University of North Carolina Press, p. 176, ISBN 0-8078-2283-3, OCLC 186744003[118]
- Chickering, Roger, et al. eds. *Great War, Total War: Combat and Mobilization on the Western Front, 1914-1918 (Publications of the German Historical Institute)* (2000). ISBN 0-521-77352-0. 584 pgs.
- Cowin, Hugh W. *German and Austrian Aviation of World War I: A Pictorial Chronicle of the Airmen and Aircraft That Forged German Airpower* (2000). Osprey Pub Co. ISBN 1-84176-069-2. 96 pgs.
- Cruttwell, C.R.M.F. *A History of the Great War: 1914-1918* (1935) ch 15-29 online free[119]
- Cross, Wilbur (1991), *Zeppelins of World War I*, ISBN 1-55778-382-9
- Herwig, Holger H. *The First World War: Germany and Austria-Hungary 1914-1918* (1996), mostly military
- Horne, John, ed. *A Companion to World War I* (2012)
- Hubatsch, Walther; Backus, Oswald P (1963), *Germany and the Central Powers in the World War, 1914–1918*, Lawrence, Kansas: University of Kansas, OCLC 250441891[120]

- Kitchen, Martin. *The Silent Dictatorship: The Politics of the German High Command under Hindenburg and Ludendorff, 1916–1918* (London: Croom Helm, 1976)
- Morrow, John. *German Air Power in World War I* (U. of Nebraska Press, 1982); Contains design and production figures, as well as economic influences.
- Sheldon, Jack (2005). *The German Army on the Somme: 1914 - 1916*. Barnsley: Pen and Sword Books Ltd. ISBN 1-84415-269-3.

The miltarism mean the countries need to develop military or army levels From 1880 to 1914,the military expenditure of the six bog powers(viz.Germany,Russia,Austria,Italy,France,and Britain)

Home front

- Allen, Keith. "Sharing Scarcity: Bread Rationing and the First World War in Berlin, 1914– 1923," *Journal of Social History* (1998), 32#2, pp. 371–96.
- Armeson, Robert. *Total Warfare and Compulsory Labor: A Study of the Military-Industrial Complex in Germany during World War I* (The Hague: M. Nijhoff, 1964)
- Bailey, S. "The Berlin Strike of 1918," *Central European History* (1980), 13#2, pp. 158–74.
- Bell, Archibald. *A History of the Blockade of Germany and the Countries Associated with Her in the Great War, Austria-Hungary, Bulgaria, and Turkey, 1914–1918* (London: H. M. Stationery Office, 1937)
- Broadberry, Stephen and Mark Harrison, eds. *The Economics of World War I* (2005) ISBN 0-521-85212-9. Covers France, UK, USA, Russia, Italy, Germany, Austria-Hungary, the Ottoman Empire, and the Netherlands
- Burchardt, Lothar. "The Impact of the War Economy on the Civilian Population of Germany during the First and the Second World Wars," in *The German Military in the Age of Total War,* edited by Wilhelm Deist, 111–36. Leamington Spa: Berg, 1985.
- Chickering, Roger. *Imperial Germany and the Great War, 1914–1918* (1998), wide-ranging survey
- Daniel, Ute. *The War from Within: German Working-Class Women in the First World War* (1997)
- Dasey, Robyn. "Women's Work and the Family: Women Garment Workers in Berlin and Hamburg before the First World War," in *The German Family: Essays on the Social History of the Family in Nineteenth-and Twentieth-Century Germany,* edited by Richard J. Evans and W. R. Lee, (London: Croom Helm, 1981), pp. 221–53.

- Davis, Belinda J. *Home Fires Burning: Food, Politics, and Everyday Life in World War I Berlin* (2000) online edition[121]
- Dobson, Sean. *Authority and Upheaval in Leipzig, 1910–1920* (2000).
- Domansky, Elisabeth. "Militarization and Reproduction in World War I Germany," in *Society, Culture, and the State in Germany, 1870–1930*, edited by Geoff Eley, (University of Michigan Press, 1996), pp. 427–64.
- Donson, Andrew. "Why did German youth become fascists? Nationalist males born 1900 to 1908 in war and revolution," *Social History*, Aug2006, Vol. 31, Issue 3, pp. 337–358
- Feldman, Gerald D. "The Political and Social Foundations of Germany's Economic Mobilization, 1914-1916," *Armed Forces & Society* (1976), 3#1, pp. 121–145. online[122]
- Feldman, Gerald. *Army, Industry, and Labor in Germany, 1914–1918* (1966)
- Ferguson, Niall *The Pity of War* (1999), cultural and economic themes, worldwide
- Hardach, Gerd. *The First World War 1914-1918* (1977), economics
- Herwig, Holger H. *The First World War: Germany and Austria-Hungary 1914-1918* (1996), one third on the homefront
- Howard, N.P. "The Social and Political Consequences of the Allied Food Blockade of Germany, 1918-19," *German History* (1993), 11#2, pp. 161–88 online[123]
- Kocka, Jürgen. *Facing total war: German society, 1914-1918* (1984). online at ACLS e-books[124]
- Lee, Joe. "German Administrators and Agriculture during the First World War," in *War and Economic Development*, edited by Jay M. Winter. (Cambridge University Press, 1975).
- Marquis, H. G. "Words as Weapons: Propaganda in Britain and Germany during the First World War." *Journal of Contemporary History* (1978) 12: 467–98.
- McKibbin, David. *War and Revolution in Leipzig, 1914–1918: Socialist Politics and Urban Evolution in a German City* (University Press of America, 1998).
- Moeller, Robert G. "Dimensions of Social Conflict in the Great War: A View from the Countryside," *Central European History* (1981), 14#2, pp. 142–68.
- Moeller, Robert G. *German Peasants and Agrarian Politics, 1914–1924: The Rhineland and Westphalia* (1986). online edition[125]
- Offer, Avner. *The First World War: An Agrarian Interpretation* (1991), on food supply of Britain and Germany
- Osborne, Eric. *Britain's Economic Blockade of Germany, 1914-1919* (2004)

- Richie, Alexandra. *Faust's Metropolis: a History of Berlin* (1998), pp. 234–83.
- Ryder, A. J. *The German Revolution of 1918* (Cambridge University Press, 1967)
- Siney, Marion. *The Allied Blockade of Germany, 1914–1916* (1957)
- Steege, Paul. *Black Market, Cold War: Everyday Life in Berlin, 1946-1949* (2008) excerpt and text search[126]
- Terraine, John. "'An Actual Revolutionary Situation': In 1917 there was little to sustain German morale at home," *History Today* (1978), 28#1, pp. 14–22, online
- Tobin, Elizabeth. "War and the Working Class: The Case of Düsseldorf, 1914–1918," *Central European History* (1985), 13#3, pp. 257–98
- Triebel, Armin. "Consumption in Wartime Germany," in *The Upheaval of War: Family, Work, and Welfare in Europe, 1914–1918* edited by Richard Wall and Jay M. Winter, (Cambridge University Press, 1988), pp. 159–96.
- Usborne, Cornelie. "Pregnancy Is a Woman's Active Service," in *The Upheaval of War: Family, Work, and Welfare in Europe, 1914–1918* edited by Richard Wall and Jay M. Winter, (Cambridge University Press, 1988), pp. 289–416.
- Verhey, Jeffrey. *The Spirit of 1914. Militarism, Myth and Mobilization in Germany* (Cambridge University Press 2000)
- Welch, David. *Germany and Propaganda in World War I: Pacifism, Mobilization and Total War* (IB Tauris, 2014)
- Winter, Jay, and Jean-Louis Robert, eds. *Capital Cities at War: Paris, London, Berlin 1914-1919* (2 vol. 1999, 2007), 30 chapters 1200pp; comprehensive coverage by scholars vol 1 excerpt[127]; vol 2 excerpt and text search[128]
- Winter, Jay. *Sites of Memory, Sites of Mourning: The Great War in European Cultural History* (1995)
- Ziemann, Benjamin. *War Experiences in Rural Germany, 1914-1923* (Berg, 2007) online edition[129]

Primary sources

- Gooch, P. G. *Recent Revelations Of European Diplomacy* (1940). pp3–100
- Lutz, Ralph Haswell, ed. *Fall of the German Empire, 1914–1918* (2 vol 1932). 868pp online review[130], primary sources

External links

- (in German) "Der Erste Weltkrieg"[131] (in English) "The First World War"[132] at Living Museum Online (LeMO)
- Articles relating to Germany[133] at 1914-1918 Online: International Encyclopedia of the First World War
  - Hirschfeld, Gerhard: Germany[134]
  - Fehlemann, Silke: Bereavement and Mourning (Germany)[135]
  - Bruendel, Steffen: Between Acceptance and Refusal - Soldiers' Attitudes Towards War (Germany)[136]
  - Davis, Belinda: Food and Nutrition (Germany)[137]
  - Oppelland, Torsten: Governments, Parliaments and Parties (Germany)[138]
  - Stibbe, Matthew: Women's Mobilisation for War (Germany)[139]
  - Ungern-Sternberg, Jürgen von: Making Sense of the War (Germany)[140]
  - Ullmann, Hans-Peter: Organization of War Economies (Germany)[141]
  - Gross, Stephen: War Finance (Germany)[142]
  - Altenhöner, Florian: Press/Journalism (Germany)[143]
  - Ther, Vanessa: Propaganda at Home (Germany)[144]
  - Pöhlmann, Markus: Warfare 1914-1918 (Germany)[145]
  - Löffelbein, Nils: War Aims and War Aims Discussions (Germany)[146]
  - Whalen, Robert Weldon: War Losses (Germany)[147]
- Germany and the First World War[148] article index at Spartacus Educational
- Posters of the German Military Government in the Generalgouvernement Warshau (German occupied Poland) from World War I, 1915-1916[149] From the Collections at the Library of Congress

Command Structure

Command and obedience in the Bundeswehr

The principle of **command and obedience in the Bundeswehr** (German: *Befehl und Gehorsam*), along with the concept of "citizens in uniform" (German: *Staatsbürger in Uniform*), was central to the 1953 idea of "leadership development and civic education" (official translation of German: *Innere Führung*[150]). The revised definition of military orders and obedience, as well as superior-subordinate relations by the former "Amt Blank" (Blank Agency, predecessor of the Federal Ministry of Defense), was a 1950s result of Nazi German excesses. Central aims were the reduction of power to command by superiors and a shared responsibility for obedience by subordinates.[151]

Military orders

A military order is defined in § 2 (2) of the German military penal law (German: *Wehrstrafgesetz*, WStG) as an:

- instruction for a defined behavior (*Anweisung zu einem bestimmten Verhalten*)
- given by a military superior to his subordinate
- in written, oral or other form (for example, signals or signs)
- generally, or in a single case
- with claim of obedience (*Anspruch auf Gehorsam*).[152]

An instruction might be a military order, if a soldier was a defined military superior by the Ministerial Directive Governing Superior-Subordinate Relations (German: *Vorgesetztenverordnung*). If an order was given by someone not a military superior, it would be juridically called a "military non-order" (without claim of obedience). Fundamentally, a superior is responsible for his orders and obligated to implement his instructions. He may only give orders concerning official aims and respecting international and national laws and the general directives issued by the Ministry.[153] He is fundamentally responsible for the consequences of his orders. Whenever possible, military orders should include a description of the task and its aim. This is known as *Auftragstaktik*, and would enable subordinates to act to achieve the order's aim in changed circumstances.[154]

Superior-subordinate relations

The command relationships in the Bundeswehr are defined in the Ministerial Directive Governing Superior-Subordinate Relations (official translation of German: *Verordnung über die Regelung des militärischen Vorgesetztenverhältnisses*, abbreviated *Vorgesetztenverordnung* (VorgV)). These service regulations were decreed March 19, 1956, shortly before the first soldiers joined the newly founded Bundeswehr, and went into effect June 7, 1956. They were modified by decree October 7, 1981. The *Vorgesetztenverordnung* applies only to Bundeswehr soldiers and does not apply to civilian personnel of the Bundeswehr. Superior-subordinate relations of civilian Bundeswehr members (as well as military-civilian or civilian-military superior-subordinate relations) are defined by other regulations and ordinances. The content of the *Vorgesetztenverordnung* is one of the first things that recruits are required to learn.

Superior positions

§§ 1-3 VorgV concern the assignment of a superior. It is possible for a soldier to be superior to another in several ways. The following types of superiors are defined:[155]

Who?	Whom?	When?	What?	Remarks
§ 1 **Immediate superior** (German: *Unmittelbarer Vorgesetzter*, general commanding position)				
Leader of a military unit (platoons, companies, battalions, divisions and so forth)	Soldiers of his unit	Superior: always Subordinate: always	Everything the general order authorization will include	Immediate superiors are urged not to interfere in professional affairs (see § 2 VorgV)
Example: squad leader -> soldiers of his squad Note: Superiorship according to this paragraph - somewhat confusingly called "immediate" - is the entire chain of command known from other armies, and usually consists of a team (*Trupp*) leader, a squad (*Gruppe*) leader, a platoon (*Zug*) leader, a company "chief", a bataillon or regimental commander, a brigade commander, a division commander, a corps commander (until the 1990s), the commander of the troops of the respective branch of service, the "inspector" of the respective branch of service, the "Inspector General" (chief of staff; only since 2012, even though he was even previously recognized as the highest-ranking soldier) and the Minister of Defence. President and, outside a state of defence, Chancellor are not superiors, even though they are to be saluted. It is quite acceptable to bypass the team-leader and, after basic training when no direct military field training issues are concerned, also the squad leader and deal immediately with the platoon leader.				

Command and obedience in the Bundeswehr

§ 2 Professional superior (German: *Fachvorgesetzter*, special commanding position)				
Assignment holder, who is responsible for the professional service of a unit/office	For professional-service subordinate soldiers	Superior: on duty Subordinate: on duty	Only for professional purposes	These assignments are only defined for the medical service, geographic information service (MILGEO) and military music service. Usually, the professional leader in a military unit/office is not the same as the immediate superior (§ 1 VorgV) of it.

Example:
Admiralarzt der Marine (admiral surgeon of the navy) -> Military physicians and medical soldiers of the navy, concerning medical affairs

§ 3 Superior due to a special assignment (German: *Vorgesetzter mit besonderem Aufgabenbereich*, special commanding position)				
Holder of a special defined assignment or function	Service-regulated or instruction-defined subordinate soldiers	Superior: on duty Subordinate: always	Everything necessary for task fulfillment	Such assignments or functions (which are associated with special task responsibilities) are defined in general service regulations or special working instructions. In some cases, it might be possible that a lower rank is defined as superior to a higher rank.

Figure 41: *Guard post: superior to passing soldiers due to the special defined assignment (§ 3 VorgV)*

Examples:
- Training sergeant -> trainee (also when he has an officer rank; relationship must be defined in a special working instruction)
- *Kompaniefeldwebel* (coll. *"Spieß"*, comparable to a First Sergeant) -> soldiers of the same unit with ranks up to Hauptfeldwebel in indoor duty affairs (generally defined in Central Service Regulations)
- Guard soldier -> all soldiers within the guard responsibility area, even those who are his direct superiors (§1) in normal service, except his guard-service-superiors (the superiors within the guard platoon itself, with the officer of the guard at top; and then e. g. the barracks commandant; the commander of the battalion stationed in the barracks; and the latter's direct superiors)
- Feldjäger on duty -> other soldiers
- *Truppenarzt* (military physician, responsible for health care of a battalion/regiment) -> patient (concerning treatment)

§ 4 Superior due to rank (or rank class/group) (German: *Vorgesetzter aufgrund des Dienstgrades*, general commanding position)

see also: German Army rank insignia

§ 4 (1) In companies of equivalents, as well as internal vessel crews

Officer ranks (OF-1 - OF-9)	NCO or private ranks (OR-1 - OR-9)	companies: Superior: on duty Subordinate: on duty vessels: Superior (when also § 1 superior & crew member): always Superior (crew and non-crew members): always	Everything the general order authorization includes	
Unteroffizier mit Portepee (sergeant ranks, NCO OR-6 - OR-9)	*Unteroffizier ohne Portepee* and private ranks(OR-1 - OR-5)			
Unteroffizier ohne Portepee ranks (OR-5)	Private ranks (OR-1 - OR-4)			

§ 4 (2) In staffs and other units (differs from § 4 (1) VorgV)

Officer ranks (OF-1 - OF-9)	NCO or private ranks (OR-1 - OR-9)	Superior: on duty Subordinate: on duty	Everything the general order authorization includes	May be reduced to parts of his unit/office by a disciplinary superior of a battalion or higher

§ 4 (3) Internal (enclosed military facilities)

Officer ranks (OF-1 - OF-9)	NCO and private ranks (OR-1 - OR-9)	Superior: always Subordinate: always	Everything the general order authorization includes	"Enclosed military facilities" are barracks, office buildings and so on, posted with *Militärischer Sicherheitsbereich* (military security area) signs (not open-air training areas and so on).
NCO ranks (OR-5 - OR-9)	Private ranks (OR-1 - OR-4)			

§ 5 **Superior due to special order** (German: *Vorgesetzter aufgrund besonderer Anordnung*; special commanding position)

Superior ordered by a higher superior, who is allowed to subordinate other soldiers to him	Subordinate soldiers	Superior: on duty Subordinate: on duty	Everything necessary to fulfill the task	For the task, subordinate soldiers must be officially informed of the subordinate relationship. If essential, it might be possible to make a lower rank superior to a higher rank to fulfill a task.

Examples:
- Daily class duty in military schools is responsible to line the class for the roll call
- Leader of a military marching formation is responsible for commanding a unit from A to B

§ 6 **Superior due to own declaration** (German: *Vorgesetzter aufgrund eigener Erklärung*; coll. "emergency paragraph")

Command and obedience in the Bundeswehr

Officer/NCO self-declared to superior	Present soldiers	Defined case must be given Superior: always Subordinate: always	All essential to clear the situation	Self-declaration to superior of an officer/NCO is only possible if:
				• there is no higher rank on site
				• there is no §§ 1-3 or 5 superior on site
				• professional activities should be commanded by a qualified officer/NCO
				• one of the following cases prompts declaration of superior:
				  • situation needs emergency aid
				  • immediate action is necessary for maintenance of discipline
				  • uniform command at scene is required to clear a critical situation (although soldiers present are not hierarchically/organizationally associated)

Not mentioned in the *Vorgesetztenverordnung*, but recognized in practice (if rare), is "superiorship by consent of the subordinates": If no other superior is on site and either the situation is not an emergency, or none of those involved is at least an nco (hence cannot use § 6), then the soldier with the highest rank on site or one of them if several can command if the others don't object. (An example for this would be a group of privates off duty who, for the fun of it and perhaps for training, get the idea to march in formation to the canteen rather than simply go to it; as a march in formation needs a leader, to do so one of them must take step in as leader to march them there.)

Contradictory orders

If a subordinate receives an order contrary to an already-received order (or one which defers substantially the achievement of its aim), he must inform the superior who gave the second order of this. On the basis of this knowledge, the second superior would have (due to his order) responsibility to verify the given order and decide whether or not the subordinate had to obey his order (instead of the first received order). The subordinate must obey the last given order, if the second one is not canceled; this is necessary because the second superior may have new information about a changed situation. If a subordinate has not been able to execute the first order (or to attain the expected aim) because of the second order, he must inform the first superior as soon as possible. The subordinate is immune from punishment by him, because the second superior is responsible for his order.

Prioritization (in opposing superior relationships)

It may be possible for two soldiers to be superior to each other due to differing paragraphs of the *Vorgesetztenverordnung*. For such situations the following prioritization of relationship importance is defined:

> Superior by § 5 VorgV > § 3 VorgV > § 1 VorgV > § 2 VorgV > § 4 VorgV

§ 6 VorgV is excluded because a commissioned officer (or NCO) could only declare himself superior if there was no superior to him at the scene.

Obedience and disobedience

Duty of obedience

Above all, subordinates must obey their superiors and must inform superiors of non-executed orders or unreached aims. Subordinates must execute military orders:

- with their best effort
- completely and
- immediately.[156]

Although a superior must verify his orders, the recipient must also do so. First he would have to verify whether an instruction was given by a defined military superior according to the *Vorgesetztenverordnung*. If not, it would not be a military order with claim to obedience. If he executed this "military non-order", he would be responsible for possible consequences. If the instruction is given by a military superior, he must verify whether he must obey, may obey, or must refuse to obey. Generally he has to obey. He *may but need not* obey if the order has obviously no legitimate aim (e. g. "clean my boots" in usual situations), violates the soldier's *own* human dignity (e. g. "run into the city and shout that you are a fool"), or is unconscionable (e. g. obliges the soldier to spend amounts of his own money above limits mentioned in directives). He *must not* obey if the order violates *others'* human dignity, international law or consists of a crime (including a misdemeanor). Otherwise, subordinates are guilty of their deeds if their criminal character was obvious to them. Obviously-unavoidable errors may remain unpunished.[157]

Apart from that, it is not the soldier's job to investigate the entire legitimacy of the order; e. g. whether the not obviously lacking official aim actually existed, or whether non-penal laws or directives of the Ministry were complied with. In particular, a soldier must obey to commit a contravention. In these cases, the commanding superior has the entire responsibility for the act. It might, though, be comradely to bring an error to the superior's attention, and the soldier is not to be punished for doing so.

Penalties for disobedience and insubordination

Punishment for disobedience is regulated in the *Wehrstrafgesetz* (military penal law). Germany does not have any military courts; civilian courts have jurisdiction over military law. Subordinates who do not execute military orders with claim to obedience may be punished with imprisonment up to three years (in cases with "severe consequences" up to five years). "Severe consequences" means that the result of the disobedience either would have grave consequences for the security of Germany or for the combat worthiness of the forces, or that it caused death or severe bodily harm to another person.[158] Insubordination is the oral or physical revolt against military orders or the denial (in spite of repetition) of an order, and may be punished with imprisonment up to three years. In case of an initial revolt against a military order, a court could withhold sentencing if the subordinate executed the order voluntarily and in time afterwards.[159] If subordinates avoided executing orders frivolously, they could also be sentenced to imprisonment up to two years in cases of severe consequences.[160]

German Army

German Army

	German Army *Heer*
	Logo of the German Army
Founded	1955
Country	Germany
Type	Land force
Size	60,431 (28 February 2018) 265 aircraft
Motto(s)	To protect, help, moderate, and fight *Schützen, helfen, vermitteln, kämpfen*
Colors	Green, "Sand" and White
Anniversaries	November 12, 1955
Engagements	United Nations Operations in Somalia Aftermath of the Balkan Wars 1995-1999 Operation Libelle Kosovo War Battle of Tetovo Operation Essential Harvest War in Afghanistan North Kosovo crisis

Decorations	Badge of Honour of the Bundeswehr Military Proficiency Badge Badge of Marksmanship Service Medal Flood Service Medal 2002 Flood Service Medal 2013
Website	www<wbr/>.deutschesheer<wbr/>.de[161]
Commanders	
Current commander	Lieutenant General Jörg Vollmer
Notable commanders	General Ulrich de Maizière General Ernst Ferber, COMAFCENT 1973–1975 Lieutenant General Jörg Schönbohm, later Deputy Minister President of Brandenburg

The **German Army** (German: *Deutsches Heer*) is the land component of the armed forces of Germany. The present-day German Army was founded in 1955 as part of the newly formed West German *Bundeswehr* together with the Marine (German Navy) and the Luftwaffe (German Air Force). As of 28 February 2018[162], the German Army had a strength of 60,431 soldiers.

History

Bundeswehr

Branches
(*Teilstreitkräfte*)

Heer

Luftwaffe

Marine

Organisational areas
(*Organisationsbereiche*)

Joint Medical Service

Joint Support Service

Cyber and Information Space

German Army

Overview

A German Army, equipped, organized and trained following a single doctrine, and permanently unified under one command dates from 1871, and the unification of Germany under the leadership of Prussia. From 1871 to 1919 the title *Deutsches Heer* (German Army) was the official name of the German land forces. Following the German defeat in World War I and the end of the German Empire the main army was dissolved. From 1921 to 1935 the name of the German land forces was *Reichsheer* (Army of the Realm) and from 1935 to 1945 the name *Heer* was used. The *Heer* was one of two ground forces of the Third Reich during World War II, but unlike the *Heer*, the Waffen-SS was not a branch of the Wehrmacht, but was a combat force under the Nazi Party's own *Schutzstaffel* forces. The *Heer* was formally disbanded in August 1946.[163]

After World War II Germany was split into two sovereign states and both formed their own militaries: on 12 November 1955 the first recruits began their service in the West German *Heer*, while on 1 March 1956 the East German *Landstreitkräfte der NVA* (Land Forces of the National People's Army) were founded. During the Cold War the West German Army was fully integrated into NATOs command structure, while the *Landstreitkräfte* were part of the Warsaw Pact. Following the German reunification in 1990 the *Landstreitkräfte* were partially integrated into the German Army. Since then the German Army has been employed in peacekeeping operations worldwide and since 2002 also in combat operations in Afghanistan as part of NATO's International Security Assistance Force.

While the modern German army prefers to distance itself from the World War II era, it still retains certain uniform accessories from that era and before. For example, the iconic Stahlhelm remains in service, as do the arabesque general collar tab designs. Cufftitle designs used by elite units during World War II now appear on both cuffs. The German Army also continues to use the MG3, a machine gun that looks much like the MG42 used during World War II. The East German military used uniforms that were very similar to the WWII era army uniforms.

Founding of the Army

Following World War II the Allies dissolved the Wehrmacht with all its branches on 20 August 1946. However already one year after the founding of the Federal Republic of Germany in May 1949 and because of its increasing links with the West under German chancellor Konrad Adenauer, the Consultative Assembly of Europe began to consider the formation of a European Defence Community with German participation on 11 August 1950. Former

Figure 42: *Bundeswehr soldiers with MG1 and HK G3 during a 1960s maneuver. In the background is a Schützenpanzer Kurz.*

high-ranking German Wehrmacht officers outlined in the Himmeroder memorandum a plan for a "German contingent in an international force for the defense of Western Europe." For the German land forces the memorandum envisioned the formation of a 250,000 strong army. The officers saw the need for the formation of twelve Panzer divisions and six corps staffs with accompanying Corps troops, as only armored divisions could muster a fighting force to throw back the numerically far superior forces of the Warsaw Pact.

On 26 October 1950 Theodor Blank was appointed "officer of the Federal Chancellor for the Strengthening of Allied Troops questions". This Defence Ministry forerunner was known somewhat euphemistically as the Blank Office (Amt Blank), but explicitly used to prepare for the rearmament of West Germany (Wiederbewaffnung).[164] By March 1954 the Blank Office had finished plans for a new German army. Plans foresaw the formation of six infantry, four armoured, and two mechanised infantry divisions, as the German contribution to the defense of Western Europe in the framework of a European Defence Community.[165] On 8 February 1952 the Bundestag approved a German contribution to the defense of Western Europe and on 26 February 1954 the Basic Law of the Republic was amended with the insertion of an article regarding the defence of the sovereignty of the federal government.[166] Following a decision at the London Nine Power Conference of 28 September to 3 October 1954, Germany's entry into NATO effective from 9 May 1955 was accepted as a replacement for the failed European Defence Community plan. Afterwards the Blank Office was converted to the Defence Ministry and Theodor Blank became the first Defence Minister. The nucleus of army was the so-called *V* Branch of the Department of Defence. Subdivisions included were *VA Leadership and Training*, *VB Organisation* and *VC Logistics*.

The army saw itself explicitly not as a successor to the defeated Wehrmacht, but as in the traditions of the Prussian military reformers of 1807 to 1814 and the members of the military resistance during National Socialism; such as the officers which undertook the failed 20 July plot to assassinate Adolf Hitler in 1944. Nevertheless, for lack of alternatives the officer corps was made up largely of former Wehrmacht officers. The first Chief of the Army was the former Wehrmacht General der Panzertruppe Hans Rottiger, who had been involved in the drafting of the Himmeroder memorandum.

The official date of the founding of the army is 12 November 1955 when the first soldiers began their service in Andernach. In 1956 the first troops set up seven training companies in Andernach and began the formation of schools and training centers. On 1 April 1957, the first conscripts arrived for service in the army. The first military organisations created were instructional battalions, officer schools, and the Army Academy, the forerunner to the Führungsakademie der Bundeswehr in Hamburg. In total of twelve armoured and infantry divisions were to be established by 1959, as planned in Army Structure I. To achieve this goal existing units were split approximately every six months. However the creation of all twelve divisions did not take place until 1965. At the end of 1958 the strength of the army was about 100,000 men. The army was equipped at first with American material, such as the M-47 Patton main battle tank. Three corps commands were formed beginning in 1957: the I Corps, II Corps, and the III Corps.

Also in 1957 the "Office for Territorial Defence" was established as the highest Territorial Army authority. The Office for Territorial Defence was under the direct command of the Federal Ministry of Defence and commanded the Territorial Army (Germany) (*Territorialheer*), a reserve formation. While the *Heer* along with the *Marine* and *Luftwaffe* were firmly integrated into the NATO Military Command Structure, the *Territorialheer* remained under national command. The main function of the *Territorialheer* was to maintain the operational freedom of NATO forces through providing rear area defence against saboteurs, enemy special forces, and the like. There were three Territorial Commands (*Territorialkommandos*), including North, South, and Schleswig-Holstein, and up to six *Wehrbereichskommandos* (WBKs), military regional commands.[167] By 1985 each of the WBKs had two *Heimatschutzbrigades* (HSBs, home defence brigades).

Figure 43: *M47 Patton tank in service with the Bundeswehr, 1960*

The development of Soviet tactical nuclear weapons required the development of a new Army structure even before Army Structure I was fully achieved. To minimize the effects of attacks with tactical nuclear weapons on massed forces, the 28,000 strong divisions of the *Heer* were broken up into smaller and more mobile brigades. These smaller units were also to be capable of self-sustainment on an atomic battlefield for several days, and to be capable of to move quickly from defense and to attack. The new armoured and mechanized brigades were capable of combined arms combat. Each division was composed of three brigades. The armoured brigades consisted of an armoured infantry battalion, two armoured battalions, an armoured artillery battalion and a supply battalion. The mechanized brigades consisted of a motorized infantry battalion, two mechanized infantry battalions, an armored battalion, a field artillery battalion and a supply battalion. The motorized brigades consisted of three motorized infantry battalions, an anti-tank battalion, a field artillery battalion and a supply battalion. The alpine brigades consisted of three alpine battalions, a mountain artillery battalion and a supply battalion. By 1959 the Heer consisted of 11 divisions of 27 brigades, four Panzer (armoured), four Panzergrenadier (mechanized), two Jäger (motorized), and one Gebirgsjäger (alpine).

At the end of the Cold War the German Army fielded 12 divisions with 38 brigades: six Panzer (armoured), four Panzergrenadier (mechanized), one

Figure 44: *Helicopter of the German Army Aviation Corps in Northern Iraq in 1991*

Fallschirmjäger (airborne), and one Gebirgsjäger (alpine) division. Nine divisions were grouped into three corps: I German Corps as part of NATO's Northern Army Group, II German Corps and III German Corps as part of Central Army Group. The remaining three divisions were part of Allied Forces Baltic Approaches (6th Panzergrenadier Division) and NORTHAG's I Netherlands Corps (3rd Panzer Division), while 1st Fallschirmjäger Division was assigned in peacetime to II German Corps and doubled as general staff for the ACE Mobile Force (Land).Wikipedia:Citation needed

Post Cold War

After 1990, the Heer absorbed the Nationale Volksarmee, the armed forces of East Germany. The former East German forces were initially controlled by the Bundeswehr Command East under the command of Lieutenant General Jörg Schönbohm and disbanded on 30 June 1991.[168] In the aftermath of the merger, the German Army consisted of four Corps (including IV Corps at Potsdam in the former DDR) with a manpower of 360,000 men. It was continuously downsized from this point. In 1994 III Corps was reorganised as the German Army Forces Command. In 1996, the 25th Airborne Brigade was converted into a new command leading the Army's special forces, known as the Kommando Spezialkräfte.

The 2001 onwards restructuring of the German Army saw it move to a seven division structure – 5 mechanized (each with two mechanized brigades), 1 special forces, and one air assault.

In 2003, three Corps still existed, each including various combat formations and a maintenance brigade, as well as the I. German/Dutch Corps, a joint German-Netherlands organization, used to control in peacetime the 1st Panzer and 7th Panzer Divisions as well as Dutch formations. The 1st Panzer would have reported to the corps in wartime while the 7th would be posted to the Allied Rapid Reaction Corps. II Corps was German in peacetime but would have exchanged a division with the V U.S. Corps in time of war (the 5th Panzer). The 5th Panzer was formally Division disbanded as of 30 June 2001. In peacetime it also commanded the 10th Panzer Division, which was allocated to Eurocorps and which parents the German half of the Franco-German Brigade. The 1st Mountain Division at Munich was also subordinate to this headquarters.

The IV Corps was headquartered at Potsdam in eastern Germany and controlled two Panzer-Grenadier Divisions, the 13th and 14th. The 14th Panzergrenadier Division also took control of units in Western Germany resubordinated from the 6th Panzergrenadier Division when it lost its command function. It would have made up the German contribution to the Multinational Corps Northeast in time of war. IV Corps also used to have under its command the Military District Command I, the 1st Airmobile Brigade, and the Berlin Command (de:Standortkommando Berlin).

German Army today

All corps have now been disbanded or transferred to a multinational level such as Multinational Corps North East. IV Corps was reorganized and on 31 March 2002 became an overseas deployment command, the Einsatzführungskommando der Bundeswehr, like the British Permanent Joint Headquarters. An army reorganisation in recent years has seen the disbandment of the 13th Mechanized Infantry Division headquarters, a merge of the Airmobile Operations Division and Special Operations Division headquarters, the disbandment of the 1st Airmobile Brigade, and reshuffling of units between divisions.Wikipedia:Citation needed No heavy brigades were disbanded, but the two remaining heavy divisions command three rather than two brigades.

As of 28 February 2018[162] there were a total of 61,054 soldiers on active service in the German Army. However, the quite unique German military branch of the Joint Support Service consists to a significant degree of *Heeresuniformträger* (army uniform wearing personnel).[169] This is also contributed to by the Joint Medical Service, which does have other solely-military-medical branch counterparts (such as in South Africa).

In accordance with EU working hour regulations, the regular work-week is 41 hours, although numerous exceptions exist for e.g. deployments in oversea missions, training exercises, emergencies, and similar military needs.

Modern equipment

Figure 45: *Leopard 2A6 main battle tank*

Figure 46: *PzH2000 self-propelled artillery*

Figure 47: *NH-90 transport helicopter*

Structure and organisation

File:Relief Map of Germany.svg

Locations of the army's major units

The German Army is commanded by the Inspector of the Army (*Inspekteur des Heeres*) based at the Army Command (*Kommando Heer*) in Strausberg near Berlin. The training centers are supervised by the Army Training Command in Leipzig.

The combat units of the army include two armored divisions, one rapid forces division and the Franco-German Brigade, which is under direct supervision

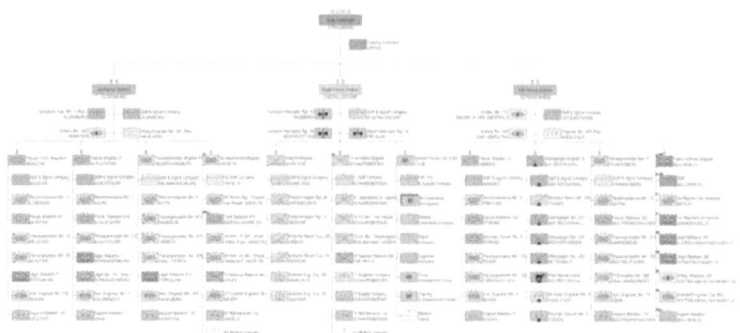

Figure 48: *Structure of the German Army with integrated allied units in 2017 (click to enlarge; for structure with only German units see: Structure of the German Army)*

Figure 49: *German Army soldiers from Paratrooper Battalion 261 on board an armoured personnel carrier in Somalia in 1993*

Figure 50: *A German Army soldier demonstrates the equipment of the IdZ program.*

of the Army Command. Unlike other European armies such as neighbouring France, regiments are not a common form of organization and are thus rare in the German army. Battalions are directly subordinate to brigades or to divisions as divisional troops. German infantry battalions field 1,000 men, considerably larger than most NATO armies, i.e. twice the size of a US Army battalion.

- **1. Panzerdivision** in Oldenburg

  - Divisional troops
  - 9th Armoured Demonstration Brigade in Munster
  - 21st Panzer Brigade at Augustdorf
  - 41st Mechanized Infantry Brigade *Vorpommern* in Neubrandenburg
  - 43rd Mechanized Brigade in Havelte, (Royal Netherlands Army)
  - 325th Artillery Demonstration Battalion

- **10. Panzerdivision** in Veitshöchheim

  - Divisional troops
  - 12th Armoured Brigade *Oberpfalz* in Cham
  - 23rd Mountain Infantry Brigade *Bayern* in Bad Reichenhall

- 37th Panzergrenadier Brigade at Frankenberg, Saxony
- Deutsch-Französische Brigade (Franco-German Brigade) in Müllheim
- 131st Artillery Battalion
- 345th Artillery Demonstration Battalion
- **Division Schnelle Kräfte (Rapid Forces Division)** in Stadtallendorf

- Divisional troops
- Kommando Spezialkräfte (KSK) (Special Forces Command) in Calw
- 1st Airborne Brigade, in Saarlouis
- 11th Airmobile Brigade, in Schaarsbergen (Royal Netherlands Army)
- 10th Transport Helicopter Regiment
- 30th Transport Helicopter Regiment
- 36th Attack Helicopter Regiment
- German elements, **Eurocorps** HQ in Strasbourg (France)

- *Command Support Brigade*
- German elements in two permanent battalions and one staff company
- **1 (German/Netherlands) Corps** in Münster

- German elements in two permanent battalions and one staff company
- **Multinational Corps North East** in Szczecin (Poland)

- Fernmeldebataillon 610 (610th Signal Battalion)
- German elements
- **Zentrales Langzeitlager** (Army Central Depot) in Herongen

- **Zentrales Langzeitlager** (Army Central Depot) in Pirmasens

- **Zentraler Mobilmachungsstützpunkt** (Central Mobilisation Base) in Brück

Truppengattungen

The German Army has eleven different branches of troops, designated as *Truppengattungen*. Each *Truppengattung* is responsible for training and readiness of its units and disposes of its own schools and centres of excellence for doing so. Optically this distinction can be made by the branch colour, called *Waffenfarbe* which is displayed by a cord attached to the rank insignia, and the colour of their beret with a specific badge attached to it.

Beret Colour (Army only and Security Units of Navy and Air Force)

- Black: Armoured Corps, Reconnaissance Corps
- Green: Mechanized Infantry and Rifles Corps
- Dark Red: Aviation Corps, Airborne Corps, Special Forces, formations assigned to airborne division
- Light Red: Combat Support Corps and Military Police
- Dark Blue: Medical Corps
- Navy Blue: Multinational Units, Officer Cadet Battalions, Navy and Air Force Security Units
- Bright Blue: Troops with United Nations Missions

Grey mountain cap (*Bergmütze*): Mountain Troops *Gebirgsjäger*

Waffenfarbe (Army and army support branch only)

- Bright Red:General ranks (only "Kragenspiegel", not "Litze"),
- Crimson: General Staff

Rank structure

The rank structure of the German army is adjusted to the rank structure of NATO. Unlike its predecessors, the modern German Army does not use the rank of Colonel General. The highest rank for an army officer is Lieutenant General, as the rank of Full General is reserved for the Armed Forces chief of staff or officers serving as NATO officers. Officer cadets do not pass through all enlisted ranks, but are directly promoted to Lieutenant after 36 months of service.

Equivalent US Army ranks are shown below according to "STANAG 2116 NSA MC LO (EDITION 6) – NATO CODES FOR GRADES OF MILITARY PERSONNEL":

Officers of the German Army						
General (*General*) Gen	Lieutenant General (*Generalleutnant*) GenLt/GL	Major General (*Generalmajor*) GenMaj/GM	Brigadier General (*Brigadegeneral*) BrigGen/BG	Colonel (*Oberst*) Oberst/-O	Lieutenant Colonel (*Oberstleutnant*) Oberstlt/OTL
OF-9	OF-8	OF-7	OF-6	OF-5	OF-4

Officers of the German Army

Major (*Major*) Maj/M	Staff Captain (*Stabshauptmann*) StHptm/SH	Captain (*Hauptmann*) Hptm/H	1st Lieutenant (*Oberleutnant*) OLt /OL	2nd Lieutenant (*Leutnant*) Lt/L
OF-3	OF-2	OF-2	OF-1	OF-1

Non-Commissioned Officers of the German Army

Sergeant Major (*Oberstabsfeldwebel*) OStFw/OSF	Master Sergeant (*Stabsfeldwebel*) StFw/SF	Sergeant 1st Class (officer cadet) (*Oberfähnrich*) OFähnr/OFR	Sergeant 1st Class (*Hauptfeldwebel*) HptFw/HF	Staff Sergeant (*Oberfeldwebel*) OFw/OF
OR-9	OR-8	OR-8	OR-7	OR-6

Non-Commissioned Officers of the German Army

Staff Sergeant (officer cadet) (*Fähnrich*) Fähnr/FR	Staff Sergeant (*Feldwebel*) Fw/F	Sergeant (*Stabsunteroffizier*) StUffz/SU	Corporal (officer cadet) (*Fahnenjunker*) Fhj/FJ	Corporal (*Unteroffizier*) Uffz/U
OR-6	OR-6	OR-5	OR-5	OR-5

Enlisted Ranks of the German Army				
Corporal Specialist (*Oberstabsgefreiter*) OStGefr/OSG	Specialist (*Stabsgefreiter*) StGefr/SG	Lance Corporal (*Hauptgefreiter*) HptGefr/HG	Private 1st Class (NCO cadet) (*Obergefreiter UA*) OGefr/OG	Private 1st Class (*Obergefreiter*) OGefr/OG
OR-4	OR-4	OR-3	OR-3	OR-3

Enlisted Ranks of the German Army				
Private 1st Class (officer cadet) (*Gefreiter OA*) Gefr/G	Private 1st Class (Sergeant cadet) (*Gefreiter FA*) Gefr/G	Private 1st Class (NCO cadet) (*Gefreiter UA*) Gefr/G	Private 1st Class (*Gefreiter*) Gefr/G	Private (*Soldat*) S
OR-2	OR-2	OR-2	OR-2	OR-1

Further reading

- Addington, Larry H. *The Blitzkrieg Era and the German General Staff, 1865-1941* (1971).
- Bartov, Omer. *Hitler's army: Soldiers, Nazis, and war in the Third Reich* (1992).
- Bull, Stephen. *German Assault Troops of the First World War: Stosstrupptaktik-The First Stormtroopers* (History Press, 2014).
- Citino, Robert M. *The Path to Blitzkrieg: Doctrine and Training in the German Army, 1920-39* (2007).
- Citino, Robert M. *Quest for Decisive Victory: From Stalemate to Blitzkrieg in Europe, 1899-1940* (2002).
- Dupuy, Trevor Nevitt. *A Genius for War: The German Army and General Staff, 1807-1945* (1977).
- Gross, Gerhard P. *The Myth and Reality of German Warfare: Operational Thinking From Moltke the Elder to Heusinger* (2016).

- Deist, Wilhelm, ed. *The German military in the age of total war* (Berg, 1985).
- Hubatscheck, Gerhard (2006), *50 Jahre Heer: Der Soldat und seine Ausrüstung*, Sulzvach: Report-Verlag, ISBN 978-3-932385-21-6
- Hughes, Daniel J. and Richard L. DiNardo, eds. *Imperial Germany and War, 1871-1918* (University Press of Kansas, 2018).
- Kelleher, Catherine M. "Fundamentals of German Security: The Creation of the Bundeswehr: Continuity and Change", in Stephen F. Szabo (ed.), *The Bundeswehr and Western Security*, St. Martin's Press, New York, 1990.
- Seaton, Albert. *The German Army: 1933-45* (1982).
- Showalter, Dennis. *Instrument of War: The German army 1914-18* (2016)
- Showalter, Dennis. *The Wars of German Unification* (2015)
- Wheeler-Bennet, Sir John (2005), *The Nemesis of Power: German Army in Politics, 1918–1945* (2nd ed.), New York: Palgrave Macmillan Publishing Company, ISBN 978-1-4039-1812-3 Online free[170]

External links

 Wikimedia Commons has media related to *Heer (Bundeswehr)*.

- Official Homepage of the German Army (Heer)[171] in German

Historical links

- German Army pre 1914[172]
- German Army 1914-1918[173]
- German Army Organization 1914[174]
- German Infantry Photographs from World War II[175] - Colour photographs of German infantry during World War II
- Gebirgsjaeger[176] - German Mountain Troops
- Axis History[177] - Axis History site including German troops.

List of modern equipment of the German Army

Modern equipment of the German Army is a list of equipment currently in service with the German Army.

Infantry weapons

Model	Image	Origin	Type	Caliber	Notes
Handguns					
Heckler & Koch USP Designated as: Pistole 8 (P8) Pistole 12 (P12)		Germany	Handgun	9×19mm Parabellum .45 ACP (11.43x23mm)	The P8 model (9×19mm) will become the standard handgun of the Bundeswehr, while the P12 model (.45 ACP/11.43x23 mm) will be used by the Special Forces.
Heckler & Koch P7		West Germany	Handgun	9×19mm Parabellum	Used by Military Police.
Heckler & Koch P30		Germany	Handgun	9×19mm Parabellum	Used by Military Police and soldiers of the special forces; replacing the P7.
Heckler & Koch P2A1		West Germany	Flare Handgun	26.5mm	
Submachine guns					
Heckler & Koch MP7		Germany	Submachine Gun	HK 4.6×30mm	Replacing the UZI to become the standard submachine gun of the German Army.
Heckler & Koch MP5		West Germany	Submachine Gun	9×19mm Parabellum	In use with the Special Forces - Kommando Spezialkräfte, the military police and the German Navy.
Rifles					
Heckler & Koch HK417		Germany	Battle Rifle	7.62×51mm NATO	Bundeswehr designation "G27"

Heckler & Koch G36		Germany	Assault Rifle	5.56×45mm NATO	Standard assault rifle of the German Army since 1997, replacing the old G3. The G36 will be replaced by a new standard service rifle.
Heckler & Koch G38 / Heckler & Koch G95		Germany	Assault Rifle	5.56×45mm NATO	Special forces only. HK416 A5 designated as 'G38'. HK416 A7 designated as 'G95'
Heckler & Koch G3		West Germany	Battle Rifle	7.62×51mm NATO	Was the standard rifle of the West German Army with the last active use in the Afghan War, since then all weapons are in reserve with batches being given away to friendly forces, like the Peshmerga.
Karabiner 98k		Nazi Germany	Carbine	7.92×57mm Mauser	Retained for ceremonial use only.
Machine guns					
Heckler & Koch MG4		Germany	Light machine gun	5.56×45mm NATO	Standard light machine gun of the German Army.
Rheinmetall MG3		West Germany	General-purpose machine gun	7.62×51mm NATO	Standard general-purpose machine gun of the German Army; it was derived from MG42. Will be replaced by the MG5.
Heckler & Koch MG5		Germany	General-purpose machine gun	7.62×51mm NATO	Will become the new standard general-purpose machine gun of the German Army; replacing the MG3
M2 Browning		United States	Heavy machine gun	12.7×99mm NATO	Standard heavy machine gun German Army. Bundeswehr designation "Maschinengewehr Kaliber .50". Used mostly as vehicle armament, for example on the LIV (SO) Serval.
Sniper rifles					

List of modern equipment of the German Army 101

Accuracy International AWM		United Kingdom	Sniper Rifle	.300 Winchester Magnum	Bundeswehr Designation "G22".
Heckler & Koch G28		Germany	Designated Marksman Rifle	7.62×51mm NATO	Based on the HKMR308.
M107/-M107A1		United States	Anti-materiel rifle	12.7×99mm NATO	Bundeswehr designation "G82/-G82A1".
Haenel RS9		Germany	Sniper Rifle	.338 Lapua Magnum	Bundeswehr designation "G29", in service with the special forces; replacing the G22

Shotguns

Heckler & Koch FABARM FP6		Germany/ Italy	Shotgun	12 gauge	
Remington Model 870		United States	Shotgun	12 gauge	Now being replaced by the FP6.

Grenades & Grenade launchers

DM51		Germany	Fragmentation grenade		
Heckler & Koch AG36		Germany	grenade launcher	40×46mm	Replacing the HK69A1. Bundeswehr designation "AG-40 2"
Heckler & Koch HK69A1		West Germany	grenade launcher	40×46mm	Bundeswehr designation "AG40 A1"
Heckler & Koch GMG		Germany	automatic grenade launcher	40×53mm	Bundeswehr designation "Granatmaschinenwaffe 40mm". Sometimes used as vehicle armament on vehicles such as the TPz Fuchs, Mungo ESK, Boxer (armoured fighting vehicle) or Fennek.

Anti-tank weapons

Panzerfaust 3		Germany	Rocket Propelled Grenade	60mm	Standard infantry AT weapon.

MATA-DOR		Israel / Germany / Singapore	Rocket launcher	90mm	Designation "RGW90".
Carl Gustav		Sweden	Recoilless Rifle	84mm	Former standard AT weapon of West Germany, now used only for firing signal ammunition in training scenarios. Bundeswehr designation "Schwere Panzerfaust 84 mm/Leuchtbüchse 84 mm".
EUROSPIKE		Israel	Anti-tank Missile	152mm	
MILAN		France/West Germany	Anti-tank Missile	115mm	

Vehicles

Model	Image	Origin	Type	Number	Notes
Armoured vehicles					
Leopard 2		Germany	Main Battle Tank	328 Active. 104 Reserve	Leopard 2A6/-2A7. The number of tanks in active service will possibly be increased to 328. On 20 May 2017 it was announced on DefenceIndustry Daily that 104 Leopard 2's would be taken out of storage and upgraded to be put back into service and an additional 32 new tanks would be built by Krauss Maffei.

List of modern equipment of the German Army

Marder		West Germany	Infantry Fighting Vehicle	357	200 to be upgraded; will remain in service until the Puma becomes fully operational by 2024
Puma		Germany	Infantry Fighting Vehicle	190 (of 350)	Replacing Marder. 190 Puma IFVs delivered by January 2018
TPz Fuchs		West Germany	Armoured personnel carrier	898 active 668 available 532 operational	267 upgraded to the latest A8 version
GTK Boxer		Germany Netherlands	Armoured personnel carrier	272 (of 403)	Replacing TPz Fuchs Fleet partly.
BV 206S		Sweden	Specialist vehicle	379	Protected all-terrain vehicle.
Wiesel 1/2		Germany	Armored fighting vehicle	272	
Eagle IV/Eagle V		Switzerland	MRAP	495 +176 Eagle V	495 ordered, 20 will be armored ambulances
Enok		Germany	Armored car	331	

Dingo 1/2		Germany	Infantry mobility vehicle	725	
Fennek		Germany Netherlands	Light armored reconnaissance vehicle	217 (of 248)	148 reconnaissance, 24 combat engineer, 50 joint fire support teams (JFST). Total number to be increased to 248.[178]
KMW Grizzly		Germany Italy	MRAP		
AGF Serval		Germany	Light armored utility vehicle		
DURO III		Switzerland	MRAP		
Mungo ESK		Germany	MRAP, NBC vehicle	> 400	
YAK		Germany	MRAP, various roles	296	Based on DURO III.
Artillery and air defence					
M270 MLRS		United States	Multiple rocket launcher	38	38 are planned to remain in service.

List of modern equipment of the German Army

PzH 2000		Germany	Self-propelled artillery	123 active 61 available 41 operational	101 are planned to remain in service.
Tampella		Finland	Mortar	86[179]	120mm mortar based artillery.

Engineering vehicles

Dachs		West Germany	Engineering vehicle		Based on Leopard 1 chassis.
Büffel		Germany	Armoured recovery vehicle		Based on Leopard 2 chassis.
Keiler		Germany	Mine-clearing vehicle		
Biber		West Germany	Armoured vehicle-launched bridge		

Leguan		Germany	Armoured vehicle-launched bridge	7 ordered	Replacing the Biber.
M3 Amphibious Rig		Germany	Amphibious Bridgelayer		
Logistics					
SLT 50 Elefant		Germany	Tank transporter		
RMMV HX		Germany	Truck		2,271 on order. Replacing KAT1
RMMV TG MIL		Austria Germany	Truck		
Zetros		Germany	Truck		
Unimog		Germany	Truck	18,000	
MAN KAT1		Germany	Truck		

List of modern equipment of the German Army 107

		Utility		
Volkswagen T3/T4			Germany	Utility van
Mercedes-Benz 250 GD "Wolf"			Germany	Utility car

Aircraft

Type	Origin	Class	Role	Introduced	In service	Total	Notes
H135	France/-Germany	Rotorcraft	Trainer		14		
Tiger	Germany	Rotorcraft	Attack		47 (-1)		8 more on order. 40 will remain in service and updated to AS-GARD configuration. Rest used for training, tests and spare parts. One lost in Mali, July 2017.
NHI NH90 TTH	Multinational	Rotorcraft	Transport		47		35 more on order.
UH-1D Iroquois	USA	Rotorcraft	Utility		115		

German Navy

German Navy

	German Navy *Deutsche Marine*
Founded	2 January 1956
Country	Germany
Type	Navy
Size	16,333 personnel (as of 9 February 2017) 65 ships 55 aircraft
Part of	Bundeswehr
Headquarters of the German Navy	Rostock (Navy Command)
Motto(s)	Wir. Dienen. Deutschland. (*We. Serve. Germany.*)
March	"Gruß an Kiel"
Anniversaries	14 June

Engagements	• Operation Sharp Guard (1993–96) • Operation Enduring Freedom • Combined Task Force 150 (2002–) • Operation Active Endeavour • UNIFIL II • Operation ATALANTA
Website	www<wbr/>.marine<wbr/>.de[180]
Commanders	
Inspector of the Navy	Vice Admiral Andreas Krause
Deputy Inspector of the Navy	Vice Admiral Rainer Brinkmann
Chief of Staff	Rear Admiral Thorsten Kähler
Notable commanders	• Friedrich Ruge • Günter Luther
Insignia	
Naval ensign	

German Navy
Deutsche Marine

German Navy

Components
Organization
Ships
Naval Air Arm
Kampfschwimmer

Command
Navy Command

Equipment
Ship Classes

History and Traditions
Prussian Navy
North German Federal Navy
Imperial German Navy
Reichsmarine
Kriegsmarine
Volksmarine

Awards, Decorations and Badges
Badge of Honour of the Bundeswehr
Military Proficiency Badge
Badge of Marksmanship
Deployment Medal
Flood Service Medal 2002
Flood Service Medal 2013

The **German Navy** (German: ***Deutsche Marine*** or simply German: ***Marine***— listen Wikipedia:Media helpFile:De-Marine-pronunciation.ogg) is the navy of Germany and part of the unified *Bundeswehr* ("Federal Defense"), the German Armed Forces. The German Navy was originally known as the *Bundesmarine* ("Federal Navy") from 1956 until 1995 when *Deutsche Marine* ("German Navy") became the official name with respect to the 1990 incorporation of the East German *Volksmarine* ("People's Navy"). It is deeply integrated into the NATO alliance. Its primary mission is protection of Germany's territorial waters and maritime infrastructure as well as sea lines of communication. Apart from this, the German Navy participates in peacekeeping operations, and renders humanitarian assistance and disaster relief. They also participate in Anti-Piracy operations.[181]

History

The German Navy traces its roots back to the *Reichsflotte* (Imperial Fleet) of the revolutionary era of 1848–52. The Reichsflotte was the first German navy to sail under the black-red-gold flag. Founded on 14 June 1848 by the orders of the democratically elected Frankfurt Parliament, the Reichsflotte's brief existence ended with the failure of the revolution and it was disbanded on 2 April 1852; thus, the modern day navy celebrates its birthday on 14 June.

Between May 1945 and 1956, the German Mine Sweeping Administration and its successor organizations, made up of former members of Nazi Germany's *Kriegsmarine* ("War Navy"), became something of a transition stage for the navy, allowing the future *Marine* to draw on recently experienced personnel upon its formation. Also, from 1949-52 the US Navy had maintained the Naval Historical Team in Bremerhaven. This group of former Kriegsmarine officers acting as historical and tactical consultants to the Americans, was significant in establishing a German element in the NATO senior naval staff. In 1956, with West Germany's accession to NATO, the *Bundesmarine* ("Federal Navy"), as the navy was known colloquially, was formally established. In the same year the East German *Volkspolizei See* (literally "People's Police Sea") became the *Volksmarine* ("People's Navy"). During the Cold War all of the German Navy's combat vessels were assigned to NATO's Allied Forces Baltic Approaches's naval command NAVBALTAP.

With the accession of East Germany to the Federal Republic of Germany in 1990 the Volksmarine along with the whole National People's Army (*Nationale Volksarmee*, NVA) became part of the Bundeswehr. Since 1995 the name *German Navy* is used in international context, while the official name since 1956 remains *Marine* without any additions. As of 16 December 2016, the strength of the navy is 16,137 men and women.

A number of naval forces have operated in different periods. See

- Preußische Marine (Prussian Navy), 1701–1867
- Reichsflotte (Fleet of the Realm), 1848–52
- North German Federal Navy, 1867–71
- Imperial German Navy (*Kaiserliche Marine*), 1871–1919
- Reichsmarine, 1919–35
- Kriegsmarine, 1935–45
- German Mine Sweeping Administration, 1945–48
- Volksmarine the navy of East Germany (GDR) 1956–90
- *Marine*, 1956–present (*Bundesmarine*, colloquially)
- German Navy, 1995–present (international contexts)

Current operations

German warships permanently participate in all four *NATO Maritime Groups*. The German Navy is also engaged in operations against international terrorism such as Operation Enduring Freedom and NATO Operation Active Endeavour.

Presently the largest operation the German Navy is participating in is UNIFIL off the coast of Lebanon. The German contribution to this operation is two frigates, four fast attack craft, and two auxiliary vessels. The naval component of UNIFIL has been under German command.

The navy is operating a number of development and testing installations as part of an inter-service and international network. Among these is the Centre of Excellence for Operations in Confined and Shallow Waters (COE CSW), an affiliated centre of Allied Command Transformation. The COE CSW was established in April 2007 and officially accredited by NATO on 26 May 2009.[182] It is co-located with the staff of the German Flotilla 1 in Kiel whose Commander is double-hatted as Director, COE CSW.

Equipment

Ships and submarines

In total, there are about 65 commissioned ships in the German Navy, including; 10 frigates, 5 corvettes, 3 minesweepers, 10 minehunters, 6 submarines, 11 replenishment ships and 20 miscellaneous auxiliary vessels. The displacement of the navy is 220,000 tonnes. In addition, the German Navy and the Royal Danish Navy are in cooperation in the "Ark Project". This agreement made the Ark Project responsible for the strategic sealift of German armed forces where the full-time charter of three roll-on-roll-off cargo and troop ships are ready for deployments. In addition, these ships are also kept available for the use of the other European NATO countries.

The three vessels have a combined displacement of 60,000 tonnes. Including these ships, the total ships' displacement available to the Deutsche Marine is 280,000 tonnes.

A total of five Joint Support Ships, two JSS800 and three JSS400, were planned during the 1995–2010 period but the programme appears now to have been abandoned, not having been mentioned in two recent defence reviews. The larger ships would have been tasked for strategic troop transport and amphibious operations, and were to displace 27,000 to 30,000 tons for 800 soldiers. The German Navy will use the Joint Support Ship HNLMS Karel Doorman (A833) of the Royal Netherlands Navy as part of the integration of the German Navy Marines (Seebatallion) in the Royal Netherlands Marine Corps as of 2016.

Aircraft

The naval air arm of the German Navy is called the *Marinefliegerkommando*. The Marinefliegerkommando operate 55 aircraft.

Type	Origin	Class	Role	Introduced	In service	Total	Notes
Camcopter S-100	Austria	UAV	ISR				6 on order.
Dornier Do 228	Germany	Propeller	Pollution control		5^{183}		
H135	Germany	Rotorcraft	Trainer		2		
Lockheed P-3C Orion – CUP	USA	Propeller	MPA		8		Former Royal Netherlands Navy
NH90 Sea Lion	Germany	Rotorcraft	SAR/-transport				18 on order.
Westland Lynx	UK	Rotorcraft	Attack		22		
Westland Sea King Mk.41	UK	Rotorcraft	SAR/-transport		21		

Structure

The German Navy is commanded by the Inspector of the Navy (*Inspekteur der Marine*) supported by the Navy Command (*Marinekommando*) in Rostock.

Formations

- HQ German Navy (*Marinekommando*), Rostock
    - Einsatzflottille 1 (HQ Kiel)
        - 1st Corvette Squadron (*1. Korvettengeschwader*), Warnemünde
        - 1st Submarine Squadron (*1. Ubootgeschwader*), Eckernförde
            - Submarine Training Centre (*Ausbildungszentrum Unterseeboote*), Eckernförde
        - 3rd Minesweeping Squadron (*3. Minensuchgeschwader*), Kiel
        - 5th Minesweeping Squadron (*5. Minensuchgeschwader*), Kiel
        - 7th Fast Patrol Boat Squadron (*7. Schnellbootgeschwader*), Warnemünde
        - Naval Force Protection Battalion, (*Seebataillon*), Eckernförde

Figure 51: *Westland WG-13 Super Lynx Mk88a of the German Navy*

Figure 52: *A German Navy boarding team member assigned to the frigate Augsburg (F213) provides security with a P8 pistol for the remainder of his team as they board a local cargo hold by fast rope to conduct a search of the vessel*

Figure 53: *Naval Academy Mürwik*

- Naval Special Forces Command, (*Kommando Spezialkräfte Marine*), Eckernförde
- Naval Base Command Kiel (*Marinestützpunktkommando Kiel*)
- Naval Base Command Eckernförde
- Naval Base Command Warnemünde
- Einsatzflottille 2, Wilhelmshaven
  - HQ 2nd Flotilla
  - 2nd Frigate Squadron (*2. Fregattengeschwader*), Wilhelmshaven
  - 4th Frigate Squadron (*4. Fregattengeschwader*), Wilhelmshaven
  - Auxiliary Squadron (*Trossgeschwader*), Wilhelmshaven
  - Naval Base Command Wilhelmshaven
- Naval Aviation Command (*Marinefliegerkommando*), Nordholz
  - Naval Air Wing 3 (*Marinefliegergeschwader 3*), Nordholz
  - Naval Air Wing 5 (*Marinefliegergeschwader 5*), Nordholz
- Naval Support Command (*Marineunterstützungskommando — MUKdo*)
- Naval Medical Institute (*Schiffahrtsmedizinisches Institut*), Kiel
- Naval Academy (*Marineschule Mürwik*), Flensburg
- Petty Officer School (*Marineunteroffiziersschule*), Plön
- Engineering School (*Marinetechnikschule*), Parow, near Stralsund

- Naval Operations School (*Marineoperationsschule*), Bremerhaven
- Naval Damage Control Training Centre (*Ausbildungszentrum für Schiffssicherung*), Neustadt in Holstein

Ranks

Officers

German Navy

NATO code	Germany (Edit)			
OF-10	No equivalent			
OF-9				Admiral
OF-8				Vizeadmiral
OF-7				Konteradmiral
OF-6				Flotillenadmiral
OF-5				Kapitän zur See
OF-4				Fregattenkapitän
OF-3				Korvettenkapitän
OF-2				Stabskapitänleutnant
OF-1				Kapitänleutnant
				Oberleutnant zur See
				Leutnant zur See
OF(D)				Oberfähnrich zur See
				Fähnrich zur See
				Seekadett
Student officer	Enlisted rank plus a star indicating cadet's career			

German Navy

- Seekadett – Officer Cadet
- Fähnrich zur See – Midshipman
- Oberfähnrich zur See – Midshipman / Ensign
- Leutnant zur See – Ensign / Lieutenant Junior Grade / Sublieutenant
- Oberleutnant zur See – Lieutenant Junior Grade / Sublieutenant
- Kapitänleutnant – Lieutenant / Lieutenant Commander
- Stabskapitänleutnant – senior to *Kapitänleutnant*, same pay grade as *Korvettenkapitän*, for specialist officers only
- Korvettenkapitän – Corvette Captain
- Fregattenkapitän – Frigate Captain
- Kapitän zur See – Ship-of-the-line Captain
- Flottillenadmiral – Rear Admiral lower half
- Konteradmiral – Rear Admiral upper half / Counter Admiral
- Vizeadmiral – Vice Admiral
- Admiral

Petty officers and enlisted seamen

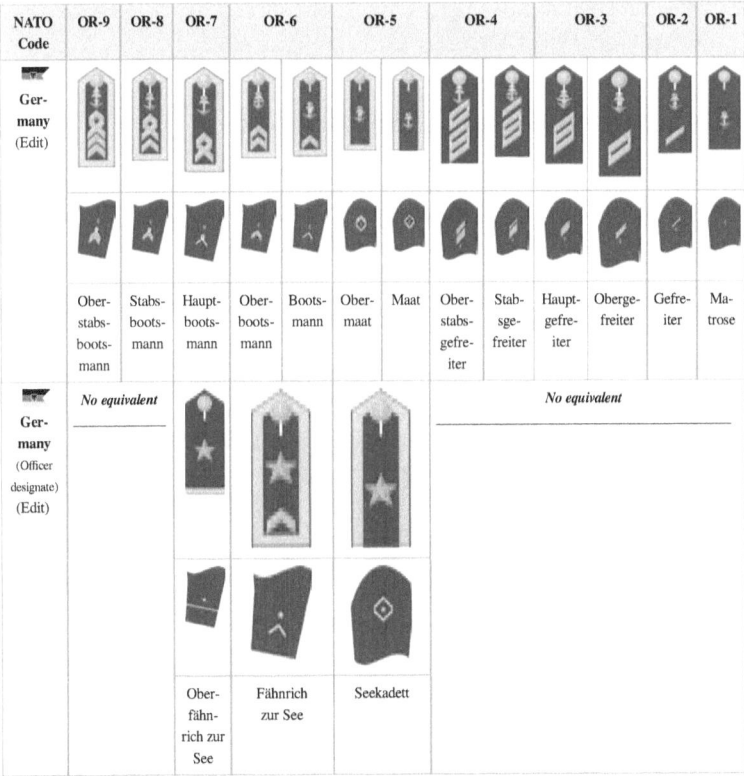

- Matrose – Seaman Recruit
- Gefreiter – Seaman Apprentice
- Gefreiter-UA – Seaman Apprentice E2 – Petty Officer 2nd Class Candidate
- Gefreiter-BA – Seaman Apprentice E2 – Petty Officer 1st Class Candidate
- Gefreiter-OA – Seaman Apprentice E2 – Officer Candidate
- Obergefreiter – Seaman
- Hauptgefreiter – Seaman
- Stabsgefreiter – Petty Officer 3rd Class
- Oberstabsgefreiter – Petty Officer 3rd Class
- Maat – Petty Officer 2nd Class
- Maat-BA – Petty Officer 2nd Class – Probationary Petty Officer 1st Class
- Obermaat – Petty Officer 2nd Class
- Bootsmann – Petty Officer 1st Class
- Oberbootsmann – Petty Officer 1st Class
- Hauptbootsmann – Chief Petty Officer
- Stabsbootsmann – Senior Chief Petty Officer
- Oberstabsbootsmann – Master Chief Petty Officer, Command/Fleet/Force Master Chief Petty Officer

Radio and communication stations

- DH038
- DHJ58
- DHJ59

Future developments

- A first batch of four frigates of the F125 class (*Baden-Württemberg* class) specialised for persistent stabilization missions is planned to replace all eight *Bremen* class guided-missile frigates. Each F125 will have two crews. They are expected to enter service between 2016 and 2018.
- Six large surface combat ships are planned under the name 'Mehrzweckkampfschiff 180' (MKS 180), a multi-mission frigate
- Two more Type 212A submarines will be procured within the next decade.
- Five additional Braunschweig class corvettes will be procured from 2019–2023.
- 18 NH90 NFH Helicopters ordered to replace Lynx in ASW/AsuW role, originally ordered by the German Army as NH90 TTH variant.

- 12 Medium Sized Helicopters are planned to replace the current 22 *Sea King* helicopters of Naval Air Wing 5 in SAR & ship-based Transport Role (VertRep)
- A first batch of six Camcopter S-100 UAVs for the use on the Braunschweig class corvettes has been ordered (more being planned). Deliveries took place in 2013.
- Integration of the German Navy Marines (Seebatallion) in the Netherlands Marine Corps and use of the Amphibious ships of the Royal Netherlands Navy such as the Joint Support Ship HNLMS Karel Doorman (A833) as of 2016.
- In May 2013 it was announced by both Ministers of Defence that the German- & Dutch Navy agreed to integrate submarine operations, training and design for future replacements.

Further reading (COE CSW)

- Jan Wiedemann: COE CSW celebrates fifth anniversary; in: NAVAL FORCES III/2014 p. 90 f.
- Hans-Joachim Stricker: Centre of Excellence for Operations in Confined and Shallow Waters COE CSW – Das COE als Ausdruck unserer besonderen nationalen Fähigkeiten im Bündnis; in: Marineforum 6-2007 p. 3 f.
- Fritz-Rudolf Weber: Centre of Excellence for Operations in Confined and Shallow Waters – Think Tank für die NATO; in: Marineforum 1/2-2010 p. 11 ff.
- Hans Georg Buss, Stefan Riewesell: Maritime C-IED and Harbour Protection: A Joint Effort; in: The Transformer Fall 2013 Vol 9 Issue 2 p. 18

External links

 Wikimedia Commons has media related to *Navy of Germany*.

- Official website[180]
- The German Navy — Facts and Figures, 12th Edition, February 2013[184]
- Uniforms[185]

List of active German Navy ships

This is a **list of active German Navy ships** as of December 2016. There are approximately 65 ships in commission including; 10 frigates, 5 corvettes, 3 minesweepers, 10 minehunters, 6 submarines, 11 replenishment ships and 20 miscellaneous auxiliary vessels.

Current ships

Class	Picture	Type	Ships	Displacement	Note
Submarines (6 in service)					
Type 212		Attack submarine	S181 *U31* S182 *U32* S183 *U33* S184 *U34* S185 *U35* S186 *U36*	1,830 tonnes	Two more planned by 2030.
Frigates (10 in service)					
Baden-Württemberg		General-purpose frigate	F222 *Baden-Württemberg*	7,200 tonnes	3 more fitting out. 1 returned to builder.
Sachsen		Air-defense frigate	F219 *Sachsen* F220 *Hamburg* F221 *Hessen*	5,800 tonnes	Generally considered a destroyer internationally due to size, armament, and role.
Brandenburg		Anti-Submarine Warfare frigate	F215 *Brandenburg* F216 *Schleswig-Holstein* F217 *Bayern* F218 *Mecklenburg-Vorpommern*	4,900 tonnes	
Bremen		General-purpose frigate	F213 *Augsburg* F214 *Lübeck*	3,680 tonnes	To be replaced by four Baden-Württemberg-class frigates.
Corvettes (5 in service)					
Braunschweig		General-purpose corvette	F260 *Braunschweig* F261 *Magdeburg* F262 *Erfurt* F263 *Oldenburg* F264 *Ludwigshafen am Rhein*	1,840 tonnes	5 more vessels planned by 2023.
Mine countermeasures (12 in service)					

List of active German Navy ships

Ensdorf		Minesweeper	M1090 *Pegnitz* M1098 *Siegburg*	650 tonnes	
Frankenthal		Minehunter	M1063 *Bad Bevensen* M1061 *Rottweill* M1064 *Grömitz* M1068 *Datteln* M1065 *Dillingen* M1069 *Homburg* M1062 *Sulzbach-Rosenberg* M1058 *Fulda* M1059 *Weilheim* M1067 *Bad Rappenau*	650 tonnes	
Replenishment (11 in service)					
Berlin		Replenishment oiler	A1411 *Berlin* A1412 *Frankfurt am Main* A1413 *Bonn*	20,240 tonnes	
Rhön		Replenishment oiler	A1443 *Rhön* A1442 *Spessart*	14,169 tonnes	
Elbe		Tender	A511 *Elbe* A512 *Mosel* A513 *Rhein* A514 *Werra* A515 *Main* A516 *Donau*	3,586 tonnes	
Miscellaneous (18 in service)					
Oste		Electronic surveillance	A52 *Oste* A50 *Alster* A53 *Oker*	3,200 tonnes	
Wangerooge		Ocean tugboat	A1451 *Wangerooge* A1452 *Spiekeroog*	798 tonnes	
Helgoland		Salvage tugboat	A1458 *Fehmarn*	1,310 tonnes	
Nordstrand		Harbor tugboat	Y817 *Nordstrand* Y819 *Langeness* Y816 *Vogelsand* Y812 *Lütje Hörn* Y815 *Scharhörn* Y814 *Knechtsand*		
Bottsand		Pollution control	Y1643 *Bottsand* Y1644 *Eversand*	650 tonnes	
Schwedeneck		Trials ship	Y861 *Kronsort* Y862 *Helmsand*	1,000 tonnes	

Planet		Research ship	A1437 *Planet*	3,500 tonnes	
Gorch Fock		Sail training ship	A60 *Gorch Fock*	1,760 tonnes	

External links

- Official Website of German Navy in English[186]
- Die Flotte 2006 - official fleet listing and presentation in German and English[187]

Figure 54: *Naval ensign of Germany*

German Air Force

German Air Force

	**German Air Force** *Luftwaffe*
	Logo of the German Air Force
Founded	1956
Country	Germany
Type	Air force
Role	Aerial warfare
Size	27,704 personnel (30 June 2018) 467 aircraft
Nickname(s)	Team Luftwaffe
Motto(s)	*Immer im Einsatz (Always in action)*
Colors	Blue, Grey and White
Anniversaries	9 January 1956
Engagements	Operation Deliberate Force Kosovo War War in Afghanistan Military intervention against ISIL Northern Mali conflict
Website	www<wbr/>.luftwaffe<wbr/>.de[188]
	**Commanders**
Inspector of the Air Force	Generalleutnant Ingo Gerhartz
Ceremonial chief	Generalleutnant Dieter Naskrent

Colonel of the Regiment	Generalmajor Günter-Erhard Giesa
Notable commanders	• General Josef Kammhuber • General Johannes Steinhoff • Generalleutnant Günther Rall • Oberst Erich Hartmann
Insignia	
Roundel	
Aircraft flown	
Attack	Tornado IDS
Electronic warfare	Tornado ECR
Fighter	Eurofighter Typhoon
Helicopter	AS532, H145M, CH-53
Trainer	Grob G-120, T-6 Texan II, T-38 Talon
Transport	Global Express 5000, A310, A400M, A319, A340, C-160, C-130J

The **German Air Force** (German: *Luftwaffe* (German pronunciation: [ˈlʊftvafə] (listen)), the German-language generic term for *air force*) is the aerial warfare branch of the Bundeswehr, the armed forces of Germany. With a strength of 27,704 personnel (30 June 2018), it is the fourth largest air force within the European Union, after the air forces of the United Kingdom, France and Italy. Although its budget has been significantly reduced since the end of the Cold War in 1989–1990, the Luftwaffe is still among the best-equipped air forces in the world.

The German Air Force (as part of the Bundeswehr) was founded in 1956 during the era of the Cold War as the aerial warfare branch of the armed forces of then West Germany. After the reunification of West and East Germany in 1990, it integrated parts of the air force of the former German Democratic Republic, which itself had been founded in 1956 as part of the National People's Army. There is no organizational continuity between the current German Air Force and the former Luftwaffe of the Wehrmacht combined forces founded in 1935, which was completely disbanded in 1945/46 after World War II. The term *Luftwaffe* that is used for both the historic and the current German air force is the German-language generic designation of any air force.

The commander of the German Air Force is Lieutenant General Karl Müllner. In 2015 the Air Force uses eleven air bases, two of which host no flying units. Furthermore, the Air Force has a presence at three civil airports. In 2012,

Figure 55: *This Canadair CL-13 is preserved at the Military History Museum in Berlin.*

the Air Force had an authorized strength of 28,475 active soldiers and 4,914 reservists.[189]

History

After World War II, German aviation was severely curtailed, and military aviation was completely forbidden after the *Luftwaffe* of the Third Reich had been disbanded by August 1946 by the Allied Control Commission. This changed in 1955 when West Germany joined NATO, as the Western Allies believed that Germany was needed to counter the increasing military threat posed by the Soviet Union and its Warsaw Pact allies. Therefore, on 9 January 1956, a new German Air Force called *Luftwaffe* was founded as a branch of the new *Bundeswehr*.

Many well-known fighter pilots of the *Luftwaffe* of the Wehrmacht in World War II joined the new post-war air force and underwent refresher training in the USA before returning to West Germany to upgrade on the latest U.S.-supplied hardware. These included Erich Hartmann, Gerhard Barkhorn, Günther Rall and Johannes Steinhoff. Steinhoff became commander-in-chief of the *Luftwaffe*, with Rall as his immediate successor. Another pilot of World War II,

Josef Kammhuber, also made a significant career in the post-war *Luftwaffe*, retiring in 1962 as *Inspekteur der Luftwaffe* (Chief Inspector of the Air Force). Despite the partial reliance of the new air force on soldiers who had served in the Wehrmacht's air arm, there was no organizational continuity between the old and the new Luftwaffe. This is in line with the policy of the Bundeswehr on the whole, which does not consider itself a successor of the Wehrmacht and does not follow the traditions of any other previous German military organization.

First years

The first volunteers of the Luftwaffe arrived at the Nörvenich Air Base in January 1956. In the same year, the Luftwaffe was provided with its first aircraft, the US-made Republic F-84 Thunderstreak. At first, the Luftwaffe was divided into two operational commands, one in Northern Germany, aligned with the British-led Second Allied Tactical Air Force, and the other in Southern Germany, aligned with the American-led Fourth Allied Tactical Air Force.

In 1957, the Luftwaffe took command of the Army Air Defence Troops located in Rendsburg and began the expansion of its own air defence missile capabilities. The first squadron to be declared operational was the 61st Air Transport Squadron at Erding Air Base, followed by the 31st Fighter-Bomber Squadron at Büchel Air Base. In 1958, the Luftwaffe received its first conscripts. In 1959 the Luftwaffe declared the 11th Missile Group in Kaufbeuren armed with MGM-1 Matador surface-to-surface tactical nuclear cruise missiles operational. The same year *Jagdgeschwader 71* (Fighter Wing 71) equipped with North American F-86 fighters became operational at Ahlhorner Heide Air Base. All aircraft sported—and continue to sport—the Iron Cross on the fuselage, harking back to the pre-March 1918 days of World War I, while the national flag of West Germany is displayed on the tail.

Cold War

In 1963, the Luftwaffe saw its first major reorganization. The two operational Air Force Group Commands – Command North and Command South were both split into two mixed Air Force divisions containing flying and air defence units and one Support division. Additionally a 7th Air Force division was raised in Schleswig-Holstein containing flying units, missile units, support units and the German Navy's naval aviation and placed under command of Allied Forces Baltic Approaches.

In 1960, the Luftwaffe received it first Lockheed F-104 Starfighter jets. The Starfighter remained in service for the entire duration of the Cold War, with the last being taken out of service in 1991. The Luftwaffe received a total of 916

Starfighters, 292 of which crashed resulting in the deaths of 116 pilots. The disastrous service record of the Starfighter led to the Starfighter crisis in 1966 as a reaction to 27 Starfighter crashes with 17 casualties in 1965 alone. The West German public referred to the Starfighter as the *Witwenmacher* (widow-maker), *fliegender Sarg* (flying coffin), *Fallfighter* (falling fighter) and *Erdnagel* (tent peg, literally "ground nail").

On 25 August 1966 the German Defence Minister Kai-Uwe von Hassel relieved the *Inspekteur der Luftwaffe* Generalleutnant Werner Panitzki, and transferred the Colonel Erich Hartmann, commanding officer of the 71st Fighter Squadron, as both had publicly criticized the acquisition of the Starfighter as a "purely political decision". On 2 September 1966 Johannes Steinhoff, with Günther Rall as deputy, became the new *Inspekteur der Luftwaffe*. Steinhoff and his deputy Günther Rall noted that the non-German F-104s proved much safer. The Americans blamed the high loss rate of the *Luftwaffe* F-104s on the extreme low-level and aggressive flying of German pilots rather than any faults in the aircraft. Steinhoff and Rall went to America to learn to fly the Starfighter under Lockheed instruction and noted some specifics in the training (a lack of mountain and foggy-weather training), combined with handling capabilities (rapidly initiated, high G turns) of the aircraft that could cause accidents. Steinhoff and Rall therefore changed the training regimen for the F-104 pilots, and the accident rates fell to those comparable or better than other air forces. They also brought about the high level of training and professionalism seen today throughout the *Luftwaffe*, and the start of a strategic direction for *Luftwaffe* pilots to engage in tactical and combat training outside of Germany. However, the F-104 never lived down its reputation as a "widow-maker", and was replaced by the Luftwaffe with the McDonnell Douglas F-4 Phantom II fighter and the Panavia Tornado fighter-bomber in many units much earlier than in other national air forces.

On Steinhoff's initiative the Luftwaffe opened the German Air Force Command USA/Canada (*Deutsches Luftwaffenkommando USA/Kanada*) in Fort Bliss, where the Luftwaffe trained its missile and air defence troops, as well as pilots received their basic training. At the same time the Luftwaffe opened a Tactical Training Command in Beja, Portugal, where pilots trained Close Air Support missions.

Between 1967 and 1970, the Luftwaffe undertook a major reorganization of its forces. The two operational commands were disbanded and the four mixed Air Force divisions were divided into two flying divisions and two air defence divisions. The remainder of the units were divided into functional commands:

- Air Force Operation Command (*Luftwaffenführungsdienstkommando*), with the signal regiments, the radar, and the signals intelligence units

Figure 56: *An Alpha Jet A in 1996*

Figure 57: *One of 212 Panavia Tornado IDSs delivered to the Luftwaffe*

- Air Force Training Command (*Luftwaffenausbildungskommando*), with the schools and training regiments
- Air Force Support Command (*Luftwaffenunterstützungskommando*), with all logistical, maintenance and repair units, and the Material Office of the Air Force
- Air Force Transport Command (*Lufttransportkommando*), with the air transport squadrons.

Over the next decade, the Luftwaffe received large amounts of new equipment including in 1968 the first C-160 Transall transport planes, in 1974 the F-4 Phantom II fighter-bombers, in 1978 the first Alpha Jet Version A light attack jets and in 1979 the first of 212 Panavia Tornado fighters.

The air defense forces began to replace their Nike Hercules missile systems in 1986 with state of the art surface-to-air missile systems: first to arrive was the MIM-104 Patriot system, followed one year later by Roland short range missile system.

Nuclear sharing

Germany is participating in NATO's nuclear sharing concept. Nuclear sharing is a concept, which involves member countries without nuclear weapons of their own in the planning for the use of nuclear weapons by NATO, and in particular provides for the armed forces of these countries to be involved in delivering these weapons in the event of their use.

Soon after its founding the German Air Force began to train with the US Seventeenth Air Force in handling, arming and delivering nuclear weapons. At first the F-104 Starfighter was intended to be used solely as a nuclear delivery platform, armed with nuclear air-to-air and air-to-surface missiles, as well as nuclear bombs. The Tornado was the second plane the air force fielded capable of delivering nuclear ammunition, although it was limited to deliver B61 nuclear bombs.

From 1965 through 1970, the Missile Wing 1 and Missile Wing 2 fielded 16 Pershing 1 missile systems with nuclear warheads under U.S. Army custody. In 1970, the system was upgraded to Pershing 1a with 72 missiles. Although not directly affected by the 1988 Intermediate-Range Nuclear Forces Treaty, the *Luftwaffe* unilaterally removed the Pershing 1a missiles from its inventory in 1991, and the missiles were destroyed. At the end of the Cold War more than 100,000 soldiers served in the Luftwaffe.

The United States still lends nuclear weapons for hypothetical use by the Luftwaffe under the nuclear sharing agreement. In 2007, 22 B61 nuclear bombs

were still kept in Germany, stored at the Büchel Air Base for use with Tornado IDS fighter-bombers of Jagdbombergeschwader 33. The American nuclear weapons formerly stored at Nörvenich Air Base, Ramstein Air Base and Memmingen Air Base were all withdrawn from Germany during the mid-and-late-1990s.

By international treaties between Germany and the "Big Four" powers in Europe (that formerly occupied Germany), East Germany is a nuclear-free zone. The Big Four powers are the United States, Russia, the United Kingdom, and France, and with the latter three having no nuclear weapons in Germany anymore.

Reunification

After German reunification in October 1990, the aircraft and personnel of the former GDR air force, the *Luftstreitkräfte der NVA* were taken. The remnants of the East German Air Force were placed under the newly formed *5. Luftwaffendivision* (5th Air Force Division) in Strausberg. In 1993 the division was renamed *3. Luftwaffendivision*, moved to Gatow in Berlin and in 1995 assigned to NATO. Already in 1990 the East German plane markings were replaced by the Air Force Iron Cross, the first time Soviet-built aircraft had served in a NATO air force. However, as the *Luftstreitkräfte der NVA* were supplied exclusively with Eastern Bloc-produced aircraft such as the Sukhoi Su-17, MiG-21, MiG-23 and MiG-29 fighters, most of the equipment was not

Figure 58: *Luftwaffe MiG-29UB*

compatible with the West German NATO equipment and therefore taken out of service and sold or given to new members of NATO in Eastern Europe, such as Poland and the Baltic states.

An exception to this was the *Jagdfliegergeschwader 3* "Vladimir Komarov" (Fighter Wing 3 "Vladimir Komarov") in Preschen Air Base. The *Jagdfliegergeschwader 3* flew brand new MiG-29 fighters. On 1 June 1993 the wing was renamed *Jagdgeschwader 73* (Fighter Wing 73) and on 1 October 1994 completed its move to its new home at Laage Air Base. The pilots of JG 73 were some of the most experienced MiG-29 pilots in the world. One of their primary duties was to serve as aggressor pilots, training other pilots in dissimilar combat tactics. The United States sent a group of fighter pilots to Germany during the *Red October* exercise to practice tactics against the aircraft they were most likely to meet in real combat. The MiG-29s of JG 73 were fully integrated into the Luftwaffe's air defence structure and the first Soviet Bloc aircraft to be declared operational within NATO.[190] With the introduction of the Eurofighter Typhoon imminent, the decision was taken to withdraw the MiG-29. All German MiG-29, save one, were sold to Poland for the symbolic price of €1 apiece. On 9 August 2004 the last MiG-29s landed in Poland where they continue to serve in the 41st Tactical Squadron of the Polish Air Force.

The Balkans

The Luftwaffe experienced combat action for first time since World War II during September 1995 in the course of Operation Deliberate Force, when six IDS Tornado fighter-bombers, equipped with forward looking infrared devices, and escorted by eight ECR Tornados, supported NATO's artillery missions on positions of the Bosnian Serbs around Sarajevo, Bosnia & Herzegovina.[191,192]

In March 1999, the *Luftwaffe* became involved in direct combat role as part of the Kosovo War along with the other NATO powers. This event was noted as significant in the British press with *The Sun* running the headline *"Luftwaffe and the RAF into battle side by side"*. The *Luftwaffe* sent in the Fighter Bomber Wing 32, equipped with ECR Tornadoes, and this unit flew missions to suppress enemy air defences in and around Kosovo.

These fighter-bombers were equipped with an electronic countermeasures pod, one AIM-9 Sidewinder air-to-air missile for self-defence, and an AGM-88 HARM air-to-ground missile (anti-radar). The bomber wing flew 2108 hours and 446 sorties, firing 236 HARM missiles at hostile targets. No manned Luftwaffe planes were lost in combat during this campaign.

Figure 59: *A Luftwaffe Tornado ECR during the air campaign over Kosovo (1999)*

2000s

In 2005 and 2008, *Luftwaffe* F-4F *Phantom II* fighter planes took part in the Baltic Air Policing operation (of NATO), and these fighters were supplemented in 2009 by units flying the *Typhoon*.

In 2006, to support military operations in Afghanistan, the *Luftwaffe* sent over several Panavia Tornado reconnaissance planes from *Aufklärungsgeschwader* 51 "Immelmann" (the 51st Reconnaissance Wing "Immelmann"), stationed in Mazar-i-Sharif, Northern Afghanistan. There have also been assorted German Army helicopters flying from the *Luftwaffe* Air Base in Mazar-i-Sharif. Also, Luftwaffe C-160 Transall have flown transport plane missions in and around Afghanistan.

Since the 1970s, the *Luftwaffe* of West Germany and later the reunited Germany (as well as many other European air forces) has actively pursued the construction of European internationally made warplanes such as the Panavia Tornado and the Eurofighter Typhoon introduced into the *Luftwaffe* in 2006.

On 13 January 2004, the Minister of Defence, Peter Struck, announced major changes in the future of the German armed forces. A major part of this announcement was a plan to cut the number of fighter planes from 426 in early

Figure 60: *A Luftwaffe Eurofighter Typhoon (single-seater version)*

2004, to 265 by 2015. Assuming that the plans to order 180 Typhoons is carried out in full, and all of the F-4 Phantoms are removed from service, this would cut the number of Tornado fighter-bombers down to just 85.

In the past, the Bundesmarine's naval air wing (the *Marineflieger*) received 112 Tornado IDS planes. However, during late 2004, the last unit of Bundesmarine Tornadoes was disbanded. All of the maritime combat role was assigned to the *Luftwaffe*, and one unit of this has had its Tornadoes fighters equipped to carry Kormoran II missiles and American HARM missiles.

2010s

As of 2014, a significant proportion of Germany's military aircraft were reported to be unserviceable. It has been reported that the Sea Lynx helicopters have experienced cracking in their tails, that around half of the Eurofighters and Tornadoes are not currently airworthy, and that the aging C-160 fleet remains in limited service while waiting for the introduction of the Airbus A400M, the first of which was delivered in December 2014. Ursula von der Leyen admitted that due to the poor state of the Bundeswehr's equipment, Germany was no longer able to fulfill its NATO commitments.

The German Air Force was one of the founding members of the European Air Transport Command headquartered in Eindhoven - The Netherlands and most of the Transport & Tanker assets have been transferred under EATC management. Replacement of the current 4 Airbus A310 MRTT by the Airbus A330

Figure 61: *Luftwaffe Eurofighter Typhoon 30+68 with painting "60 years of Luftwaffe" (2016)*

MRTT was approved in 2018 by joining the acquisition of 4 by the Royal Netherlands Air Force.

Future plans are the replacement of the ageing Sikorsky CH-53 Sea Stallion acquired since the 1970s by 40-70 Boeing CH-47 Chinook or Sikorsky CH-53K King Stallion from 2022 onwards.

The German Air Force is working with Airbus to define requirements for a replacement of the Tornado, called FCAS (Future Combat Air System) in the 2035 timeframe, under the Next-Generation Weapon System (NGWS) future fighter programme. It is envisioned as a networked system of systems, working with UAVs, complementing the Eurofighter and could be optionally manned. A possible alternative under evaluation is the procurement of Lockheed Martin F-35 fighters.

The German Luftwaffe participated in the Israeli Air Force exercise "Blue Flag", the country's largest international air combat exercise, designed to simulate extreme combat scenarios. The German Air Force six Eurofighter Typhoon fighter jets of the tactical air force squadron 73 Steinhoff from Rostock. It is the first German participation in the Blue Flag exercise.

The German military needs a "fifth-generation" replacement for its Tornado fighter jets that is hard to detect on enemy radars and can strike targets from a great distance, the chief of staff of the air force said on November 8, 2017. Lieutenant General Karl Muellner's comments are his clearest public statements to date on the Tornado replacement program. They indicate a preference for Lockheed Martin Corp's F-35 fighter jet, the only Western aircraft that

Figure 62: *German Air Force MIM-104 Patriot system*

meets those requirements. In 2018, the Air Force issued a request for information from manufacturers about four potential aircraft to replace the Tornado - the Eurofighter Typhoon, F-15 Advanced Eagle, F/A-18E/F Super Hornet and F-35 Lightning.

Due to the problems with the A400M and in service limitations, the German Air Force will acquire 3 * C130J Super Hercules Transport and 3 * KC-130J Tanker Aircraft (delivery planned 2020-2021) which will be jointly operated with the French Air Force the 2 * C-130J and 2 * KC-130J Aircraft (delivery planned 2018-2019).

Structure

The current commander of the German Air Force is Lieutenant General Karl Müllner. Upon the retirement of Lieutenant General Aarne Kreuzinger-Janik on 30 April 2012, Müllner became the 15th Inspector of the Air Force (*Inspekteur der Luftwaffe*). The Inspector of the Air Force is the commander of Air Force Command (*Kommando Luftwaffe*), a body created in 2013 by the merger of the Air Force Office (*Luftwaffenamt*), German Air Staff (*Führungsstab der Luftwaffe*), and Air Force Forces Command (*Luftwaffenführungskommando*). Similar to the Air Staff of the United States Air Force,

Figure 63: *Büchel Air Base*

the German Air Force Command is a force providing command, not an operational command. The Air Force Command is tasked with ensuring the combat readiness of the German Air Force combat units, which during operations would either be commanded by a NATO command or the Joint Operations Command of the Bundeswehr. The Air Force command directly controls three higher commands.[193]

The creation of the Air Force Command was part of a reorganization of the Bundeswehr as a whole, announced by Thomas de Maizière in 2011, which also involved the Air Force shrinking to 23,000 soldiers and thus undergoing major restructuring at all levels. In addition to the higher command authorities, the three air divisions, the Air Force Training Command, and Air Force Weapon Systems Command, were disbanded. The three surface-to-air missile units will merge into a single wing in Husum in Northern Germany. The wing fields 14 MIM-104 Patriot and 4 MANTIS systems. The three air transport wings will be merged into a single wing based at Wunstorf Air Base, which will field 40 A400M Atlas transport planes. The Luftwaffe will field three Multirole Eurofighter Wings, each with two squadrons for a total of 143 Eurofighter Typhoon.[194] A fighter-bomber wing fielding Panavia Tornado IDS planes remains in service at Büchel Air Base. The Reconnaissance Wing 51 will remain in service at Schleswig Air Base and add one drone squadron to its Panavia Tornado ECR squadron.

The Kommando Luftwaffe has two main elements subordinate to it:

- Air Operations Center (*Zentrum Luftoperationen der Luftwaffe*), responsible for providing command and control to air operations
- Air Force Forces Command (*Luftwaffentruppenkommando*)

Individual units of the Air Force are either part of the Air Force Operational Forces Command or the Support Forces Command. They only fall under the command of the Air Operations Center when on deployments or attached to EU or NATO organizations.

Air Operations Center

File:Relief Map of Germany.svg

German Air Force radar stations, and control and reporting centers
- HR-3000 (HADR) radar station
- GM 406F radar station
- RRP-117 radar station
- Control and Reporting Center

The main subordinate elements of the Air Operations Center are:

- **Air Operations Center** (NATO CAOC Uedem), in Uedem, responsible for NATO's Integrated Air Defense System North of the Alps
- Air Force Support Group (Luftwaffenunterstützungsgruppe), in Kalkar
- Control and Reporting Center 2 (Einsatzführungsbereich 2), in Erndtebrück
  - Operations Squadron 21, in Erndtebrück
  - Operations Support Squadron 22, in Erndtebrück
    - Sensor Platoon I, in Lauda
      - Remote Radar Post 240 "Loneship", in Erndtebrück with GM 406F
      - Remote Radar Post 246 "Hardwheel", on Erbeskopf with HADR
      - Remote Radar Post 247 "Batman", in Lauda with GM 406F
      - Remote Radar Post 248 "Coldtrack", in Freising with GM 406F
      - Remote Radar Post 249 "Sweet Apple", in Meßstetten with HADR
    - Sensor Platoon II, in Auenhausen
      - Remote Radar Post 241 "Crabtree", in Marienbaum with Hughes HR-3000
      - Remote Radar Post 242 "Backwash", in Auenhausen with GM 406F
      - Remote Radar Post 243 "Silver Cork", in Visselhövede with GM 406F
      - Remote Radar Post 244 "Round up", in Brockzetel with HADR
      - Remote Radar Post 245 "Bugle", in Brekendorf with GM 406F
  - Control and Reporting Training Inspection 23, in Erndtebrück
    - Education and Training Center, in Erndtebrück
    - Education, Test and Training Group, in Erndtebrück
- Control and Reporting Center 3 (Einsatzführungsbereich 3), in Schönewalde
  - Operations Squadron 31, in Schönewalde
  - Operations Support Squadron 32, in Schönewalde

- Sensor Platoon III, in Cölpin
  - Remote Radar Post 351 "Matchpoint", in Putgarten with RRP-117
  - Remote Radar Post 352 "Mindreader", in Cölpin with RRP-117
  - Remote Radar Post 353 "Teddy Bear", in Tempelhof with RRP-117
  - Remote Radar Post 356 "", in Elmenhorst with RRP-117
- Sensor Platoon IV, in Regen
  - Remote Radar Post 354 "Blackmoor", in Döbern with RRP-117
  - Remote Radar Post 355 "Royal Flash", in Gleina with RRP-117
  - Remote Radar Post 357 "", on Döbraberg with RRP-117
  - Remote Radar Post 358 "Snow Cap", on Großer Arber with RRP-117
- Deployable Control and Reporting Centre, in Schönewalde
- Air Force Command Support Center (Führungsunterstützungszentrum der Luftwaffe), in Köln-Wahn
- German Representation at NATO's Allied Air Command, at Ramstein Air Base
- German Representation at Joint Air Power Competence Centre, in Kalkar
- German Representation at European Air Transport Command, in Eindhoven Air Base
- German Representation at NATO Airborne Early Warning & Control Force Command, at NATO Air Base Geilenkirchen
- German Representation at Alliance Ground Surveillance, in Sigonella Air Base

Air Force Forces Command

The main subordinate elements of the Air Force Operational Forces Command are:

Directly subordinated institutions:

- Air Force Air and Space Medicine Center, at Köln-Wahn Air Base

Subordinated flying units:

- Tactical Air Force Wing 31 "Boelcke", at Nörvenich Air Base, with Eurofighter Typhoon
- Tactical Air Force Wing 33, at Büchel Air Base, with Tornado IDS

German Air Force

- Tactical Air Force Wing 51 "Immelmann", at Schleswig Air Base, with Tornado ECR
- Tactical Air Force Wing 71 "Richthofen", at Wittmundhafen Air Base, with Eurofighter Typhoon
- Tactical Air Force Wing 73 "Steinhoff", at Laage Air Base, with Eurofighter Typhoon
- Tactical Air Force Wing 74, at Neuburg Air Base, with Eurofighter Typhoon
- Air Transport Wing 62, at Wunstorf Air Base with A400M Atlas
- Air Transport Wing 63, at Hohn Air Base with C-160 Transall
- Helicopter Wing 64, at Laupheim Air Base and Holzdorf Air Base
  - Flying Group, at Laupheim Air Base with CH-53 Sea Stallion and H145M LUH SOF
  - Air Transport Group, at Holzdorf Air Base with CH-53 Sea Stallion
- Federal Defence Ministry Transport Wing, at Köln-Wahn and Berlin-Tegel airports with A310, A319CJ, A340-300, Global 5000 and AS532 U2 Cougar
- Air Force Tactical Training Command USA, Holloman AFB, New Mexico, with Tornado IDS
  - German Representation at Euro NATO Joint Jet Pilot Training, Sheppard AFB, Texas with T-6 Texan II and T-38C Talon
  - German Air Force Training Squadron 2, at NAS Pensacola, Florida
  - German Air Force Training Squadron 3, at Phoenix Goodyear Airport, Arizona
- Electronic Warfare Flying Weapon Systems Center, in Kleinaitingen

Subordinated ground based units:

- Air Defence Missile Wing 1 "Schleswig-Holstein", in Husum Air Base
  - Air Defence Missile Group 21, in Sanitz and Prangendorf with MIM-104 Patriot
  - Air Defence Missile Group 24, in Bad Sülze with MIM-104 Patriot
  - Air Defence Missile Group 26, in Husum Air Base with MIM-104 Patriot
  - Air Defence Missile Group 61, in Todendorf with MANTIS (joined the Royal Netherlands Army's Joint Land-based Air Defense Command in April 2018)
  - Air Defence Missiles Tactical Training and Instruction Center, in Fort Bliss, Texas
  - Air Defence Missiles Training Center, in Husum
- Air Force Regiment "Friesland", at Jever Air Base
  - Battalion I (Infantry), at Jever Air Base
  - Battalion II (Logistics, Sappers, Firefighters), at Diepholz Air Base

- Air Force Officer School, in Fürstenfeldbruck
- Air Force Non-Commissioned Officer School, in Appen and Heide
- Air Force Training Battalion, in Germersheim
- Air Force Support Group, at Köln-Wahn Air Base

Subordinated support units:

- Weapon System Support Center 1, at Erding Air Base
  - Maintenance Center 11, at Erding Air Base
  - Maintenance Center 12, in Ummendorf
  - Maintenance Center 13, at Landsberg/Lech Air Base
  - Maintenance Center 14, at Ingolstadt/Manching Air Base
- Weapon System Support Center 2, at Diepholz Air Base
  - Maintenance Center 21, at Diepholz Air Base (will move to Holzdorf Air Base)
  - Maintenance Center 23, at Wunstorf Air Base
  - Maintenance Center 24, at Trollenhagen Air Base (will move to Laage Air Base)
  - Maintenance Center 25, in Erndtebrück
  - Maintenance Center 26, at Wunstorf Air Base
- Air Force Technical Training Center, at Faßberg Air Base
  - Air Force Technical Training Center North, at Faßberg Air Base
  - Air Force Technical Training Center South, at Kaufbeuren Air Base
  - Air Force Professional College, at Faßberg Air Base
- German Representation at the NATO Programming Center, in Glons, Belgium

North American training centers

In light of the destroyed infrastructure of West Germany post–World War II, the restrictions on aircraft production placed on Germany and the later restrictive flying zones available for training pilots, the reconstructed *Luftwaffe* trained most of its pilots tactically away from Germany, mainly in the United States and Canada where most of its aircraft were sourced.

During the 1960s and 1970s, a very large number of Luftwaffe jet crashes—the *Luftwaffe* suffered a 36 percent crash rate for F-84F Thunderstreaks and an almost 30 percent loss of F-104 Starfighters—created considerable public demand for moving Luftwaffe combat training centers away from Germany.

As a result, the *Luftwaffe* set up two tactical training centres: one, like those of many of the NATO forces, at the Royal Canadian Air Force base at Goose Bay; and the second in a unique partnership with the United States Air Force at Holloman Air Force Base in New Mexico (F-104 pilots had already been trained at Luke Air Force Base, Arizona, since 1964). Both facilities provide

Figure 64: *Luftwaffe Panavia Tornados at CFB Goose Bay*

access to large unpopulated areas, where tactical and combat training can take place without danger to large populations.

On 1 May 1996, the *Luftwaffe* established the German Air Force Tactical Training Center (TTC) in concert with the United States Air Force 20th Fighter Squadron at Holloman Air Force Base in New Mexico, which provides aircrew training in the F-4F Phantom II. The TTC serves as the parent command for two German air crew training squadrons. The F-4 Training Squadron oversees all German F-4 student personnel affairs and provides German instructor pilots to cooperate in the contracted F-4 training program provided by the U.S. Air Force (20th Fighter Squadron). A second TTC unit, the Tornado Training Squadron, provides academic and tactical flying training, by German air force instructors, for German Tornado aircrews.

The first contingent of Tornado aircraft arrived at Holloman in March 1996. More than 300 German air force personnel are permanently assigned at Holloman to the TTC, the only unit of its kind in the United States. The German Air Force Flying Training Center activated on 31 March 1996, with German Air Force Chief of Staff Gen. Portz and U.S. Air Force Chief of Staff Gen. Michael Ryan present. The *Luftwaffe* has since stationed up to 800 personnel at Holloman for training exercises, due to limited training space in Europe.

In September 2004, the Luftwaffe announced a reduction in its training program by about 20%. By the end of 2006, 650 Luftwaffe personnel and 25 Tornado aircraft were assigned to Holloman.

Figure 65: *F-4Es of the 1st GAFTS.*

Air bases

In 2018 the Air Force uses 16 air bases, six of which host no flying units. Furthermore, the Air Force has a presence at two civil airports:

Name[195]	Major Tenants	ICAO-Code	IATA-Code	Runways Code			Year	Nearest City	State
				Direction	Cover	Size			
Berlin Tegel Airport	MOD Transport Wing	EDDT	TXL	08L/-26R	Asphalt	3022x45	1948	Berlin	Berlin
				08R/-26L	Asphalt	2427x45			
Büchel Air Base	Tactical Wing 33	ETSB	–	03/-21	Asphalt	2507x45	1955	Büchel	Rhineland-Palatinate
Cologne Bonn Airport	MOD Transport Wing	EDDK	CGN	14L/-32R	Asphalt	3815x60	1938	Cologne	North Rhine-Westphalia
				06/-24	Concrete	2459x45			
				14R/-32L	Asphalt	1863x45			

German Air Force

Erding Air Base	Maintenance Regiment 1	ETSE	–	08/-26	Concrete	2521x30	1935	Erding	Bavaria
Hohn Air Base	Air Transport Wing 63	ETNH	–	08/-26	Concrete	2440x30		Hohn	Schleswig-Holstein
Holzdorf Air Base	Helicopter Wing 64	ETSH	–	09/-27	Asphalt	2419x30	1974	Holzdorf	Saxony-Anhalt
Landsberg-Lech Air Base		ETSA	–	07/-25	Concrete	2066x30	1935	Landsberg	Bavaria
Lechfeld Air Base		ETSL	–	03/-21	Concrete	2678x30	1912	Klosterlechfeld	Bavaria
Neuburg Air Base	Tactical Wing 74	ETSN	–	09/-27	Asphalt	2440x30	1960	Neuburg	Bavaria
Nörvenich Air Base	Tactical Wing 31	ETNN	QOE	07/-25	Asphalt	2439x45	1954	Nörvenich	North Rhine-Westphalia
Rostock-Laage Airport	Tactical Wing 73	ETNL	RLG	10/-28	Concrete	2500x45	1984	Laage	Mecklenburg-Vorpommern
Schleswig Air Base	Tactical Wing 51	ETNS	WBG	05/-23	Asphalt	2439x30		Schleswig	Schleswig-Holstein
Wittmundhafen Air Base	Tactical Wing 71	ETNT	–	08/-26	Asphalt	2440x30	1951	Wittmund	Lower Saxony
Wunstorf Air Base	Air Transport Wing 62	ETNW	–	08/-26	Asphalt	1877x46,5	1936	Wunstorf	Lower Saxony
				03/-21	Asphalt	1699x47,5			
				08/-26	Grass	1088x40			

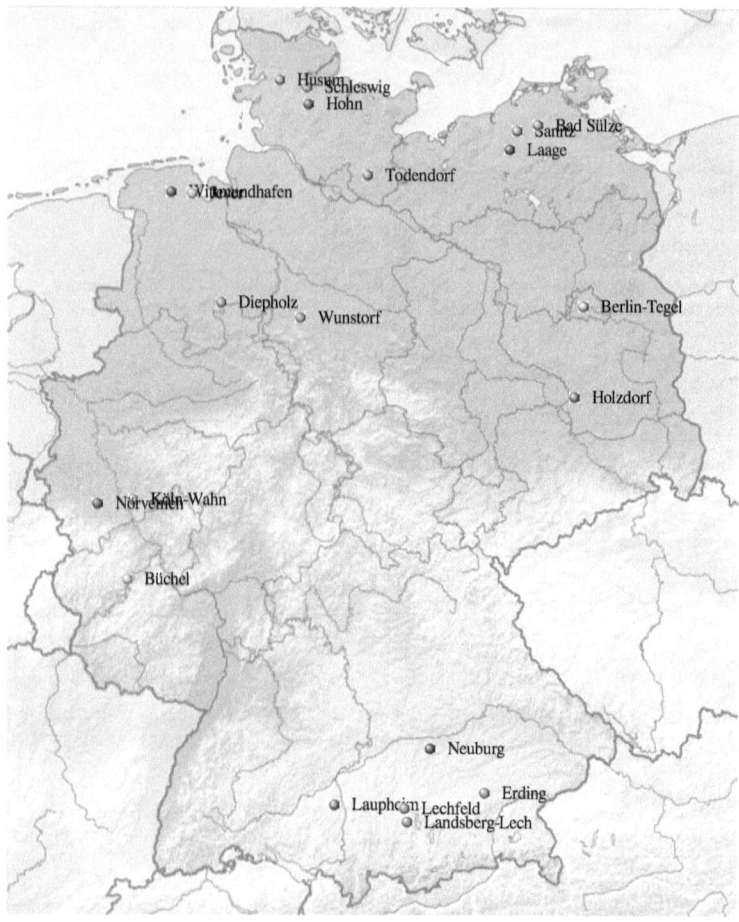

File:Relief Map of Germany.svg

Air bases of the German Air Force

- Eurofighter Typhoon
- Tornado IDS
- Tornado ECR & IDS
- A400M Atlas
- C-160 Transall
- CH-53 Sea Stallion
- VIP Transport
- Air Force Regiment
- Air Defence Missile Wing 1
- Bases without flying units

Figure 66: *A preserved Fokker D.VII with original-style Balkenkreuz of 1918*

Personnel

In 2012, the Air Force had an authorized strength of 44,565 active soldiers and 4,914 reservists. The civil personnel within the Air Force is being reduced to 5,950 officials and employees. Most of the civilian employees work in maintenance and the Air Force Fire Department. On 20 September 2011 defense minister Thomas de Maizière announced that the Air Force would shrink to 23,000 soldiers.[196]

Training

The Luftwaffe has set up a total of 5 training institutions, namely the Offizierschule der Luftwaffe, Unteroffizierschule der Luftwaffe, Luftwaffenausbildungsbataillon, Fachschule der Luftwaffe and Technische Ausbildungszentrum der Luftwaffe, for training catering both personnel in active service and civilians willing to enter the Luftwaffe.

Symbols, emblems and uniform

Roundel and serial number

Originally German Air Force aircraft carried an Iron Cross — appearing to be closely modeled on that used by the 1916-17 era Imperial German Luftstreitkräfte through the spring of 1918, but no longer having the white border around the crosses' "ends" (thusly resembling the straight white "flanks" of

Figure 67: *Air Force dress uniform*

the earlier, 1918-1945 era *Balkenkreuz* national marking) — as an identifying feature on all four wing positions and on both sides on the rear of the fuselage and a small German flag painted on the vertical stabilizer. Each aircraft also carried a serial number consisting of 2 letters, which identified the service and combat wing, followed by three numbers identifying the squadron and the number of the plane within the squadron, almost graphically resembling the USAF's own buzz numbers of the same period.

This system was changed in 1968. The large Iron Cross and serial numbers have since been replaced on all aircraft by a four number registration code, appearing somewhat in the manner of the earlier alphanumeric *Geschwaderkennung* code characters used by their World War II predecessor — separated by an Iron Cross in the middle: the first two numbers identify the type of aircraft and the second two numbers are a sequential for each type. When writing the registration number the Iron Cross is written as a "+". I.e. the Tornado IDS of the Air Force are numbered from 43+01 to 46+22, while the Tornado ECR of the Air Force are numbered from 46+23 to 46+57. The numbers from 30+01 to 33+99 are being used for the Eurofighter.

Figure 68: *A Eurofighter Typhoon during exercise Frisian Flag*

Uniform

The ranks of the Air Force are identical to the ranks of the German Army. The Air Force field dress is the same as the army field dress. The dress uniform of the Air Force is dark blue with gold-yellow wings as collar patches. As headdress a dark blue side cap or dark blue peaked cap can be worn. Members of the German Air Force Regiment wear a dark blue beret.

Aircraft

Current inventory

Aircraft	Origin	Type	Variant	In service	Notes
Combat Aircraft					
Panavia Tornado	Multi-national[197]	multirole	IDS	87	employs variable-sweep wing design
Eurofighter Typhoon	Multi-national[198]	multirole		132	
Electronic Warfare					
Panavia Tornado	Multi-national	SEAD	ECR	28	
Tanker					

Airbus A310 MRTT	Multi-national[199]	aerial refueling / transport		4	
Transport					
Airbus A310	Multi-national	VIP	A310-304	1	
Airbus A319	Multi-national[200]	VIP	A319CJ	2	
Airbus A321	Multi-national[201]	VIP	A321-200		1 on order
Airbus A340	Multi-national	VIP	A340-300	2	
Airbus A400M	Multi-national[202]	tactical airlift		19[203]	34 on order
Global Express	Canada	VIP	Global 5000	4	
Transall C-160	Multi-national[204]	transport	C-160D	29[205]	
Helicopter					
Sikorsky CH-53	United States[206]	heavy lift	CH-53G[207]	72	
Eurocopter EC145	Multi-national[208]	light utility	H145M	15	use for Special Operations Forces
Eurocopter AS532	Multi-national[209]	VIP	AS532 U2	3	
Trainer aircraft					
Eurofighter Typhoon	Multi-national	conversion trainer		24	2 on order
Panavia Tornado	Multi-national	conversion trainer	IDS	7	
UAVs					
MQ-4C Triton	United States	SIGINT / surveillance			4 on order[210]
IAI Heron TP	Israel	surveillance		3[211]	

Four Airbus A330 MRTT's are on order to support NATO's Multinational Multi-Role Tanker Transport Fleet, which includes Germanys contribution to the program.

Selected bibliography

Hundreds of books, magazines and articles have been written about the Luftwaffe. A select few are listed here.

- Amadio, Jill (2002), *Günther Rall: A Memoir*, Seven Locks Press. ISBN 0-9715533-0-0.

Figure 69: *A CH-53G in flight over ILA Berlin 2016*

Figure 70: *A Luftwaffe A400M on its maiden flight*

- Philpott, Bryan (1986), *History of the German Air Force*, Hamlyn. ISBN 0-600-50293-7.

External links

 Wikimedia Commons has media related to *Air force of Germany*.

- Official website[188] (in German)
- Luftwaffe museum[212] (in German) & (in English)

Special Forces

German special forces

The **German special forces** include the Special Operations Command (*Kommando Spezialkräfte*, KSK) of the German Army and the Naval Special Forces Command (*Kommando Spezialkräfte Marine*, KSM) of the German Navy. Both are regular units and fully integrated in the branches of the German Armed Forces. During operations, special forces are led by the special operations division of the Bundeswehr Joint Operations Command (*Einsatzführungskommando der Bundeswehr*) in Potsdam, which belongs to the Joint Support Service (*Streitkräftebasis*).

Beside KSK and KSM, there is a numerous of specialized units which are able to support special forces operations.

Special Forces

Army Special Forces

Most German special forces are part of the **Kommando Spezialkräfte** (KSK) which was founded in 1996. The KSK is a brigade level unit and stationed in Calw. It is under the command of the Rapid Response Forces Division (*Division Schnelle Kräfte*) and made up of around 1.100 soldiers. Most of them serve in the support forces department.

- **Kommando Spezialkräfte**
  - HQ KSK
    - Psychological Service
    - Language Service
  - Force Development Group
  - *Operational Forces*
    - 1st Commando Company
    - 2nd Commando Company

- 3rd Commando Company
- 4th Commando Company
- Special Commando Company
- Training Centre
- *Support Forces*
  - HQ & Support Company
  - Signal Company
  - Support Company
  - Medial Centre

Naval Special Forces

The **Kommando Spezialkräfte Marine** (KSM) was founded in 2014 and built around the Commando Frogmen Company (*Kampfschwimmerkompanie*), the oldest German special forces unit. The KSM is based in Eckernförde and is part of the 1st Flotilla (*Einsatzflottille 1*) in Kiel.

- **Kommando Spezialkräfte Marine**
  - HQ KSM
    - S1 - Personnel
    - S2/6 - Intelligence/Communications
    - S3 - Operations
    - S4 - Logistics
      - Operations Support Team Air (*Einsatzgruppe Luft*)
      - Diver Depot
      - Vehicle Repair Squad
    - Analysis & Development Group
    - Special Operation Medial Support Team (SOMST)
  - Commando Frogmen Company
    - Commando Frogmen Teams (*Kampfschwimmereinsatzteams*, KSET)
    - Operations Support Team Sea (*Einsatzgruppe See*)
  - Tactics and Training Group (*Gruppe Grundlagen, Verfahren, Taktik und Ausbildung*, GVTA)

Special Forces Aviation

The KSK is currently supported by the German Army Aviation Corps and - since reorientation of the Bundeswehr in 2010 - by the helicopter force of the German Air Force. From 2015, the KSK gets its own aviation component made up of 15 EC645 T2 utility helicopters. They will be part of the Helicopter Wing 64 at the Holzdorf Air Base.

The KSM is supported by the Naval Air Wing 5 in Nordholz which operates the Westland Lynx and Westland Sea King.

Specialized Forces

Special Operations Training Centre

Originally established in 1979 as an international school for long-range reconnaissance patrol team, the **Ausbildungszentrum Spezielle Operationen** is responsible for initial and further training of special and specialized forces. The centre has the size of a regiment, is subordinate to Army Training Commando and based in Pfullendorf.

Special Forces Support Units

In order to support the KSK, the Germany Army developed a concept of specialized forces (*Spezialierte Kräfte des Heeres mit erweiteter Grundgefähigung für spezielle Operationen*, EGB). This includes a numerous of army units, mostly airborne forces. A distinction is made between the main operational forces and support forces. All of them are independent units respectively part of regular formations.

In 2013, the operational forces consists of:

- 4 x Fallschirmjäger companies with each 4 platoons
- 4 x Fallschirmjäger pathfinder platoons
- 1 x Longe Range Reconnaissance Patrol Company
- 2 x airborne engineer platoons
- 2 x HUMINT HQ Squads
- 4 x HUMINT Squads

The support force are made up of:

- 2 x airborne reconnaissance companies
- 4 x K9 platoons of the Fallschirmjäger
- 1 x Mountain Leader Platoon of the Gebirgsjäger reconnaissance company
- 4 x Fallschirmjäger Joint Fire Support Coordination Teams
- 4 x Fallschirmjäger Joint Fire Support Teams
- 1 x electronic warfare platoon
- several units, e.g. medics and PSYOPS

Fleet Protection Forces

From 1997 until spring 2014, both naval special forces (commando frogmen) and naval specialized forces (mine clearance divers and boarding trained naval infantry men) were organized into the Naval Specialized Deployment Forces, a battalion-sized unit with four companies. The ideas was to combine all specialized skills into one single formation. At the beginning, it was planned to create a force protection company beside the Boarding Company to support operations of the commando frogmen.

Through the reorientation of the Bundeswehr, the commando frogmen got their own battaillon while naval infantry (including HUMINT experts) and mine clearance divers were summarized into the Naval Force Protection Battalion (*Seebataillon*) in Eckernförde. The formation is often described as the "multi tool of the German Navy". So, the battalion is able to support special forces operations.

Counter-Terrorism

Grenzschutzgruppe 9 der Bundespolizei (Border Protection Group 9 of the Federal Police), commonly abbreviated GSG 9, is the Police Tactical Unit of the German federal police. Their counterparts on the state level are the Special Deployment Commandos.

Appendix

References

[1] http://www.bundeswehr.de
[2] //en.wikipedia.org/w/index.php?title=Bundeswehr&action=edit
[3] Fritz Erler, 'Politik und nicht Prestige,' in Erler and Jaeger, Sicherheit und Rustung, 1962, p.82-3, cited in Julian Lider, Origins and Development of West German Military Thought, Vol. I, 1949–1966, Gower Publishing Company Ltd, Aldershot/Brookfield VT, 1986, p.125
[4] Aberheim, 'The Citizen in Uniform: Reform and its Critics in the Bundeswehr,' in Szabo, (ed.), The Bundeswehr and Western Security, St. Martin's Press, New York, 1990, p.39.
[5] Donald Aberheim, 1990, p.37; Donald Aberheim, 'German Soldiers and German Unity: Political Foundations of the German Armed Forces,' California Naval Postgraduate School, 1991, p.14, cited in Artur A Bogowicz, ' Polish Armed Forces of 2000: Demands and Changes http://oai.dtic.mil/oai/oai?verb=getRecord&metadataPrefix=html&identifier=ADA376462,' NPGS Thesis, March 2000, and Obituary for General Ulrich de Maizière, The Times, 13 September 2006
[6] Large, David Clay *Germans to the Front West German rearmament in the Adenauer era* University of North Carolina Press 1996 pp244-5
[7] John Lewis Gaddis, 'The Cold War – a New History', Penguin Books, London, 2005, p.220
[8] Large op.cit. pp263-4
[9] Duffield, John: *World Power Forsaken: Political Culture, International Institutions, and German Security Policy After Unification*, p. 32
[10] Madeline Chambers (3 December 2015), More assertive Germany considers bigger army as Syria vote looms https://www.reuters.com/article/us-mideast-crisis-germany-idUSKBN0TM25A20151203 *Reuters*.
[11] A soldier's joke about this situation runs thus: "The service uniform is called service uniform because it's not worn on service, while the field uniform is called field uniform because it's not worn in the field." (In the field they wear the battle uniform ("Gefechtsanzug"), an extended version of the field uniform.)
[12] Bei jedem Wetter, zu jeder Zeit: Neue Tarnung für die Truppe https://www.bundeswehr.de bundeswehr.de. Erding, Bayern, 9 February 2016.
[13] http://hdl.loc.gov/loc.gdc/cntrystd.de
[14] http://www.bundeswehr.de/
[15] http://www.bmvg.de/portal/poc/bmvg?uri=ci%3Abw.bmvg&lg=en
[16] http://www.bwb.org/
[17] http://www.it-amtbw.de/
[18] https://web.archive.org/web/20060127005113/http://www.terrwv.bundeswehr.de/
[19] http://www.y-magazin.de/
[20] http://www.if-zeitschrift.de/
[21] https://archive.is/20130106080254/http://www.readersipo.de/
[22] //en.wikipedia.org/w/index.php?title=Template:History_of_Germany&action=edit
[23] John M. Jeep, *Medieval Germany: An Encyclopedia* (2001) covers AD 500 to 1500
[24] Henryk Sienkiewicz and Miroslaw Lipinski, eds. *The Teutonic Knights* (1996)
[25] David Nicolle and Graham Turner, *Teutonic Knight: 1190-1561 (Warrior)* (2007)
[26] Stephen Turnbull and Angus McBride, *The Hussite Wars 1419-36* (Men-at-Arms, 2004)
[27] Douglas Miller and Angus McBride, *Armies of the German Peasants' War 1524-26* (Men-at-Arms series) (2003)
[28] Peter H. Wilson, *The Thirty Years War: Europe's Tragedy* (2009)
[29] Dennis E. Showalter, *The Wars of Frederick the Great* (1996)
[30] Robert Asprey, *Frederick the Great: The Magnificent Enigma* (2007) pp 425-560
[31] Franz A.J. Szabo, *The Seven Years War in Europe: 1756-1763* (2007)
[32] Robert P. Goetz, *1805: Austerlitz: Napoleon And The Destruction Of The Third Coalition* (2005)

[33] David Gates, *The Napoleonic Wars 1803-1815* (1997)
[34] Charles Edward White, *The Enlightened Soldier: Scharnhorst and the Militarische Gesellschaft in Berlin, 1801-1805* (1988)
[35] Roger Parkinson, *The Hussar General: The Life of Blucher, Man of Waterloo* (2000)
[36] Jon Tetsuro Sumida, "The Relationship of History and Theory in On War: The Clausewitzian Ideal and Its Implications," *Journal of Military History* Vol. 65, No. 2 (Apr., 2001), pp. 333-354 in JSTOR https://www.jstor.org/stable/2677163
[37] Dennis E. Showalter, *The wars of German unification* (2004)
[38] Michael Howard, *The Franco-Prussian War: The German Invasion of France 1870-1871* (1961) excerpt and text search https://www.amazon.com/dp/0415266718/
[39] Robert K Massie, *Dreadnought: Britain, Germany and the coming of the Great War*, (1991) is popular
[40] Paul M. Kennedy, *The Rise of the Anglo-German Antagonism: 1860-1914* (1980) is advanced
[41] Holger H. Herwig, *The First World War: Germany and Austria-Hungary 1914-1918* (2009)
[42] Paul Halpern, *A Naval History of World War I* (1994) ch 10-13 excerpt and text search https://www.amazon.com/Naval-History-World-War/dp/0870212664/
[43] Bruce I. Gudmundsson, *Stormtroop Tactics: Innovation in the German Army, 1914-1918* (1995)
[44] Alexander Turner and Peter Dennis, *Cambrai 1917: The birth of armoured warfare* (2007)
[45] Phil Tomaseli, *Lys 1918: Estaires And Givenchy, The: German Spring Offensives* (2011)
[46] William Mulligan, *The Creation of the Modern German Army: General Walther Reinhardt and the Weimar Republic, 1914-1930* (2004)
[47] James S. Corum, *The Roots of Blitzkrieg: Hans von Seeckt and German Military Reform* (1994)
[48] Kevin W. Farrell, "Recent Approaches to the German Army of World War II: Is the Topic More Accessible after 65 Years?" *Global War Studies* (2010) 7#2 pp 131-156 online http://www.ingentaconnect.com/content/gws/gws/2010/00000007/00000002/art00004
[49] Andrew Roberts, *The Storm of War: A New History of the Second World War* (2011) pp 29-42
[50] Robert A. Doughty, *The Breaking Point: Sedan and the Fall of France, 1940* (1990) ch 1
[51] Alistair Horne, *To Lose a Battle: France 1940* (1969) pp 646-66
[52] Anthony J. Cumming, "Did Radar Win the Battle of Britain?" *Historian*, 2007 69#4 pp 688-705
[53] Civilian deaths were 300 to 600 a day, plus 1000 to 3000 injured. London was not a factory city and aircraft production went up.
[54] Arnold D. Harvey, "The Battle of Britain, in 1940 and 'Big Week,' in 1944: A Comparative Perspective," *Air Power History* (2012) 59#1 pp 34-45
[55] M. P. Barley, "Contributing to its Own Defeat: The Luftwaffe and the Battle of Britain," *Defence Studies*, Autumn 2004, Vol. 4#3 pp 387-411
[56] Robert M. Kennedy, *Hold the Balkans!: German Antiguerrilla Operations in the Balkans 1941-1944* (2001)
[57] Ian Kershaw, *Fateful Choices: Ten Decisions That Changed the World, 1940-1941* (2007)
[58] Gerhard L. Weinberg, *A World at Arms: A Global History of World War II* (1994) ch 5
[59] Weinberg, *A World at Arms: A Global History of World War II* (1994) pp 122-86
[60] David M. Glantz, *Operation Barbarossa: Hitler's Invasion of Russia 1941* (2011)ch 1
[61] Mark Healy, *Kursk 1943: The Tide Turns In The East* (1992) ch 6
[62] Dennis E. Showalter, *Patton And Rommel: Men of War in the Twentieth Century* (2006) ch 1
[63] Ian V. Hogg, *German Secret Weapons of World War II* (2006)ch 1
[64] Antony Beevor, *The Fall of Berlin 1945* (2003) ch 1
[65] A. J. Birtle, *Rearming the Phoenix: U.S. Military Assistance to the Federal Republic of Germany, 1950-1960* (1991), 131-249.
[66] Ingo Wolfgang Trauschweizer, "Learning with an Ally: The U.S. Army and the Bundeswehr in the Cold War," *Journal of Military History* (2008) 72#2 pp 477-508 online http://muse.jhu.edu/journals/journal_of_military_history/v072/72.2trauschweizer.html
[67] Emily O. Goldman and Leslie C. Eliason, *The diffusion of military technology and ideas* (2003) p 132
[68] Alan L. Nothnagle, *Building the East German myth* (1999) p 176
[69] Dale Roy Herspring, *Requiem for an army: the demise of the East German military* (1998) p 2

[70] Vincent Morelli and Paul Belkin, *NATO in Afghanistan: A Test of the Transatlantic Alliance* (Congressional Research Service, 2009) p. 22

[71] Canada gives Afghanistan warning http://www.afghannews.net/index.php?action=show&type=news&id=1355, afghannews.net

[72] https://www.amazon.com/dp/0195179455/

[73] https://www.amazon.com/dp/0700616241/

[74] https://www.amazon.com/dp/0195002571/

[75] https://www.amazon.com/Rise-Fall-Luftwaffe-Hauptmann-Hermann/dp/1781550069/

[76] https://www.amazon.com/Tirpitz-Imperial-German-Patrick-Kelly/dp/0253355931/

[77] https://www.amazon.com/Hitlers-Armies-history-Machine-Military/dp/1849086478/

[78] https://www.amazon.com/Cross-Iron-German-Machine-1918-1945/dp/0805083219/

[79] http://tigger.uic.edu/~rjensen/military.html

[80] http://www.military.com/Resources/HistorySubmittedFileView?file=History_Maps.htm

[81] http://europeanhistory.about.com/gi/dynamic/offsite.htm?site=http%3A%2F%2Fwww.fordham.edu%2Fhalsall%2Fmod%2Fgermanunification.html

[82] http://www.clausewitz.com/index.htm

[83] http://www.lib.byu.edu/~rdh/eurodocs/germ/1871.html

[84] https://web.archive.org/web/20050205071414/http://home.versatel.nl/gerardvonhebel/germit1859.htm

[85] https://web.archive.org/web/20051016000600/http://www.allempires.com/articles/hussite/hussite1.htm

[86] //en.wikipedia.org/w/index.php?title=Template:History_of_Germany&action=edit

[87] Jeffrey Verhey, *The Spirit of 1914: Militarism, Myth and Mobilization in Germany* (Cambridge U.P., 2000).

[88] N.P. Howard, "The Social and Political Consequences of the Allied Food Blockade of Germany, 1918-19," *German History* (1993), 11#2, pp. 161-88 online http://libcom.org/files/blockade%20Germany_0.pdf p. 166, with 271,000 excess deaths in 1918 and 71,000 in 1919.

[89] Jeff Lipkes, *Rehearsals: The German Army in Belgium, August 1914* (2007)

[90] Barbara Tuchman, *The Guns of August* (1962)

[91] Fred R. Van Hartesveldt, *The Battles of the Somme, 1916: Historiography and Annotated Bibliography* (1996), pp. 26-27.

[92] C.R.M.F. Cruttwell, A History of the Great War: 1914-1918 (1935) ch 15-29

[93] Holger H. Herwig, *The First World War: Germany and Austria-Hungary 1914-1918* (1997) ch. 4-6.

[94] Bruce I. Gudmundsson, *Stormtroop Tactics: Innovation in the German Army, 1914-1918* (1989), pp. 155-70.

[95] David Stevenson, *With Our Backs to the Wall: Victory and Defeat in 1918* (2011), pp. 30-111.

[96] C.R.M.F. Cruttwell, *A History of the Great War: 1914-1918* (1935), pp. 505-35r.

[97] Roger Chickering, *Imperial Germany and the Great War, 1914-1918* (1998) p. 14

[98] Richie, *Faust's Metropolis*, pp. 272-75.

[99] D. G. Williamson, "Walther Rathenau and the K.R.A. August 1914-March 1915," *Zeitschrift für Unternehmensgeschichte* (1978), Issue 11, pp. 118-136.

[100] Hew Strachan, *The First World War: Volume I: To Arms* (2001), pp. 1014-49 on Rathenau and KRA.

[101] Feldman, Gerald D. "The Political and Social Foundations of Germany's Economic Mobilization, 1914-1916," *Armed Forces & Society* (1976), 3#1, pp. 121-145. online http://afs.sagepub.com/content/3/1/121

[102] Keith Allen, "Sharing scarcity: Bread rationing and the First World War in Berlin, 1914-1923," *Journal of Social History*, (1998), 32#2, pp. 371-93, quote p. 380.

[103] N. P. Howard, "The Social and Political Consequences of the Allied Food Blockade of Germany, 1918-19," *German History*, April 1993, Vol. 11, Issue 2, pp. 161-188.

[104] Roger Chickering, *Imperial Germany and the Great War, 1914-1918* (2004) p. 141-42

[105] David Welch, *Germany, Propaganda and Total War, 1914-1918* (2000) p.122

[106] Chickering, *Imperial Germany*, pp. 140-145.

[107] Keith Allen, "Sharing scarcity: Bread rationing and the First World War in Berlin, 1914-1923," *Journal of Social History* (1998) 32#2, 00224529, Winter98, Vol. 32, Issue 2

[108] Alexandra Richie, *Faust's Metropolis* (1998), pp. 277-80.
[109] A. J. Ryder, *The German Revolution of 1918: A Study of German Socialism in War and Revolt* (2008)
[110] Wilhelm Diest and E. J. Feuchtwanger, "The Military Collapse of the German Empire: the Reality Behind the Stab-in-the-Back Myth," *War in History,* April 1996, Vol. 3, Issue 2, pp. 186-207.
[111] Leo Grebler and Wilhelm Winkler, *The Cost of the World War to Germany and Austria-Hungary* (Yale University Press, 1940)
[112] N.P. Howard, N.P. "The Social and Political Consequences of the Allied Food Blockade of Germany, 1918-19," *German History* (1993) p 162
[113] Bernd Ulrich and Benjamin, ed., Ziemann, *German Soldiers in the Great War: Letters and Eyewitness Accounts* (Pen and Sword Military, 2010). This book is a compilation of German soldiers' letters and memoirs. All the references come from this book.
[114] *German Soldiers in the Great War*, 77.
[115] *German Soldiers in the Great War*, 64.
[116] *German Soldiers in the Great War*, 51.
[117] https://www.amazon.com/Ring-Steel-Germany-Austria-Hungary-World-ebook/dp/B00JZBA9MO/
[118] //www.worldcat.org/oclc/186744003
[119] https://archive.org/details/in.ernet.dli.2015.57902
[120] //www.worldcat.org/oclc/250441891
[121] https://www.questia.com/read/100891395/home-fires-burning-food-politics-and-everyday-life
[122] http://afs.sagepub.com/content/3/1/121
[123] http://libcom.org/files/blockade%20Germany_0.pdf
[124] http://quod.lib.umich.edu/cgi/t/text/text-idx?c=acls;idno=heb01301
[125] https://www.questia.com/read/9325146/german-peasants-and-agrarian-politics-1914-1924
[126] https://www.amazon.com/Black-Market-Cold-War-1946-1949/dp/0521745179/
[127] https://www.amazon.com/Capital-Cities-War-1914-1919-Cultural/dp/052166814X/
[128] https://www.amazon.com/gp/reader/0521870437/
[129] https://www.questia.com/PM.qst?a=o&d=118216477
[130] https://academic.oup.com/ahr/article-abstract/39/1/130/26876/Fall-of-the-German-Empire-1914-1918-Selected-and?redirectedFrom=fulltext
[131] http://www.dhm.de/lemo/html/wk1/
[132] https://www.dhm.de/en/lemo/kapitel/first-world-war.html
[133] https://encyclopedia.1914-1918-online.net/regions/Germany
[134] https://encyclopedia.1914-1918-online.net/article/germany
[135] https://encyclopedia.1914-1918-online.net/article/bereavement_and_mourning_germany
[136] https://encyclopedia.1914-1918-online.net/article/between_acceptance_and_refusal_-_soldiers_attitudes_towards_war_germany
[137] https://encyclopedia.1914-1918-online.net/article/food_and_nutrition_germany
[138] https://encyclopedia.1914-1918-online.net/article/governments_parliaments_and_parties_germany
[139] https://encyclopedia.1914-1918-online.net/article/womens_mobilisation_for_war_germany
[140] https://encyclopedia.1914-1918-online.net/article/making_sense_of_the_war_germany
[141] https://encyclopedia.1914-1918-online.net/article/organization_of_war_economies_germany
[142] https://encyclopedia.1914-1918-online.net/article/war_finance_germany
[143] https://encyclopedia.1914-1918-online.net/article/pressjournalism_germany
[144] https://encyclopedia.1914-1918-online.net/article/propaganda_at_home_germany
[145] https://encyclopedia.1914-1918-online.net/article/warfare_1914-1918_germany
[146] https://encyclopedia.1914-1918-online.net/article/war_aims_and_war_aims_discussions_germany
[147] https://encyclopedia.1914-1918-online.net/article/war_losses_germany
[148] http://spartacus-educational.com/GERfww.htm
[149] http://hdl.loc.gov/loc.rbc/eadrbc.rb014001

[150] *Zentrale Dienstvorschrift 10/1 "Innere Führung"* http://www.bmvg.de/fileserving/PortalFiles/ C1256EF40036B05B/W27HUAGQ114INFOEN/ZDv+10-1+Englisch.pdf, (Joint Service Regulation 10/1 "leadership development and civic education").

[151] *Die Konzeption der Inneren Führung* http//www.innerefuehrung.bundeswehr.de (German), Zentrum Innere Führung (Center of Leadership Development and Civic Education)

[152] § 2 (2) WStG "Begriffsbestimmungen"http://bundesrecht.juris.de/wstrg/__2.html (German)

[153] § 10 SG "Duties of a superior" http://www.buzer.de/gesetz/2246/a31646.htm

[154] *Befehl und Gehorsam* http://treff.bundeswehr.de/C1256FC400421173/CurrentBaseLink/ W26BCF3M203DEVVDE (German), treff.bundeswehr.de.

[155] Vorgesetztenverordnung http://bundesrecht.juris.de/svorgesv/, content in German

[156] § 11 SG "Obedience" http://www.buzer.de/gesetz/2246/a31647.htm

[157] § 22 WStG Bindingness of an order, error http://www.gesetze-im-internet.de/wstrg/__22.html

[158] § 19 WStG Disobedience http://www.gesetze-im-internet.de/wstrg/__19.html

[159] § 20 WStG Insubordination http://www.gesetze-im-internet.de/wstrg/__20.html

[160] § 21 WStG Non-execution of orders with levity http://www.gesetze-im-internet.de/wstrg/__21.html

[161] http://www.deutschesheer.de

[162] //en.wikipedia.org/w/index.php?title=German_Army&action=edit

[163] Large, David Clay (1996). *Germans to the Front: West German Rearmament in the Adenauer Era*, p. 25

[164] See Frederick Zilian Jr., 'From Confrontation to Cooperation: The Takeover of the National People's (East German) Army by the Bundeswehr,' Praeger, Westport, Conn., 1999, , p.40–41, for a discussion of this period

[165]

[166] Zilian, p.41

[167] Isby and Kamps 1985, 228-229.

[168] See Jorg Schonbohm, 'Two Armies and One Fatherland', Berghahn Books, Providence & Oxford, 1996

[169] German Bundestag - Annual Disarmament Report 2013 http://dip21.bundestag.de/dip21/btd/ 18/009/1800933.pdf, bundestag.de, page 63

[170] https://archive.org/details/nemesisofpowerge00whee

[171] http://www.deutschesheer.de/

[172] https://web.archive.org/web/20050205193544/http://users.hunterlink.net.au/~maampo/ militaer/milindex.html

[173] http://www.worldwar1.com/sfgarmy.htm

[174] https://web.archive.org/web/20050330111634/http://www.tulipacademy.org/gew/ddhob/

[175] http://www.ww2incolor.com/gallery/germans

[176] http://www.gebirgsjager.de/

[177] http://www.axishistory.com/

[178] http://www.janes.com/article/57554/germany-plans-eur130-billion-military-investment. January 28, 2016 Defence News

[179]

[180] http://www.marine.de/

[181] http//www.marine.de

[182] Deutsche Marine – press release: Neues Nato-Expertenzentrum an der Kieler Förde nimmt Fahrt auf; Faermann, 2009

[183] http://www.flugrevue.de/militaerluftfahrt/streitkraefte/die-flugzeugflotte-der-bundesmarine-dornier-do-228-212/721768?seite=2

[184] http://www.marine.de/portal/poc/marine?uri=ci%3Abw.mar.multimedia.downloads.broschueren.flotte

[185] https//web.archive.org

[186] http://www.marine.de/en

[187] http://www.marine.de/02DB070000000001/vwContentByKey/W26V5JNM814INFODE/ $File/Flotte_Nr_9_060926.pdf

[188] http://www.luftwaffe.de

[189] The Military Balance 2012, p.118

[190] MiG-29s leave Luftwaffe http://www.flug-revue.rotor.com/FRHeft/FRHeft04/FRH0404/FR0404c.htm – Flug Revue, April 2004
[191] Owen, Robert (2000). *Deliberate Force: a case study in effective air campaigning*. DIANE Publishing, p. 246.
[192] Trevor, Findlay (1996). *Challenges for the new peacekeepers*. Oxford University Press, p. 41.
[193] Orbats - Scramble http://www.scramblemagazine.nl/orbats/germany/airforce. Scramblemagazine.nl. Retrieved on 2013-08-16.
[194] "Eurofighter Typhoon Marks Delivery of 400th Aircraft" http://www.eurofighter.com/news-and-events/2013/12/eurofighter-typhoon-marks-delivery-of-400th-aircraft December 04, 2013
[195] DoD Information Publication (Enroute) Supplement Europe, North Africa and Middle East
[196] "The Military Balance 2013". http://www.tandfonline.com/toc/tmib20/current, March 14, 2013.
[197] Assembled in Germany from parts built across Tornado partner factories
[198] Assembled in Germany from parts built across Eurofighter partner factories
[199] Assembled in France from parts built across Airbus partner factories
[200] Assembled in Germany from parts built across Airbus partner factories
[201] Assembled in Germany from parts built across Airbus partner factories
[202] Assembled in Spain from parts built across Airbus partner factories
[203] http://www.airbus.com/content/dam/corporate-topics/publications/o&d/2018-05_MRS_GEN_Ord-Deliv-by-country.pdf
[204] Assembled in Germany from parts built across Transall partner factories
[205] http://augengeradeaus.net/2018/02/materiallage-der-bundeswehr-mehr-uebungen-mehr-beanspruchung-weniger-einsatzbereit/
[206] licence built by VFW-Fokker
[207] Sikorsky H-53 Sea Stallion http://www.uswarplanes.net/seastallion.html, Retrieved 28 April 2012.
[208] Assembled in Germany from parts built across Eurocopter partner factories
[209] Assembled in France from parts built across Eurocopter partner factories
[210] http://www.dsca.mil/major-arms-sales/germany-mq-4c-triton-unmanned-aircraft-systems-uas
[211] Rheinmetall and IAI Offering Heron TP for Bundeswehr SAATEG Program http://www.deagel.com/news/Rheinmetall-and-IAI-Offering-Heron-TP-for-Bundeswehr-SAATEG-Program_n000004324.aspx. Deagel.com (2008-06-02). Retrieved on 2013-08-16.
[212] http://www.luftwaffenmuseum.de/

Article Sources and Contributors

The sources listed for each article provide more detailed licensing information including the copyright status, the copyright owner, and the license conditions.

Bundeswehr *Source:* https://en.wikipedia.org/w/index.php?oldid=851448082 *License:* Creative Commons Attribution-Share Alike 3.0 *Contributors:* 1990'sguy, Aflis, Aldis90, And93hil, Antiochus the Great, Arnoutf, Aro88, BB-PB, Bacon27, Boczi, Brufnus, Captintuna99, Cgschmidt3169, Chris-Gualtieri, ClueBot NG, Coltsfan, CommonsDelinker, Cplakidas, DH85868993, DagosNavy, David Biddulph, DavisAndrew416, Dcirovic, Denniss, Derek R Bullamore, DerwahreStinkstiefel, Didym, Donner60, DragonRainbow, Equord, EricSerge, FCBayern786, Fabian Schraps, Fixer88, Flor!an, GERMAN LUNATIC, GHab6, Gadget850, Genderforschung, GermanJoe, Graham11, Gray62, HDLShrsmn, HIDECCHI001, HLachman, Haage42, Headbomb, Hibernian, Htews, Hubon, I dream of horses, Iceonthemoon, Ickerbocker, Irul 901, JMRAMOS0109, Jarble, Jcfrommn, Jmertel23, JoeSperrazza, John of Reading, Johnpacklambert, Jprg1966, Jtle515, K.e.coffman, Kaloyan34-FR, Karawane 71, Keith D, KiloByte1337, KuK, L1A1 FAL, Le Anh-Huy, Levimanthys, Loose eel, Lost Boy, Lotje, Lupus in Saxonia, MER-C, Magioladitis, Marco11m22, Marek69, Mauls, MilborneOne, MisterBee1966, Mogism, Nedrutland, Nicolas Perrault III, Niet-0-leuk, Nihiltres, Noclador, Noq, ObscureReality, PMLF, PedalFuriously!, PhainetaiMoi, Pit0711, QuartierLatin1968, Quercus solaris, Rautamiekka, Red Director, Redalert2fan, Redonebird, Reenem, RicJac, Rich Farmbrough, Rumiton, SantiLak, Sca, Sfgiants1995, Sirtywell, Sitacuisses, Solarislv, Spartiate, SpencerHill, Ssolbergj, Steeletrap, SteveStrummer, Supreme Dragon, Sweat BoyX8, Syron Till, TU-nor, TehShyster, The Happy New Yorker, The PIPE, TillF, TiltuM, Tony1, Tpbradbury, Transphasic, Vermehrt, Vernemman101, Vinz7679, Vrac, Wiae, Widr, WikiPK, Wikid77, WilhelmIIdoorn, Wimmiden, Xyzzyva, ÄDA - DÄP, 156 anonymous edits 1

Military history of Germany *Source:* https://en.wikipedia.org/w/index.php?oldid=850939162 *License:* Creative Commons Attribution-Share Alike 3.0 *Contributors:* 16@r, 1990'sguy, Aldis90, Allen3, Allgaiar, Anne-theater, Anthonyvas, Averscha, Axt, BD2412, Barticus88, Bender235, BilCat, BokicaK, CaptainVindaloo, Carl Logan, Charles Matthews, Chris the speller, Chwyatt, Clicketyclack, ClueBot NG, Cmdrjameson, CommonsDelinker, Courcelles, Cplakidas, DadaNeem, Darkone, Dead Mary, Dekimasu, Director, Domino theory, Dreamafter, Droyselich, Dugell, Dwane E Anderson, Ekki01, Excirial, Flyer22 Reborn, Foghawk, Gdr, Ghirlandajo, Gilliam, Gogafax, GoingBatty, Graham87, Grahamdubya, Grandiose, Gryffindor, HMSSolent, Hchc2009, Hlover01, Hmains, Hohum, Howcheng, Hyperboreios, IRISZOOM, IronGargoyle, Italia2006, JeremyA, Jodosma, John of Reading, Joshdboz, Jt, K.e.coffman, Katich5584, Kejo13, Kevin Murray, Khazar2, Lars T., Levimanthys, Like tears in rain, Linnell, LudicrousTripe, Luna Santin, Magioladitis, Manxruler, Matthead, Melesse, Mhardcastle, Mifter, Mister-trona, MisterBee1966, Molobo, Narratorq, Nasa-verve, Nehrams2020, Niceguyedc, Nv8200pa, Octane, Olegwiki, Olessi, Pariah24, Patrick87, PeterWD, Petri Krohn, Phaedriel, R'n'B, RJHall, RandomHumanoid, Raprat0, Raven in Orbit, Rcbutcher, Rex Germanus, Rjensen, Roger Davies, Roke, Ross Uber, Rshu, Semilanceata, Skinmeister, Smoove Z, Stoni, Stryn, Super48paul, The Land, Theinstantmatrix, TimBentley, Tosh.0fag, TrebleSeven, TyA, Vanished user 90345uifj983j4toi234k, Velella, Vikasafc, Warofdreams, WereSpielChequers, Widr, WikiCopter, YUL89YYZ, Yvwv, ZeWrestler, Zscout370, ÄDA - DÄP, Ранко Николић, 大司马大将军 , 163 anonymous edits 27

History of Germany during World War I *Source:* https://en.wikipedia.org/w/index.php?oldid=847882231 *License:* Creative Commons Attribution-Share Alike 3.0 *Contributors:* 1989, 331dot, Acroterion, AdamMH, AgnosticPreachersKid, Anbu121, Anotherclown, Arjayay, BD2412, Ballsacklicker47, Bender235, Bettymnz4, Bmusician, Brigade Piron, Buffbills7701, CLCStudent, Chewings72, Clifford Mill, ClueBot NG, ContributerB, DanielJosephEyre, DavidOrtegong, Deunanknute, Discospinster, Donner60, Drm310, EagerToddler39, Editor2020, EnglishTea4me, EnigmaMcmxc, Eno Lirpa, Epbr123, Ephemeratta, Excirial, FredSmith69, Fycafterpro, Fæ, GHab6, Gareth Griffith-Jones, GeekinB3AST, Gilliam, Golgofrinchian, Grafen, GünniX, HJ Mitchell (default), HaeB, Handel85, Hmains, Ira Leviton, Iridescent, Italia2006, J36miles, JamesBWatson, Jcocecl, Jim1138, Just Chilling, K.e.coffman, K6ka, Keith-264, Keithbob, Kintetsubuffalo, KylieTastic, Leutha, Look2See1, Mackensen, Manimony, Manul, Maphisto86, Marcocapelle, Marek69, Mark Arsten, Materialscientist, Matthewrbowker, Mike Rosoft, Millennium bug, Mononomic, Mulhollant, Nick Levine, No1lakersfan, Oldmangreg, Optakeover, Orphan Wiki, Oshwah, Parkwells, Pharaoh of the Wizards, Pinethicket, R'n'B, Rhone, Riverhugger, Rjensen, Rrburke, Sdeddeh13, Serols, Slightsmile, Smalljim, Snooganssnoogans, Tabletop, Terrythometz, Tobby72, Vctrbarbieri, Vrenator, WW1Historian, WereSpielChequers, Widr, Wywin, 230 anonymous edits 53

Command and obedience in the Bundeswehr *Source:* https://en.wikipedia.org/w/index.php?oldid=832745942 *License:* Creative Commons Attribution-Share Alike 3.0 *Contributors:* Barticus88, BillFlis, Gamsbart, Jak86, JustJust51, Khazar2, Kwiki, Lacrimosus, LilHelpa, Miniapolis, Ospalh, Phuzion, Pixelfire, SchreiberBike, Shadowjams, TallNapoleon, WikHead, 20 anonymous edits 73

German Army *Source:* https://en.wikipedia.org/w/index.php?oldid=850333506 *License:* Creative Commons Attribution-Share Alike 3.0 *Contributors:* AVG1998, Ace of Spades, AlexTheWhovian, Alonso de Mendoza, America789, Anotherclown, Antiochus the Great, Aro88, BD2412, Beloki, Bermicourt, Bobrayner, BrxBrx, Bssv11, Buckshot06, Chris the speller, ClueBot NG, CommonsDelinker, ComradeDaryl, DVdm, DagosNavy, David.moreno72, Dekomori, Denniss, Deor, Dewritech, Dirkbb, DocWatson42, Donner60, Dormskirk, Dthomsen8, Ego White Tray, Ekki01, EricSerge, Feminist, Flor!an, Garuda28, Gavbadger, Ghostninja151, Gidonb, Gilliam, HDLShrsmn, HHaeckel, HMSLavender, Hammersfan, HeathIsling, Hellbert, High Contrast, Hohum, Ickerbocker, Illegitimate Barrister, Innotata, Iridescent, JWHBerlin, Jarble, JesseRafe, JezzaV, John of Reading, Jpowell3404, Jprg1966, K.e.coffman, Keith D, Khazar2, Korporaal1, Kullmann1, L1A1 FAL, Levimanthys, Lugia2453, MBlaze Lightning, MarksmanWonder, Materialscientist, MaxSmith777, MaxxL, Mean as custard, Mischakoo, MisterBee1966, Niceguyedc, Niet-0-leuk, Niko67000, Noclador, Number 57, OJSlaughter, ObscureReality, Ogbader, Optimist on the run, Parsley Man, Pixelfire, Pockekesa, Quercus solaris, Rjensen, Royalcourtier, SchreiberBike, Shaw Knowledge, ShelfSkewed, Sirtywell, Slightsmile, Snow Blizzard, Solarislv, Sonaz, SpencerHill, Steinsplitter, StjJackson, TUBS, TYelliot, Tadeusz Nowak, The Illusive Man, The PIPE, Tilmanh85, TiltuM, Tim!, Tom.Reding, Ubiquity, Utcursch, Vidarfe, Waterthrower, Winner 42, Woohookitty, Xanzzibar, XavierItzm, Xyl 54, ∼riley, ÄDA - DÄP, 光文天皇 , 178 anonymous edits 81

List of modern equipment of the German Army *Source:* https://en.wikipedia.org/w/index.php?oldid=852288696 *License:* Creative Commons Attribution-Share Alike 3.0 *Contributors:* Adavidb, AirWave 800S1, America789, Anotherclown, Antiochus the Great, Aro88, Bakedbaconbread, Blablubbs, Carlosleb99, Catlemur, Chrissymad, CommonsDelinker, Dominicleusing, Donner60, DragonRainbow, EditorDB, EsEinsteinium, Faceless Enemy, Feminist, Fireinacrowdedtheatre, Follgramm3006, Fuortu, Fuzheado, Gavbadger, Glevum, HH58, Hawkeye Ridgesaw Summer, Hmains, Hohum, Innotata, JV Roy, JessPavarocks, KatnissEverdeen, KylieTastic, LibyanMercenary, LordHello1, M'SYA Malaya, MORNINGSIDE, Marco11m22, MarksmanWonder, MilAK, Molinaro787, Mr.Strat Starky, Nguyen QuocTrung, Nickel nitride, Noclador, Patoska, Peacemaker er, ReneDens, Rurickovich, Shaunak patel, Stratocaster27, Tczk, Tilmanh85, TiltuM, Towelie the Towel, Tritario, Underlying lk, ZUKAGRAD, Zoupan, ÄDA - DÄP, 木の枝 , 186 anonymous edits 99

German Navy *Source:* https://en.wikipedia.org/w/index.php?oldid=846884435 *License:* Creative Commons Attribution-Share Alike 3.0 *Contributors:* A. B., Aldis90, Angmering, Anotherclown, Anthony Appleyard, Antiochus the Great, Aro88, Arpingstone, Arthur Rubin, Aumnamahashiva, Avicennasis, BDD, BHenry1969, BilCat, Bro5990, Bthebest, Buckshot06, Bungert55, Cdjp1, Chilrreh, ChrisGualtieri, Cobatfor, CommonsDelinker, DPdH, DagosNavy, De728631, DePiep, Dead Mary, Derek R Bullamore, DerwahreStinkstiefel, Dewritech, DexDor, DocWatson42, Donner60, Dpaajones, Dr Gangrene, Dragnadh, Editorjohn112, Ellittico, Eumolpo, Favonian, Fry1989, Gamgee, Garuda28, Gbawden, GermanJoe, GiW, Glaisher, Graham87, GroveGuy, HaeB, Hayden120, Hgrosser, Hibernian, Horodna, Huon, IAC-62, Illegitimate Barrister, Imladros, Innotata, JMRAMOS0109, Jdaloner, Joshbaumgartner, Karawane 71, Keith D, KuK, Kwamikagami, Leeshore1966, Lotje, LtNOWIS, Lux-hibou, Maggus989, Magioladitis, Magus732, Marquardtika, Mccapra, MilborneOne, Monart, Moonraker, Niet-0-leuk, Noclador, ObscureReality, Oshwah, Ospalh, Parsecboy, Philipp1984, PrairieKid, Quercus solaris, R'n'B, Rademire2, Rich Farmbrough, Rjensen, Roukee, Seabas57, Shem1805, Sigehelmus, SpencerHill, Spitfire, Stars999, StraussInTheHouse, Suneditor, Superzohar, TBR001, TaBOT-zerem, The ed17, Thewolfchild, Travelbird, Uldra, Ulf Heinsohn, Waggers, Whoop whoop pull up, Wiae, Xaark, Xeeron, Xufanc, ÄDA - DÄP, Äpplarö, زرشک, 192 anonymous edits 109

List of active German Navy ships *Source:* https://en.wikipedia.org/w/index.php?oldid=852518105 *License:* Creative Commons Attribution-Share Alike 3.0 *Contributors:* Ahndg3285, Aldis90, Anotherclown, Antiochus the Great, Argovian, Battleship Sailor, BegbertBiggs, BobNesh, Brianm358, Chris the speller, Colonies Chris, DerwahreStinkstiefel, Dpaajones, Dricherby, Ein Dahmer, Griffinofwales, GünniX, Horodna, Imladros, Imthebombliketicktick, Kistara, Languid Scientist, Nick Moyes, Noclador, Num1dgen, ObscureReality, Plastikspork, Rob984, The Bushranger, Tomdo08, Ul1-82-2, WikHead, Z0, ÄDA - DÄP, 97 anonymous edits 122

German Air Force *Source:* https://en.wikipedia.org/w/index.php?oldid=852873211 *License:* Creative Commons Attribution-Share Alike 3.0 *Contributors:* 07Sepp Dietrich, 21lima, 72, Ahunt, Antiochus the Great, Aquilosion, Arado, Aro88, Arpingstone, BLyda97112, Beitsefer, Bergfex2011, BilCat, Catlemur, Chris the speller, ClueBot NG, Crown-job, DagosNavy, Denniss, DonoZ5, Duboka, EDV1969, FOX 52, Finnusertop, Garuda28, Gavbadger, GermanJoe, Gilliam, GraemeLeggett, GünniX, HH58, Hammersfan, Helmy oved, Ibrahim Husain Meraj, Illegitimate Barrister, Iridescent, J.K Nakkila, Jprg1966, Julian Herzog, K.e.coffman, Khananel, LordHello1, Lovetravel86, Lukasz Lukomski, Magicman0361, MatthewHaywood, MilborneOne, Mistral535, Molinaro787, Muffin Wizard, NYKTNE, Nbpillai380, NebY, Niet-0-leuk, Noclador, Nyttend, Quercus solaris, Ras67, Realn3rd, Redalert2fan, ScrapIronIV, Ser Amantio di Nicolao, Shaw Knowledge, Sitacuisses, Sweepy, TAnthony, Tadeusz Nowak, The PIPE, TheChampionMan1234 alt, Thewolfchild, Tom.Reding, TomStar81, Uhlemanns, Uli Elch, WOSlinker, Yankee starbase, ÄDA - DÄP, בר, 149 anonymous edits 127

German special forces *Source:* https://en.wikipedia.org/w/index.php?oldid=843951449 *License:* Creative Commons Attribution-Share Alike 3.0 *Contributors:* Feminist, Fury 1991, Innotata, Jodosma, LilHelpa, Melbguy05, Narky Blert, Polybos∼enwiki, Saturne160, TheTruthiness, Unician, Vyom25, Ykhwong, ÄDA - DÄP, 3 anonymous edits 157

Image Sources, Licenses and Contributors

The sources listed for each image provide more detailed licensing information including the copyright status, the copyright owner, and the license conditions.

Image *Source:* https://en.wikipedia.org/w/index.php?title=File:Bundeswehr_Kreuz_Black.svg *License:* Public Domain *Contributors:* Fry1989, Kresspahl, Marseille77, Milgesch, Parsecboy, Wester, Yumenghan, Zscout370, 1 anonymous edits ... 1

Image *Source:* https://en.wikipedia.org/w/index.php?title=File:Bundeswehr_Logo_Heer_with_lettering.svg *License:* Public Domain *Contributors:* Bundeswehr ... 1

Image *Source:* https://en.wikipedia.org/w/index.php?title=File:Bundeswehr_Logo_Marine_with_lettering.svg *License:* Public Domain *Contributors:* Entwurf: unbekannt ... 1

Image *Source:* https://en.wikipedia.org/w/index.php?title=File:Bundeswehr_Logo_Luftwaffe_with_lettering.svg *License:* Public Domain *Contributors:* Bundeswehr ... 1

Image *Source:* https://en.wikipedia.org/w/index.php?title=File:Bundeswehr_Logo_Streitkraeftebasis_with_lettering.svg *License:* Public Domain *Contributors:* PS2801 ... 1

Image *Source:* https://en.wikipedia.org/w/index.php?title=File:Bundeswehr_Logo_Sanitaetsdienst_with_lettering.svg *License:* Public Domain *Contributors:* PS2801 ... 1

Image *Source:* https://en.wikipedia.org/w/index.php?title=File:Flag_of_Europe.svg *License:* Public Domain *Contributors:* User:Verdy p, User:-xfi-, User:Paddu, User:Nightstallion, User:Funakoshi, User:Jeltz, User:Dbenbenn, User:Zscout370 ... 2

Image *Source:* https://en.wikipedia.org/w/index.php?title=File:Flag_of_the_United_States.svg *License:* Public Domain *Contributors:* Anomie, Jo-Jo Eumerus, MSGJ, Mr. Stradivarius ... 2

Image *Source:* https://en.wikipedia.org/w/index.php?title=File:Loudspeaker.svg *License:* Public Domain *Contributors:* User:Dbenbenn, User:Optimager, User:Tsca, User:Dbenbenn, User:Optimager, User:Tsca, User:Dbenbenn, User:Optimager, User:Tsca ... 2

Figure 1 *Source:* https://en.wikipedia.org/w/index.php?title=File:Großer_Zapfenstreich_Ramstein_Air_Base_2002.jpg *License:* Public Domain *Contributors:* MSGT JOHN P. SNOW, USAF ... 4

Figure 2 *Source:* https://en.wikipedia.org/w/index.php?title=File:NATO-2002-Summit.jpg *License:* Public Domain *Contributors:* Adam Zábranský, Aschroet, Counny, Emijrp, Er Komandante, Henxter, OgreBot 2, PhElias, Rimshot, Shizhao, Sinigagl, Spiritia, 6 anonymous edits ... 5

Figure 3 *Source:* https://en.wikipedia.org/w/index.php?title=File:Leopard_2_A5_der_Bundeswehr.jpg *License:* Creative Commons Attribution 2.0 *Contributors:* Bundeswehr-Fotos ... 6

Figure 4 *Source:* https://en.wikipedia.org/w/index.php?title=File:Mikoyan_mig29.jpg *License:* GNU Free Documentation License *Contributors:* Jo Mitchell ... 7

Figure 5 *Source:* https://en.wikipedia.org/w/index.php?title=File:Bundeskader_-_Sportfördergruppe_der_Bundeswehr_-_Trainingsanzug_der_Bundeswehr_-_Frauen.jpg *Contributors:* User:Lupus in Saxonia ... 9

Figure 6 *Source:* https://en.wikipedia.org/w/index.php?title=File:Bundeswehr_Logo.svg *License:* Public Domain *Contributors:* Bundeswehr ... 11

Figure 7 *Source:* https://en.wikipedia.org/w/index.php?title=File:Von_der_Leyen_2010.jpg *License:* Creative Commons Attribution-Sharealike 3.0 Germany *Contributors:* Laurence Chaperon ... 11

Figure 8 *Source:* https://en.wikipedia.org/w/index.php?title=File:Fregatte_Mecklenburg-Vorpommern_F218.jpg *License:* GNU Free Documentation License *Contributors:* Alureiter~commonswiki, Btr, Darkone, Indeedous, MGA73bot2, Stunteltje, 2 anonymous edits ... 12

Figure 9 *Source:* https://en.wikipedia.org/w/index.php?title=File:ATF_Dingo_in_German_service_(Afghanistan).jpg *License:* Creative Commons Attribution 2.0 *Contributors:* ISAF Headquarters Public Affairs Office ... 13

Figure 10 *Source:* https://en.wikipedia.org/w/index.php?title=File:Auslandseinsätze_der_Bundeswehr.svg *License:* Creative Commons Attribution-Sharealike 3.0 *Contributors:* Alexrk2 ... 14

Figure 11 *Source:* https://en.wikipedia.org/w/index.php?title=File:Fregatte_Karlsruhe.jpg *License:* Public Domain *Contributors:* U.S. Navy photo 15

Image *Source:* https://en.wikipedia.org/w/index.php?title=File:Flag_of_Afghanistan.svg *Contributors:* 5ko, Ahmad2099, Alex Great, Alkari, Amateur55, Andres gb.ldc, Ankry, Antonsusi, Avala, Bastique, BotMultichill, BotMultichillT, Cycn, Dancingwombatsrule, Dbenbenn, Denelson83, Denniss, Domhnall, Duduziq, Erlenmeyer, F l a n k e r, Farhod, Frigotoni, Fry1989, Gast32, Golden Bosnian Lily, GoldenRainbow, Happenstance, Henriquebachelor, Herbythyme, Homo lupus, Ilfga, Illegitimate Barrister, Jarekt, Jebulon, JoaoPedro10029, Khwahan, Klemen Kocjancic, Koefbac, Kookaburra, Lokal Profil, Ludger1961, Lumia1234, MPF, Mattes, MrPanyGoff, Myself488, Neq00, Nersy, Nightstallion, O, Orange Tuesday, Palosirkka, Prev, RainbowSilver, Rainforest tropicana, Reisio, Ricordisamoa, Rocket000, Sangjinhwa, Sarang, Sarilho1, SiBr4, Smaug the Golden, Smooth O, Sojah, Solar Police, Stasyan117, SteveGOLD, Stewi101015, Supreme Dragon, TFerenczy, Tabasco~commonswiki, Tcfc2349, Unma.af, Zscout370, \\'arrior 786, Şêr, ,ייהלייזיושמר 李煊洋 567, 33 anonymous edits ... 14

Image *Source:* https://en.wikipedia.org/w/index.php?title=File:Flag_of_Kosovo.svg *License:* Public Domain *Contributors:* Cradel (current version), earlier version by Ningyou ... 14

Image *Source:* https://en.wikipedia.org/w/index.php?title=File:Flag_of_South_Sudan.svg *License:* Public Domain *Contributors:* User:Achim1999 14

Image *Source:* https://en.wikipedia.org/w/index.php?title=File:Flag_of_Sudan.svg *License:* Public Domain *Contributors:* Vzb83 ... 14

Image *Source:* https://en.wikipedia.org/w/index.php?title=File:Flag_of_Lebanon.svg *License:* Public Domain *Contributors:* Traced based on the CIA World Factbook with some modification done to the colours based on information at Vexilla mund ... 15

Image *Source:* https://en.wikipedia.org/w/index.php?title=File:Flag_of_Mali.svg *License:* Public Domain *Contributors:* User:SKopp ... 15

Image *Source:* https://en.wikipedia.org/w/index.php?title=File:Flag_of_Senegal.svg *License:* Public Domain *Contributors:* Original upload by Nightstallion ... 15

Image *Source:* https://en.wikipedia.org/w/index.php?title=File:Flag_of_Somalia.svg *License:* Public Domain *Contributors:* see upload history . 15

Image *Source:* https://en.wikipedia.org/w/index.php?title=File:Flag_of_Iraq.svg *License:* Public Domain *Contributors:* User:Hoshie, User:Militaryace ... 16

Figure 12 *Source:* https://en.wikipedia.org/w/index.php?title=File:NH-90_ILA-2006_2.jpg *License:* Creative Commons Attribution-ShareAlike 3.0 Unported *Contributors:* Igge ... 17

Figure 13 *Source:* https://en.wikipedia.org/w/index.php?title=File:GTK_Boxer_side.jpg *License:* Public Domain *Contributors:* Heldt ... 17

Figure 14 *Source:* https://en.wikipedia.org/w/index.php?title=File:54+01_German_Air_Force_Airbus_A400M_ILA_Berlin_2016_12.jpg *License:* GNU Free Documentation License *Contributors:* Julian Herzog ... 18

Figure 15 *Source:* https://en.wikipedia.org/w/index.php?title=File:Bundeswehr_-_10th_Anniversary_of_Multinational_Corps_Northeast.jpg *License:* Creative Commons Attribution-Sharealike 2.0 *Contributors:* w?odi from Szczecin, Poland ... 18

Figure 16 *Source:* https://en.wikipedia.org/w/index.php?title=File:040610-N-1823S-348_G36andpracticenade.jpg *License:* Public Domain *Contributors:* Photographer's Mate 2nd Class George Sisting, U.S. Navy ... 19

Figure 17 *Source:* https://en.wikipedia.org/w/index.php?title=File:Trageweise_(Heer_+_Luftwaffe).svg *License:* Creative Commons Zero *Contributors:* Flor!an ... 21

Figure 18 *Source:* https://en.wikipedia.org/w/index.php?title=File:Ulrike_Flender.jpg *License:* Public Domain *Contributors:* U.S. Air Force photo 22

Figure 19 *Source:* https://en.wikipedia.org/w/index.php?title=File:Gen_Wolfgang_Schneiderhan.jpg *License:* Public Domain *Contributors:* Artic-seahorse, Flor!an, GT1976, GeorgHH, GrummelJS, Indeedous, Innotata, Sciss~commonswiki, TUBS, 1 anonymous edits ... 23

Image *Source:* https://en.wikipedia.org/w/index.php?title=File:PD-icon.svg *License:* Public Domain *Contributors:* Alex.muller, Anomie, Anonymous Dissident, CBM, Jo-Jo Eumerus, MBisanz, PBS, Quadell, Rocket000, Strangerer, Timotheus Canens, 1 anonymous edits ... 25

Image *Source:* https://en.wikipedia.org/w/index.php?title=File:Commons-logo.svg *License:* logo *Contributors:* Anomie, Callanecc, CambridgeBayWeather, Jo-Jo Eumerus, RHaworth ... 26

Image *Source:* https//en.wikipedia.org *License:* Public Domain *Contributors:* Aschroet, Mattes, OlafJanssen, Rudolph Buch ... 27

Image *Source:* https://en.wikipedia.org/w/index.php?title=File:Flag_of_Germany.svg *License:* Public Domain *Contributors:* Anomie, Jo-Jo Eumerus 28

Figure 20 *Source:* https://en.wikipedia.org/w/index.php?title=File:Germanic_limes.jpg *License:* GNU Free Documentation License *Contributors:* Theutatis ... 29

Figure 21 *Source:* https://en.wikipedia.org/w/index.php?title=File:Gustave_dore_crusades_death_of_frederick_of_germany.jpg *License:* Public Domain *Contributors:* Bender235, G.dallorto, Gryffindor, Kilom691, Mhmrodrigues, Shakko, Soerfm, Warburg, 3 anonymous edits ... 30

Figure 22 *Source:* https://en.wikipedia.org/w/index.php?title=File:Austerlitz-baron-Pascal.jpg *License:* Public Domain *Contributors:* -Strogoff-, ALE!, Alborzagros, Anne97432, Aubry Gérard, B dash, Blaue Max, BotMultichill, Bukk, Coyau, Equendil, Flominator, Goldfritha~commonswiki, Hazhk, Hohum, Jastrow, Jed, Man vyi, MarcusBritish, Mattes, Pierpao, Rama, Shakko, Sixflashphoto, Soerfm, Trzęsacz, Z7504, 2 anonymous edits ... 34

Figure 23 *Source:* https://en.wikipedia.org/w/index.php?title=File:IK_1813.jpg *License:* GNU Free Documentation License *Contributors:* User:Husnock from en.wiki ... 35

Figure 24 *Source:* https://en.wikipedia.org/w/index.php?title=File:BismarckArbeitszimmer1886rest.jpg *License:* GNU Free Documentation License *Contributors:* Julien Then ... 36

Figure 25 *Source:* https://en.wikipedia.org/w/index.php?title=File:Battle-Mars-Le-Tour-large.jpg *License:* Public Domain *Contributors:* AnRo0002, Batke, Fred.th, Man vyi, Martin H., Redtony, Shyam, YUL89YYZ ... 37

Figure 26 *Source:* https://en.wikipedia.org/w/index.php?title=File:Deutsche_Soldaten_an_der_Front.jpg *License:* GNU Free Documentation License *Contributors:* CalJW, Roke ... 39

Figure 27 *Source:* https://en.wikipedia.org/w/index.php?title=File:Guerre_14-18-Artillerie_de_campagne_allemande-1914.JPG *License:* Public Domain *Contributors:* FSII, Innotata, Jordi, Lotje, Rcbutcher, Semnoz, Tangopaso, Wolfmann, 6 anonymous edits ... 39

Figure 28 *Source:* https://en.wikipedia.org/w/index.php?title=File:Second_world_war_europe_1941-1942_map_en.png *License:* GNU Free Documentation License *Contributors:* User:ArmadniGeneral, User:San Jose ... 45

Figure 29 *Source:* https://en.wikipedia.org/w/index.php?title=File:Besatzungszonen_ohne_text.gif *Contributors:* - ... 46

Figure 30 *Source:* https://en.wikipedia.org/w/index.php?title=File:Corps_sectors_in_NATO's_Central_Region.jpg *License:* Public Domain *Contributors:* CIA ... 47

Figure 31 *Source:* https://en.wikipedia.org/w/index.php?title=File:Bundesarchiv_Bild_146-1974-118-18,_Mobilmachung.jpg *License:* Creative Commons Attribution-Sharealike 3.0 Germany *Contributors:* BotMultichill, Rcbutcher, Thib Phil, Wolfmann, 1 anonymous edits ... 55

Figure 32 *Source:* https//en.wikipedia.org *License:* anonymous-EU *Contributors:* Unknown German war photographer ... 56

Figure 33 *Source:* https://en.wikipedia.org/w/index.php?title=File:Heinrich_Zille-VaddingOW.jpg *License:* Public Domain *Contributors:* Albert Krantz, Ar-ras, BotMultichill, OTFW, Wolfmann, Иван Дулин, 1 anonymous edits ... 57

Figure 34 *Source:* https://en.wikipedia.org/w/index.php?title=File:Armierungs-Bataillon.jpg *License:* Creative Commons Attribution-Sharealike 3.0,2.5,2.0,1.0 *Contributors:* Catfishmo, Milgesch, Thib Phil ... 58

Figure 35 *Source:* https://en.wikipedia.org/w/index.php?title=File:Bundesarchiv_Bild_104-0669,_Übung_deutscher_Soldaten_mit_Flammenwerfer.jpg *License:* Creative Commons Attribution-Sharealike 3.0 Germany *Contributors:* BotMultichill, Cucumber, Duch, Jarekt, Martin H., Rcbutcher, The real Marcoman, 1 anonymous edits ... 59

Figure 36 *Source:* https://en.wikipedia.org/w/index.php?title=File:Немцы_в_Киеве_март_1918.jpg *Contributors:* II Reich / Автор фото в источнике не указан / ... 61

Figure 37 *Source:* https://en.wikipedia.org/w/index.php?title=File:Kaiser_Wilhelm_II_Truppenbesuch_Ostpreußen_Lyck_1915.jpg *License:* Public Domain *Contributors:* Verlag: Hanns Konrad, k. u. k. Hoflieferant, Brüx. Nr. 183 ... 62

Figure 38 *Source:* https://en.wikipedia.org/w/index.php?title=File:PSM_V88_D237_Collecting_scrap_metal_for_the_german_war_effort.jpg *License:* Public Domain *Contributors:* Ineuw, OgreBot 2 ... 63

Figure 39 *Source:* https://en.wikipedia.org/w/index.php?title=File:Brotmarke_Bayern.jpg *License:* Public Domain *Contributors:* uploaded by NobbiP ... 65

Figure 40 *Source:* https://en.wikipedia.org/w/index.php?title=File:Bundesarchiv_Bild_183-R34275,_Berlin,_Rückkehr_deutscher_Truppen.jpg *License:* Creative Commons Attribution-Sharealike 3.0 Germany *Contributors:* Gorgo, Rcbutcher, VladiMens, 1 anonymous edits ... 66

Figure 41 *Source:* https://en.wikipedia.org/w/index.php?title=File:Wachdienst_Torposten_(43).jpg *License:* Creative Commons Attribution-Share Alike *Contributors:* TazD ... 75

Image *Source:* https://en.wikipedia.org/w/index.php?title=File:Bundeswehr_Kreuz.svg *License:* Public Domain *Contributors:* Ausir, Burts, Flamarande~commonswiki, Gunnar.offel, Knorrepoes, Kresspahl, Madden, Milgesch, Palosirkka, Steinbeisser~commonswiki, TUBS, Wschroedter, Wst, 2 anonymous edits ... 82

Image *Source:* https://en.wikipedia.org/w/index.php?title=File:Bundeswehr_Heer.jpg *License:* Public Domain *Contributors:* Madden, Pixelfire, TUBS, 3 anonymous edits ... 82

Image *Source:* https://en.wikipedia.org/w/index.php?title=File:Bundeswehr_Luftwaffe.jpg *License:* Public Domain *Contributors:* Doco, Flamarande~commonswiki, Gamsbart, Madden, Pixelfire, TUBS, 2 anonymous edits ... 82

Image *Source:* https://en.wikipedia.org/w/index.php?title=File:Bundeswehr_Marine.jpg *Contributors:* - ... 82

Figure 42 *Source:* https://en.wikipedia.org/w/index.php?title=File:Bundeswehrsoldaten_während_eines_Manövers_(1960).jpg *License:* Public Domain *Contributors:* U.S. Army ... 84

Figure 43 *Source:* https://en.wikipedia.org/w/index.php?title=File:West_German_Bundeswehr_1960.jpg *License:* Public Domain *Contributors:* Brakeet, Burts, Fallschirmjägergewehr 42, Mediatus, Nickel nitride, Patrickneil, Sanandros, Sandmann4u, Steinbeisser~commonswiki, TUBS, Wikifreund, 3 anonymous edits ... 86

Figure 44 *Source:* https://en.wikipedia.org/w/index.php?title=File:DN-ST-92-02168.jpg *Contributors:* - ... 87

Figure 45 *Source:* https://en.wikipedia.org/w/index.php?title=File:Leopard_2A6,_PzBtl_104.jpg *License:* Public Domain *Contributors:* U.S. Army Europe photo by Visual Information Specialist Markus Rauchenberger ... 89

Figure 46 *Source:* https://en.wikipedia.org/w/index.php?title=File:PzH2000_houwitser.png *License:* Creative Commons Attribution 2.0 *Contributors:* Quistnix ... 89

Figure 47 *Source:* https://en.wikipedia.org/w/index.php?title=File:NH-90_ILA-2006_2.jpg *License:* Creative Commons Attribution-ShareAlike 3.0 Unported *Contributors:* Igge ... 90

Figure 48 *Source:* https://en.wikipedia.org/w/index.php?title=File:Germany_Army_2017_with_integrated_units.png *Contributors:* User:Noclador 92

Figure 49 *Source:* https://en.wikipedia.org/w/index.php?title=File:German_UN_Soldiers_during_UNOSOM_II_1993.jpg *License:* Public Domain *Contributors:* STAFF SGT. JEFFREY T. BRADY ... 92

Figure 50 *Source:* https://en.wikipedia.org/w/index.php?title=File:Idz.jpg *License:* Public Domain *Contributors:* KrisfromGermany ... 93

Image *Source:* https://en.wikipedia.org/w/index.php?title=File:1._Panzerdivision_(Bundeswehr).svg *License:* Public Domain *Contributors:* pixelFire ... 93

Image *Source:* https://en.wikipedia.org/w/index.php?title=File:10._Panzerdivision_(Bundeswehr).svg *License:* Public Domain *Contributors:* Hilohello, Mogelzahn, Pixelfire, VIGNERON, Wikifreund ... 93

Image *Source:* https://en.wikipedia.org/w/index.php?title=File:Division_Spezielle_Operationen_(Bundeswehr).svg *License:* Public Domain *Contributors:* Bill william compton, Gunnar.offel, JotaCartas, Pixelfire ... 94

Image *Source:* https://en.wikipedia.org/w/index.php?title=File:Eurocorps_CoA.svg *Contributors:* MaxxL, Sarang, Ssolbergj ... 94

Image *Source:* https://en.wikipedia.org/w/index.php?title=File:1_(GE-NL)_Corps.svg *License:* Public Domain *Contributors:* Flor!an ... 94

Image *Source:* https://en.wikipedia.org/w/index.php?title=File:MNC_NE_(V1).svg *License:* Public Domain *Contributors:* Poznaniak ... 94

Image *Source:* https://en.wikipedia.org/w/index.php?title=File:LZLgr_Gerät_Herongen.jpg *License:* Public Domain *Contributors:* Ekki01, Erwin Lindemann, MGA73, MGA73bot2, TUBS ... 94

Image *Source:* https://en.wikipedia.org/w/index.php?title=File:LZLgr_Gerät_Pirmasens.jpg *License:* Public Domain *Contributors:* Ekki01, Erwin Lindemann, MGA73, MGA73bot2, TUBS ... 94

Image *Source:* https://en.wikipedia.org/w/index.php?title=File:ZMobStp_Brück-Neuseddin.jpg *License:* Public Domain *Contributors:* Ekki01, Erwin Lindemann, MGA73, MGA73bot2, TUBS ... 94

Image *Source:* https://en.wikipedia.org/w/index.php?title=File:Schirmmütze_heer.jpg *Contributors:* - ... 95

Image *Source:* https://en.wikipedia.org/w/index.php?title=File:Bundeswehr-OF-9-Gen.png *License:* GNU Free Documentation License *Contributors:* Odor ... 95

Image *Source:* https://en.wikipedia.org/w/index.php?title=File:Bundeswehr-OF-8-GL.png *License:* GNU Free Documentation License *Contributors:* Odor ... 95

Image *Source:* https://en.wikipedia.org/w/index.php?title=File:Bundeswehr-OF-7-GM.png *License:* GNU Free Documentation License *Contributors:* Odor ... 95

Image *Source:* https://en.wikipedia.org/w/index.php?title=File:Bundeswehr-OF-6-BG.png *License:* GNU Free Documentation License *Contributors:* Odor ... 95

Image *Source:* https://en.wikipedia.org/w/index.php?title=File:Bundeswehr-OF-5-O.png *License:* GNU Free Documentation License *Contributors:* Odor ... 95

Image *Source:* https://en.wikipedia.org/w/index.php?title=File:Bundeswehr-OF-4-OTL.png *License:* GNU Free Documentation License *Contributors:* Odor ... 95

Image *Source:* https://en.wikipedia.org/w/index.php?title=File:Bundeswehr-OF-3-M.png *License:* GNU Free Documentation License *Contributors:* Odor ... 96

Image *Source:* https://en.wikipedia.org/w/index.php?title=File:Bundeswehr-OF-2-SH.png *License:* GNU Free Documentation License *Contributors:* Odor ... 96

Image *Source:* https://en.wikipedia.org/w/index.php?title=File:Bundeswehr-OF-2-H.png *License:* GNU Free Documentation License *Contributors:* Odor ... 96

Image *Source:* https://en.wikipedia.org/w/index.php?title=File:Bundeswehr-OF-1-OL.png *License:* GNU Free Documentation License *Contributors:* Odor ... 96

Image *Source:* https://en.wikipedia.org/w/index.php?title=File:Bundeswehr-OF-1-L.png *License:* GNU Free Documentation License *Contributors:* Odor … 96

Image *Source:* https://en.wikipedia.org/w/index.php?title=File:Bundeswehr-OR-9-OSF.png *License:* GNU Free Documentation License *Contributors:* Odor … 96

Image *Source:* https://en.wikipedia.org/w/index.php?title=File:Bundeswehr-OR-8-SF.png *License:* GNU Free Documentation License *Contributors:* Odor … 96

Image *Source:* https://en.wikipedia.org/w/index.php?title=File:Bundeswehr-OR-7-OFR.png *License:* Creative Commons Attribution-Sharealike 3.0,2.5,2.0,1.0 *Contributors:* Odor … 96

Image *Source:* https://en.wikipedia.org/w/index.php?title=File:Bundeswehr-OR-7-HF.png *License:* GNU Free Documentation License *Contributors:* Odor … 96

Image *Source:* https://en.wikipedia.org/w/index.php?title=File:Bundeswehr-OR-6-OF.png *License:* GNU Free Documentation License *Contributors:* Odor … 96

Image *Source:* https://en.wikipedia.org/w/index.php?title=File:Bundeswehr-OR-6-FR.png *License:* GNU Free Documentation License *Contributors:* Odor … 96

Image *Source:* https://en.wikipedia.org/w/index.php?title=File:Bundeswehr-OR-6-F.png *License:* GNU Free Documentation License *Contributors:* Odor … 96

Image *Source:* https://en.wikipedia.org/w/index.php?title=File:Bundeswehr-OR-5-SU.png *License:* GNU Free Documentation License *Contributors:* Odor … 96

Image *Source:* https://en.wikipedia.org/w/index.php?title=File:Bundeswehr-OR-5-FJ.png *License:* GNU Free Documentation License *Contributors:* Odor … 96

Image *Source:* https://en.wikipedia.org/w/index.php?title=File:Bundeswehr-OR-5-U.png *License:* GNU Free Documentation License *Contributors:* Odor … 96

Image *Source:* https://en.wikipedia.org/w/index.php?title=File:Bundeswehr-OR-4-OSG.png *License:* GNU Free Documentation License *Contributors:* Odor … 97

Image *Source:* https://en.wikipedia.org/w/index.php?title=File:Bundeswehr-OR-4-SG.png *License:* GNU Free Documentation License *Contributors:* Odor … 97

Image *Source:* https://en.wikipedia.org/w/index.php?title=File:Bundeswehr-OR-3-HG.png *License:* GNU Free Documentation License *Contributors:* Odor … 97

Image *Source:* https://en.wikipedia.org/w/index.php?title=File:Bundeswehr-OR-3-OGUA.png *License:* GNU Free Documentation License *Contributors:* Odor … 97

Image *Source:* https://en.wikipedia.org/w/index.php?title=File:Bundeswehr-OR-3-OG.png *License:* GNU Free Documentation License *Contributors:* Odor … 97

Image *Source:* https://en.wikipedia.org/w/index.php?title=File:Bundeswehr-OR-2-GOA.png *License:* GNU Free Documentation License *Contributors:* Odor … 97

Image *Source:* https://en.wikipedia.org/w/index.php?title=File:Bundeswehr-OR-2-GFA.png *License:* GNU Free Documentation License *Contributors:* Odor … 97

Image *Source:* https://en.wikipedia.org/w/index.php?title=File:Bundeswehr-OR-2-GUA.png *License:* GNU Free Documentation License *Contributors:* Odor … 97

Image *Source:* https://en.wikipedia.org/w/index.php?title=File:Bundeswehr-OR-2-G.png *License:* GNU Free Documentation License *Contributors:* Odor … 97

Image *Source:* https://en.wikipedia.org/w/index.php?title=File:Bundeswehr-OR-1-S.png *License:* GNU Free Documentation License *Contributors:* Odor … 97

Image *Source:* https://en.wikipedia.org/w/index.php?title=File:First-year_USP_9mm_(32415150000).jpg *Contributors:* - … 99

Image *Source:* https://en.wikipedia.org/w/index.php?title=File:H&K_USP_Tactical_(29091436595).jpg *Contributors:* lifesizepotato from San Antonio, TX … 99

Image *Source:* https://en.wikipedia.org/w/index.php?title=File:HK_P7_M13_(20965360961).jpg *Contributors:* lifesizepotato from San Antonio, TX 99

Image *Source:* https://en.wikipedia.org/w/index.php?title=File:Koalorka_H&K_P30L.jpg *License:* Public domain *Contributors:* Koalorka (talk) 99

Image *Source:* https://en.wikipedia.org/w/index.php?title=File:Heckler_u_Koch_Signalpistole_P2A2.jpg *License:* Public domain *Contributors:* BotMultichill, EH101, File Upload Bot (Magnus Manske), OgreBot 2 … 99

Image *Source:* https://en.wikipedia.org/w/index.php?title=File:H&K_MP7.jpg *License:* Public Domain *Contributors:* User:KrisfromGermany . 99

Image *Source:* https://en.wikipedia.org/w/index.php?title=File:Heckler_Koch_MP5.jpg *Contributors:* Danrok, Denniss, KOKUYO, Mattes, Nemo5576, OgreBot 2, Sanandros, SantiLak, 1 anonymous edits … 99

Image *Source:* https://en.wikipedia.org/w/index.php?title=File:Combater.jpg *License:* Creative Commons Attribution-Sharealike 3.0 *Contributors:* User:Wald-Burger8 … 99

Image *Source:* https://en.wikipedia.org/w/index.php?title=File:Domok_g36.JPG *License:* GNU Free Documentation License *Contributors:* Dcoetzee, Luk∼commonswiki, MGA73bot2, Mattes, Nemo5576, Quake44, Stonda∼commonswiki, 1 anonymous edits … 100

Image *Source:* https://en.wikipedia.org/w/index.php?title=File:HK416.jpg *License:* Creative Commons Attribution-Sharealike 2.0 *Contributors:* Dybdal. … 100

Image *Source:* https://en.wikipedia.org/w/index.php?title=File:DCB_Shooting_G3_pictures.jpg *License:* Creative Commons Attribution-Sharealike 3.0 *Contributors:* Elie.georges20, GeorgHH, Interchange88, Jahobr, Nukes4Tots∼commonswiki, O (bot), OgreBot 2, Sanandros, Sixflashphoto, 2 anonymous edits … 100

Image *Source:* https://en.wikipedia.org/w/index.php?title=File:Kar_98K_-_AM.021488.jpg *License:* Public Domain *Contributors:* Armémuseum (The Swedish Army Museum) … 100

Image *Source:* https://en.wikipedia.org/w/index.php?title=File:Flag_of_German_Reich_(1935–1945).svg *Contributors:* - … 100

Image *Source:* https://en.wikipedia.org/w/index.php?title=File:BundeswehrMG3.jpg *License:* Public Domain *Contributors:* KrisfromGermany 100

Image *Source:* https://en.wikipedia.org/w/index.php?title=File:H&K_MG5_silhouette.svg *Contributors:* User:Bes-ART … 100

Image *Source:* https://en.wikipedia.org/w/index.php?title=File:M2_Browning,_Musée_de_l'Armée.jpg *License:* Creative Commons Attribution-Sharealike 2.0 *Contributors:* Rama. … 100

Image *Source:* https://en.wikipedia.org/w/index.php?title=File:Bundeswehr-Technik_01_(RaBoe).jpg *License:* Creative Commons Attribution-Sharealike 3.0 *Contributors:* Ra Boe … 101

Image *Source:* https://en.wikipedia.org/w/index.php?title=File:Flag_of_the_United_Kingdom.svg *License:* Public Domain *Contributors:* Anomie, Good Olfactory, Jo-Jo Eumerus, MSGJ, Mifter … 101

Image *Source:* https://en.wikipedia.org/w/index.php?title=File:20131223_G28_Afghanistan.jpg *Contributors:* User:Wiegold.de … 101

Image *Source:* https://en.wikipedia.org/w/index.php?title=File:G82_German_Army_Barrett_M107_variant.jpg *License:* Creative Commons Attribution-Sharealike 3.0 *Contributors:* Sonaz … 101

Image *Source:* https://en.wikipedia.org/w/index.php?title=File:H&KFabarmFP6entry.jpg *License:* Creative Commons Attribution-Sharealike 3.0 *Contributors:* Berean Hunter … 101

Image *Source:* https://en.wikipedia.org/w/index.php?title=File:Flag_of_Italy.svg *License:* Public Domain *Contributors:* Anomie, Jo-Jo Eumerus 101

Image *Source:* https://en.wikipedia.org/w/index.php?title=File:M870mcs.jpg *License:* GNU Free Documentation License *Contributors:* Original uploader was Rizuan at ms.wikipedia … 101

Image *Source:* https://en.wikipedia.org/w/index.php?title=File:DM51_Transportkoffer.JPG *License:* Public Domain *Contributors:* Steffen Gebhart 101

Image *Source:* https://en.wikipedia.org/w/index.php?title=File:GewehrAG36.jpg *License:* Public Domain *Contributors:* KrisfromGermany … 101

Image *Source:* https://en.wikipedia.org/w/index.php?title=File:HK69A1.jpg *License:* Creative Commons Attribution-Sharealike 2.0 *Contributors:* Avron, Dbenzhuser, MKFI, Mattes, Nemo5576, Sanandros … 101

Image *Source:* https://en.wikipedia.org/w/index.php?title=File:HK_GMW.jpg *License:* Creative Commons Attribution-ShareAlike 3.0 Unported *Contributors:* Anderle … 101

Image *Source:* https://en.wikipedia.org/w/index.php?title=File:Panzerfaust3.jpg *License:* GNU Free Documentation License *Contributors:* Sonaz 101

Image *Source:* https://en.wikipedia.org/w/index.php?title=File:MATADOR_Stand.jpg *License:* Creative Commons Attribution 3.0 *Contributors:* Dave1185 (talk). Original uploader was Dave1185 (talk) at en.wikipedia … 102

Image *Source:* https://en.wikipedia.org/w/index.php?title=File:Flag_of_Israel.svg *License:* Public Domain *Contributors:* "The Provisional Council of State Proclamation of the Flag of the State of Israel" of 25 Tishrei 5709 (28 October 1948) … 102

Image *Source:* https://en.wikipedia.org/w/index.php?title=File:Flag_of_Singapore.svg *License:* Public Domain *Contributors:* Various … 102

Image *Source:* https://en.wikipedia.org/w/index.php?title=File:M3E1.jpg *Contributors:* Signaleer, 木の枝 … 102

Image *Source:* https://en.wikipedia.org/w/index.php?title=File:Flag_of_Sweden.svg *License:* Public Domain *Contributors:* Anomie, Jo-Jo Eumerus, Mr. Stradivarius … 102

Image *Source:* https://en.wikipedia.org/w/index.php?title=File:SPIKE_ATGM.jpg *License:* Creative Commons Attribution 3.0 *Contributors:* Dave1185 (talk) 102
Image *Source:* https://en.wikipedia.org/w/index.php?title=File:Milan_2.jpg *License:* Creative Commons Attribution-Sharealike 3.0 *Contributors:* davric 102
Image *Source:* https://en.wikipedia.org/w/index.php?title=File:Flag_of_France.svg *License:* Public Domain *Contributors:* Anomie, Fastily, Jo-Jo Eumerus 102
Image *Source:* https://en.wikipedia.org/w/index.php?title=File:ILÜ_der_Bundeswehr_am_24.09.2012_-_Marder_vorne.jpg *License:* Creative Commons Attribution 2.0 *Contributors:* synaxonag 103
Image *Source:* https://en.wikipedia.org/w/index.php?title=File:IFV_Puma_2015_(19727694195).jpg *License:* Creative Commons Attribution-Sharealike 2.0 *Contributors:* Katzennase 103
Image *Source:* https://en.wikipedia.org/w/index.php?title=File:TPz_1_Fuchs_NBC_reconnaissance_vehicle.jpg *License:* Public Domain *Contributors:* unknow, Released to Public by US Department of Defence 103
Image *Source:* https://en.wikipedia.org/w/index.php?title=File:Flag_of_the_Netherlands.svg *License:* Public Domain *Contributors:* Zscout370 103
Image *Source:* https://en.wikipedia.org/w/index.php?title=File:Hägglunds_Bv206S_ambulance.jpg *License:* Creative Commons Attribution 2.0 *Contributors:* funky1opti 103
Image *Source:* https://en.wikipedia.org/w/index.php?title=File:Wiesel120mm2.jpg *License:* Public domain *Contributors:* File Upload Bot (Magnus Manske), Liftarn, OgreBot 2 103
Image *Source:* https://en.wikipedia.org/w/index.php?title=File:Bundeswehr_mowag_eagle_IV_front.JPG *License:* Creative Commons Attribution-Sharealike 3.0,2.5,2.0,1.0 *Contributors:* Patrick Janotta 103
Image *Source:* https://en.wikipedia.org/w/index.php?title=File:Flag_of_Switzerland.svg *License:* Public Domain *Contributors:* User:Marc Mongenet Credits: User:-xfi- User:Zscout370 103
Image *Source:* https://en.wikipedia.org/w/index.php?title=File:Bundeswehr_LAPV_Enok.png *License:* Creative Commons Attribution-Sharealike 3.0 Germany *Contributors:* Thiemo Schuff 103
Image *Source:* https://en.wikipedia.org/w/index.php?title=File:Dingo_2.jpg *Contributors:* , WVO 104
Image *Source:* https://en.wikipedia.org/w/index.php?title=File:Fennek_2.jpg *License:* Creative Commons Attribution 2.0 *Contributors:* funky1opti from Wolfsburg, Deutschland 104
Image *Source:* https://en.wikipedia.org/w/index.php?title=File:Grizzly_er.jpg *License:* Public Domain *Contributors:* Heierlon 104
Image *Source:* https://en.wikipedia.org/w/index.php?title=File:Serval_2.jpg *License:* Creative Commons Attribution-Sharealike 2.0 *Contributors:* Fotograph: Oliver Gottlob Dl1oli 104
Image *Source:* https://en.wikipedia.org/w/index.php?title=File:Kdo_DURO_M2+M1_o._2xM2+_-_Schweizer_Armee_-_Steel_Parade_2006.jpg *License:* Public Domain *Contributors:* Sandstein 104
Image *Source:* https://en.wikipedia.org/w/index.php?title=File:Krauss_Maffai_Mungo.jpg *License:* GNU Free Documentation License *Contributors:* Denniss, Heierlon, MGA73bot2, Mattes, Sonaz, Stahlkocher, TUBS 104
Image *Source:* https://en.wikipedia.org/w/index.php?title=File:Duro3_MSPO2004.jpg *License:* Creative Commons Attribution-Share Alike *Contributors:* Pibwl 104
Image *Source:* https://en.wikipedia.org/w/index.php?title=File:MARS_(MLRS)_Bundeswehr.jpg *License:* Creative Commons Attribution-Sharealike 3.0 *Contributors:* Sonaz 104
Image *Source:* https://en.wikipedia.org/w/index.php?title=File:Granatkastare_m41_Revinge_2012.jpg *License:* Creative Commons Attribution-Sharealike 3.0 *Contributors:* User:Jorchr 105
Image *Source:* https://en.wikipedia.org/w/index.php?title=File:Panzermörser_M_113_A1_G_(Links).jpg *License:* Public Domain *Contributors:* Huhu at de.wikipedia 105
Image *Source:* https://en.wikipedia.org/w/index.php?title=File:Flag_of_Finland.svg *License:* Public Domain *Contributors:* SVG drawn by Sebastian Koppehel 105
Image *Source:* https://en.wikipedia.org/w/index.php?title=File:Pionierpanzer_Dachs_(2008).jpg *License:* Creative Commons Attribution-Sharealike 2.0 *Contributors:* Luhai Wong 105
Image *Source:* https://en.wikipedia.org/w/index.php?title=File:Bergepanzer_Bueffel.jpg *License:* Creative Commons Attribution-Sharealike 2.0 *Contributors:* Sonaz 105
Image *Source:* https://en.wikipedia.org/w/index.php?title=File:Minenräumpanzer_Keiler.jpg *License:* Creative Commons Attribution-Sharealike 3.0 *Contributors:* Hedwig KlawuttkeHedwig Klawuttke (german main account) 105
Image *Source:* https://en.wikipedia.org/w/index.php?title=File:Panzerschnellbruecke_Biber_auf_Brueckenleger.jpg *License:* Creative Commons Attribution-Sharealike 3.0 *Contributors:* Sonaz 105
Image *Source:* https://en.wikipedia.org/w/index.php?title=File:Panzerschnellbrücke_Leguan.jpg *License:* Creative Commons Attribution-Sharealike 2.0 *Contributors:* Luhai Wong 106
Image *Source:* https://en.wikipedia.org/w/index.php?title=File:M3G_ferry_2.jpg *License:* Creative Commons Attribution-Sharealike 2.0 *Contributors:* Luhai Wong from Singapore, Singapore 106
Image *Source:* https://en.wikipedia.org/w/index.php?title=File:Slt_Elefant.jpg *License:* Creative Commons Attribution-Sharealike 2.0 *Contributors:* Sonaz 106
Image *Source:* https://en.wikipedia.org/w/index.php?title=File:HX81_8x8_HET_(with_IAC).JPG *Contributors:* User:UndateableOne 106
Image *Source:* https://en.wikipedia.org/w/index.php?title=File:TG_MIL_TGM.jpg *Contributors:* 1989, Jcb, Llann Wé², Ruthven, UndateableOne 106
Image *Source:* https://en.wikipedia.org/w/index.php?title=File:Flag_of_Austria.svg *License:* Public Domain *Contributors:* User:SKopp 106
Image *Source:* https://en.wikipedia.org/w/index.php?title=File:Mercedes-Benz_Zetros_GTF_6x6.JPG *License:* Creative Commons Attribution-Sharealike 3.0 *Contributors:* Sonaz 106
Image *Source:* https://en.wikipedia.org/w/index.php?title=File:Mercedes-Benz_Unimog_U_5000.jpg *License:* Creative Commons Attribution-Sharealike 3.0 *Contributors:* Sonaz 106
Image *Source:* https://en.wikipedia.org/w/index.php?title=File:MAN_gl_(6x6)_truck_-_August_2011_-_01.jpg *License:* Creative Commons Attribution 3.0 Germany *Contributors:* High Contrast 106
Image *Source:* https://en.wikipedia.org/w/index.php?title=File:VW_T5_Transporter_front_20080811.jpg *License:* Attribution *Contributors:* Rudolf Stricker 107
Image *Source:* https://en.wikipedia.org/w/index.php?title=File:Bundeswehr_MB_Wolf.jpg *License:* Creative Commons Attribution-Sharealike 2.5 *Contributors:* user:Darkone 107
Image *Source:* https://en.wikipedia.org/w/index.php?title=File:Naval_Ensign_of_Germany.svg *License:* Public Domain *Contributors:* Alkari, Anime Addict AA, Burts, Denelson83, Ein Dahmer, Erlenmeyer, Fry1989, Illegitimate Barrister, Kandschwar, Lokal Profil, Ludger1961, Mattes, Ricordisamoa, SiBr4, Stunteltje, WerWil, 5 anonymous edits 110
Image *Source:* https://en.wikipedia.org/w/index.php?title=File:Naval_ensign_of_Germany.svg *Contributors:* - 111
Figure 51 *Source:* https://en.wikipedia.org/w/index.php?title=File:Westland_WG-13_Super_Lynx_Mk88a_(code_83+25)_of_the_German_Navy_at_RIAT_Fairford_17July2017_arp.jpg *License:* Public domain *Contributors:* Myself (Adrian Pingstone). 115
Figure 52 *Source:* https://en.wikipedia.org/w/index.php?title=File:German_Navy_P8_Pistol.jpg *License:* Public Domain *Contributors:* Photographer's Mate 1st Class Bart Bauer 115
Figure 53 *Source:* https://en.wikipedia.org/w/index.php?title=File:Marineschule_Muerwik.jpg *License:* Creative Commons Attribution-ShareAlike 3.0 Unported *Contributors:* Flor!an 116
Image *Source:* https://en.wikipedia.org/w/index.php?title=File:MDS_64_Admiral_Trp.svg *License:* Creative Commons Attribution-Sharealike 3.0 *Contributors:* TUBS 118
Image *Source:* https://en.wikipedia.org/w/index.php?title=File:MDJA_64_Admiral_Trp_Lu.svg *License:* Creative Commons Attribution-Sharealike 3.0 *Contributors:* TUBS 118
Image *Source:* https://en.wikipedia.org/w/index.php?title=File:MDS_63_Vizeadmiral_Trp.svg *License:* Creative Commons Attribution-Sharealike 3.0 *Contributors:* TUBS 118
Image *Source:* https://en.wikipedia.org/w/index.php?title=File:MDJA_63_Vizeadmiral_Trp_Lu.svg *License:* Creative Commons Attribution-Sharealike 3.0 *Contributors:* TUBS 118
Image *Source:* https://en.wikipedia.org/w/index.php?title=File:MDS_62_Konteradmiral_Trp.svg *License:* Creative Commons Attribution-Sharealike 3.0 *Contributors:* TUBS 118
Image *Source:* https://en.wikipedia.org/w/index.php?title=File:MDJA_62_Konteradmiral_Trp_Lu.svg *License:* Creative Commons Attribution-Sharealike 3.0 *Contributors:* TUBS 118
Image *Source:* https://en.wikipedia.org/w/index.php?title=File:MDS_61_Flottillenadmiral_Trp.svg *License:* Creative Commons Attribution-Sharealike 3.0 *Contributors:* TUBS 118
Image *Source:* https://en.wikipedia.org/w/index.php?title=File:MDJA_61_Flottillenadmiral_Trp_Lu.svg *License:* Creative Commons Attribution-Sharealike 3.0 *Contributors:* TUBS 118
Image *Source:* https://en.wikipedia.org/w/index.php?title=File:MDS_53_Kapitän_zur_See_Trp.svg *License:* Creative Commons Attribution-Sharealike 3.0 *Contributors:* TUBS 118

Image Source: https://en.wikipedia.org/w/index.php?title=File:MDJA_53_Kapitän_zur_See_Trp_Lu.svg License: Creative Commons Attribution-Sharealike 3.0 Contributors: TUBS ... 118
Image Source: https://en.wikipedia.org/w/index.php?title=File:MDS_52_Fregattenkapitän_Trp.svg License: Creative Commons Attribution-Sharealike 3.0 Contributors: TUBS ... 118
Image Source: https://en.wikipedia.org/w/index.php?title=File:MDJA_52_Fregattenkapitän_Trp_Lu.svg License: Creative Commons Attribution-Sharealike 3.0 Contributors: TUBS ... 118
Image Source: https://en.wikipedia.org/w/index.php?title=File:MDS_51_Korvettenkapitän_Trp.svg License: Creative Commons Attribution-Sharealike 3.0 Contributors: TUBS ... 118
Image Source: https://en.wikipedia.org/w/index.php?title=File:MDJA_51_Korvettenkapitän_Trp_Lu.svg License: Creative Commons Attribution-Sharealike 3.0 Contributors: TUBS ... 118
Image Source: https://en.wikipedia.org/w/index.php?title=File:MDS_44_Stabskapitänleutnant_Trp.svg License: Creative Commons Attribution-Sharealike 3.0 Contributors: TUBS ... 118
Image Source: https://en.wikipedia.org/w/index.php?title=File:MDJA_44_Stabskapitänleutnant_Trp_Lu.svg License: Creative Commons Attribution-Sharealike 3.0 Contributors: TUBS ... 118
Image Source: https://en.wikipedia.org/w/index.php?title=File:MDS_43_Kapitänleutnant_Trp.svg License: Creative Commons Attribution-Sharealike 3.0 Contributors: TUBS ... 118
Image Source: https://en.wikipedia.org/w/index.php?title=File:MDJA_43_Kapitänleutnant_Trp_Lu.svg License: Creative Commons Attribution-Sharealike 3.0 Contributors: TUBS ... 118
Image Source: https://en.wikipedia.org/w/index.php?title=File:MDS_42_Oberleutnant_zur_See_Trp.svg License: Creative Commons Attribution-Sharealike 3.0 Contributors: CommonsDelinker, HHubi, TUBS ... 118
Image Source: https://en.wikipedia.org/w/index.php?title=File:MDJA_42_Oberleutnant_zur_See_Trp_Lu.svg License: Creative Commons Attribution-Sharealike 3.0 Contributors: TUBS ... 118
Image Source: https://en.wikipedia.org/w/index.php?title=File:MDS_41_Leutnant_zur_See_Trp.svg License: Creative Commons Attribution-Sharealike 3.0 Contributors: CommonsDelinker, HHubi, TUBS ... 118
Image Source: https://en.wikipedia.org/w/index.php?title=File:MDJA_41_Leutnant_zur_See_Trp_Lu.svg License: Creative Commons Attribution-Sharealike 3.0 Contributors: TUBS ... 118
Image Source: https://en.wikipedia.org/w/index.php?title=File:MDS_33a_Oberfähnrich_zur_See_Trp.svg License: Creative Commons Attribution-Sharealike 3.0 Contributors: TUBS ... 118
Image Source: https://en.wikipedia.org/w/index.php?title=File:MDJA_33a_Oberfähnrich_zur_See_Trp_Lu.svg License: Creative Commons Attribution-Sharealike 3.0 Contributors: TUBS ... 118
Image Source: https://en.wikipedia.org/w/index.php?title=File:MDS_31a_Fähnrich_zur_See_Trp.svg License: Creative Commons Attribution-Sharealike 3.0 Contributors: TUBS ... 118
Image Source: https://en.wikipedia.org/w/index.php?title=File:MDJA_31a_Fähnrich_zur_See_Trp_Lu.svg License: Creative Commons Attribution-Sharealike 3.0 Contributors: TUBS ... 118
Image Source: https://en.wikipedia.org/w/index.php?title=File:MDS_21a_Seekadett_Trp.svg License: Creative Commons Attribution-Sharealike 3.0 Contributors: TUBS ... 118
Image Source: https://en.wikipedia.org/w/index.php?title=File:MDJA_21a_Seekadett_Trp_Lo.svg License: Creative Commons Attribution-Sharealike 3.0 Contributors: TUBS ... 118
Image Source: https://en.wikipedia.org/w/index.php?title=File:MDS_35_Oberstaabsbootsmann_20.svg License: Creative Commons Attribution-Sharealike 3.0 Contributors: TUBS ... 119
Image Source: https://en.wikipedia.org/w/index.php?title=File:MDS_34_Staabsbootsmann_10.svg License: Creative Commons Attribution-Sharealike 3.0 Contributors: TUBS ... 119
Image Source: https://en.wikipedia.org/w/index.php?title=File:MDS_33_Hauptbootsmann_70.svg License: Creative Commons Attribution-Sharealike 3.0 Contributors: TUBS ... 119
Image Source: https://en.wikipedia.org/w/index.php?title=File:MDS_32_Oberbootsmann_60.svg License: Creative Commons Attribution-Sharealike 3.0 Contributors: TUBS ... 119
Image Source: https://en.wikipedia.org/w/index.php?title=File:MDS_31_Bootsmann_30.svg License: Creative Commons Attribution-Sharealike 3.0 Contributors: TUBS ... 119
Image Source: https://en.wikipedia.org/w/index.php?title=File:MDS_22_Obermaat_20.svg License: Creative Commons Attribution-Sharealike 3.0 Contributors: TUBS ... 119
Image Source: https://en.wikipedia.org/w/index.php?title=File:MDS_21_Maat_10.svg License: Creative Commons Attribution-Sharealike 3.0 Contributors: TUBS ... 119
Image Source: https://en.wikipedia.org/w/index.php?title=File:MDS_16_Oberstabsgefreiter_70_L.svg License: Creative Commons Attribution-Sharealike 3.0 Contributors: TUBS ... 119
Image Source: https://en.wikipedia.org/w/index.php?title=File:MDS_15_Stabsgefreiter_60_L.svg License: Creative Commons Attribution-Sharealike 3.0 Contributors: TUBS ... 119
Image Source: https://en.wikipedia.org/w/index.php?title=File:MDS_14_Hauptgefreiter_50_L.svg License: Creative Commons Attribution-Sharealike 3.0 Contributors: TUBS ... 119
Image Source: https://en.wikipedia.org/w/index.php?title=File:MDS_13_Obergefreiter_30_L.svg License: Creative Commons Attribution-Sharealike 3.0 Contributors: TUBS ... 119
Image Source: https://en.wikipedia.org/w/index.php?title=File:MDS_12_Gefreiter_20_L.svg License: Creative Commons Attribution-Sharealike 3.0 Contributors: TUBS ... 119
Image Source: https://en.wikipedia.org/w/index.php?title=File:MDS_11_Matrose_10_L.svg License: Creative Commons Attribution-Sharealike 3.0 Contributors: TUBS ... 119
Image Source: https://en.wikipedia.org/w/index.php?title=File:MDJA_35_Oberstabsbootsmann_30_Lu.svg License: Creative Commons Attribution-Sharealike 3.0 Contributors: TUBS ... 119
Image Source: https://en.wikipedia.org/w/index.php?title=File:MDJA_34_Stabsbootsmann_40_Lu.svg License: Creative Commons Attribution-Sharealike 3.0 Contributors: TUBS ... 119
Image Source: https://en.wikipedia.org/w/index.php?title=File:MDJA_33_Hauptbootsmann_50_Lu.svg License: Creative Commons Attribution-Sharealike 3.0 Contributors: TUBS ... 119
Image Source: https://en.wikipedia.org/w/index.php?title=File:MDJA_32_Oberbootsmann_70_Lu.svg License: Creative Commons Attribution-Sharealike 3.0 Contributors: TUBS ... 119
Image Source: https://en.wikipedia.org/w/index.php?title=File:MDJA_31_Bootsmann_60_Lu.svg License: Creative Commons Attribution-Sharealike 3.0 Contributors: TUBS ... 119
Image Source: https://en.wikipedia.org/w/index.php?title=File:MDJA_22_Obermaat_20_Lo.svg License: Creative Commons Attribution-Sharealike 3.0 Contributors: TUBS ... 119
Image Source: https://en.wikipedia.org/w/index.php?title=File:MDJA_21_Maat_10_Lo.svg License: Creative Commons Attribution-Sharealike 3.0 Contributors: TUBS ... 119
Image Source: https://en.wikipedia.org/w/index.php?title=File:MDJA_16_Oberstabsgefreiter_10_Lo.svg License: Creative Commons Attribution-Sharealike 3.0 Contributors: TUBS ... 119
Image Source: https://en.wikipedia.org/w/index.php?title=File:MDJA_15_Stabsgefreiter_20_Lo.svg License: Creative Commons Attribution-Sharealike 3.0 Contributors: TUBS ... 119
Image Source: https://en.wikipedia.org/w/index.php?title=File:MDJA_14_Hauptgefreiter_30_Lo.svg License: Creative Commons Attribution-Sharealike 3.0 Contributors: TUBS ... 119
Image Source: https://en.wikipedia.org/w/index.php?title=File:MDJA_13_Obergefreiter_40_Lo.svg License: Creative Commons Attribution-Sharealike 3.0 Contributors: TUBS ... 119
Image Source: https://en.wikipedia.org/w/index.php?title=File:MDJA_12_Gefreiter_50_Lo.svg License: Creative Commons Attribution-Sharealike 3.0 Contributors: TUBS ... 119
Image Source: https://en.wikipedia.org/w/index.php?title=File:MDJA_11_Matrose_81_Lo.svg License: Creative Commons Attribution-Sharealike 3.0 Contributors: TUBS ... 119
Figure 54 Source: https://en.wikipedia.org/w/index.php?title=File:Naval_Ensign_of_Germany.svg License: Public Domain Contributors: Alkari, Anime Addict AA, Buris, Denelson83, Ein Dahmer, Erlenmeyer, Fry1989, Illegitimate Barrister, Kandschwar, Lokal Profil, Ludger1961, Mattes, Ricordisamoa, SiBr4, Stunteltje, WerWil, 5 anonymous edits ... 125
Image Source: https://en.wikipedia.org/w/index.php?title=File:U_34_in_Fahrt.jpg License: Creative Commons Attribution 2.0 Contributors: Bundeswehr-Fotos ... 122
Image Source: https://en.wikipedia.org/w/index.php?title=File:BADEN-WURTTEMBERG_00257_(cropped).jpg Contributors: User:Ein Dahmer ... 122
Image Source: https://en.wikipedia.org/w/index.php?title=File:F221_Hessen-Kieler_Woche_2007.jpg License: Public domain Contributors: Cobatfor, High Contrast, Indeedous, OgreBot 2, Stunteltje ... 122

Image *Source:* https://en.wikipedia.org/w/index.php?title=File:FGS_Emden_(F210).jpg *License:* Public Domain *Contributors:* Mass Communication Specialist Seaman Apprentice Shonna Cunningham ... 122
Image *Source:* https://en.wikipedia.org/w/index.php?title=File:Korvette_Braunschweig_F260_2895.jpg *License:* Creative Commons Attribution-ShareAlike 3.0 Unported *Contributors:* Torsten Bätge ... 122
Image *Source:* https://en.wikipedia.org/w/index.php?title=File:M1098_Siegburg.jpg *License:* Public domain *Contributors:* Common Good, File Upload Bot (Magnus Manske), Indeedous, OgreBot 2, Stunteltje ... 123
Image *Source:* https://en.wikipedia.org/w/index.php?title=File:Minenjagdboot_Grömitz.JPG *License:* GNU Free Documentation License *Contributors:* Alureiter～commonswiki, D.W., Felix Stember, Indeedous, MGA73bot2, Stunteltje, WerWil ... 123
Image *Source:* https://en.wikipedia.org/w/index.php?title=File:FGS-Frankfurt-Am-Main.JPG *License:* Creative Commons Attribution-ShareAlike 3.0 *Contributors:* User:Adrignola ... 123
Image *Source:* https://en.wikipedia.org/w/index.php?title=File:20060916-Piraeus-A1443-Roen.jpg *License:* Creative Commons Attribution-ShareAlike 3.0 *Contributors:* Copyright © 2006, K. Krallis, Sv1xv ... 123
Image *Source:* https://en.wikipedia.org/w/index.php?title=File:Tender_Donau_A516.jpg *License:* Creative Commons Attribution-ShareAlike 2.5 *Contributors:* user:Darkone ... 123
Image *Source:* https://en.wikipedia.org/w/index.php?title=File:Oker_A_53_Hamburg_2261.jpg *License:* GNU Free Documentation License *Contributors:* Torsten Bätge, Hamburg ... 123
Image *Source:* https://en.wikipedia.org/w/index.php?title=File:Cuxhaven_marine_01.JPG *License:* Creative Commons Attribution-ShareAlike 2.5 *Contributors:* Ra Boe ... 123
Image *Source:* https://en.wikipedia.org/w/index.php?title=File:Neue_Jadewerft.jpg *License:* Creative Commons Attribution 3.0 *Contributors:* Laupf ... 123
Image *Source:* https://en.wikipedia.org/w/index.php?title=File:KNECHTSAND_2271.jpg *License:* Creative Commons Attribution-ShareAlike 3.0 *Contributors:* User:Ein Dahmer ... 123
Image *Source:* https://en.wikipedia.org/w/index.php?title=File:Ölauffangschiff_Bottsand.jpg *License:* Public domain *Contributors:* , ... 123
Image *Source:* https://en.wikipedia.org/w/index.php?title=File:Helmsand_Schiff_2010_02_(RaBoe).jpg *License:* Creative Commons Attribution-ShareAlike 3.0 *Contributors:* © Ra Boe / Wikipedia ... 123
Image *Source:* https://en.wikipedia.org/w/index.php?title=File:Neue_Planet_von_vorn.jpg *License:* Creative Commons Attribution-ShareAlike 2.0 *Contributors:* Dr. Lothar Ginzkey ... 124
Image *Source:* https://en.wikipedia.org/w/index.php?title=File:Gorch_Fock_unter_Segeln_Kieler_Foerde_2006.jpg *License:* Creative Commons Attribution-ShareAlike 2.5 *Contributors:* Felix Koenig (King) ... 124
Image *Source:* https://en.wikipedia.org/w/index.php?title=File:Roundel_of_the_German_Air_Force_(with_Border).svg *License:* Creative Commons Attribution-ShareAlike 3.0 *Contributors:* User:Wrekin762 ... 128
Figure 55 *Source:* https://en.wikipedia.org/w/index.php?title=File:Airforce_Museum_Berlin-Gatow_43.JPG *License:* Public Domain *Contributors:* RosarioVanTulpe ... 129
Figure 56 *Source:* https://en.wikipedia.org/w/index.php?title=File:German_Air_Force_(41+71)_Dassault-Dornier_Alpha_Jet_A.jpg *License:* Creative Commons Attribution 2.0 *Contributors:* Gerard van der Schaaf ... 132
Figure 57 *Source:* https://en.wikipedia.org/w/index.php?title=File:Panavia_Tornado_IDS_of_Luftwaffe,_static_display,_Radom_AirShow_2005,_Poland.jpg *License:* Creative Commons Attribution-ShareAlike 2.5 *Contributors:* Przemyslaw "Blueshade" Idzkiewicz ... 132
Image *Source:* https://en.wikipedia.org/w/index.php?title=File:Emblem_of_aircraft_of_NVA_(East_Germany).svg *License:* Public Domain *Contributors:* diese Datei: Jwnabd ... 134
Figure 58 *Source:* https://en.wikipedia.org/w/index.php?title=File:MiG-29_Fulcrum_B_Luftwaffe.jpg *License:* Public Domain *Contributors:* Camera Operator: TSGT GARY TOMOYASU ... 135
Figure 59 *Source:* https://en.wikipedia.org/w/index.php?title=File:AGM-88_and_AIM-9_on_Tornado.jpg *License:* Public Domain *Contributors:* U.S. Air Force ... 137
Figure 60 *Source:* https://en.wikipedia.org/w/index.php?title=File:2010-06-11_Eurofighter_Luftwaffe_31+21_EDDB_02.jpg *Contributors:* GT1976, High Contrast, Wo st 01 ... 138
Figure 61 *Source:* https://en.wikipedia.org/w/index.php?title=File:30+68_German_Air_Force_Eurofighter_Typhoon_EF2000_ILA_Berlin_2016_06.jpg *License:* GNU Free Documentation License *Contributors:* A.Savin, Daniel Case, Joshbaumgartner, Julian Herzog ... 139
Figure 62 *Source:* https://en.wikipedia.org/w/index.php?title=File:Patriot_System_2.jpg *License:* Creative Commons Attribution-ShareAlike 2.5 *Contributors:* Aka, Bukvoed, Clpo13, Darkone, GeorgHH, Hayden120, Heierlon, High Contrast, Homo lupus, MB-one, PMG, Steinbeisser～commonswiki, TUBS ... 140
Figure 63 *Source:* https://en.wikipedia.org/w/index.php?title=File:Büchel_Fliegerhorst.jpg *License:* GNU Free Documentation License *Contributors:* Stahlkocher ... 141
Image *Source:* https://en.wikipedia.org/w/index.php?title=File:Red_ff0000_pog.svg *License:* Creative Commons Zero *Contributors:* User:One Salient Oversight ... 143
Image *Source:* https://en.wikipedia.org/w/index.php?title=File:Blue_0080ff_pog.svg *License:* Creative Commons Zero *Contributors:* Antonsusi, One Salient Oversight, Pierpao, Sarang, YLSS ... 143
Image *Source:* https://en.wikipedia.org/w/index.php?title=File:Orange_pog.svg *License:* Public Domain *Contributors:* User:Andux ... 143
Image *Source:* https://en.wikipedia.org/w/index.php?title=File:Lightgreen_pog.svg *License:* Public Domain *Contributors:* Davide101 ... 143
Figure 64 *Source:* https://en.wikipedia.org/w/index.php?title=File:Luftwaffe_Goose_Bay.jpg *License:* Creative Commons Attribution-ShareAlike 3.0 Unported *Contributors:* User:JcPollock ... 147
Figure 65 *Source:* https://en.wikipedia.org/w/index.php?title=File:F-4Es_1GAFTS_9FS_Holloman_1992.JPEG *License:* Public Domain *Contributors:* Photographer: MSgt. Michael Haggerty, USAF ... 149
Image *Source:* https://en.wikipedia.org/w/index.php?title=File:Red_pog.svg *License:* Public Domain *Contributors:* Andux, Antonsusi, Bdk, Chenspec, ChrisiPK, Cuthbertwong, Davepape, Doodledoo, Er Komandante, Grolltech, Herbythyme, Körnerbrötchen, LNICOLAS, LX, Nagy, Penubag, Pieter Kuiper, Pimke, Rlevse, STyx, Saibo, Sarang, Siebrand, Steinsplitter, Trixt, TwoWings, YLSS, 46 anonymous edits ... 150
Image *Source:* https://en.wikipedia.org/w/index.php?title=File:Yellow_pog.svg *License:* Public Domain *Contributors:* Amalthea ... 150
Image *Source:* https://en.wikipedia.org/w/index.php?title=File:Purple_pog.svg *License:* Public Domain *Contributors:* User:Andux ... 150
Image *Source:* https://en.wikipedia.org/w/index.php?title=File:Steel_pog.svg *License:* Public Domain *Contributors:* derivative work: Mareklug talk Red_pog.svg: Andux ... 150
Image *Source:* https://en.wikipedia.org/w/index.php?title=File:Black_pog.svg *License:* Public Domain *Contributors:* Andux, Antonsusi, Gutten på Hemsen, Juiced lemon, Lzhl, Mattes, STyx, Sarang, TwoWings, Via null, YLSS ... 150
Image *Source:* https://en.wikipedia.org/w/index.php?title=File:Green_pog.svg *License:* Public Domain *Contributors:* Andux, Antonsusi, Jcb, Juiced lemon, Nixón, Pd4u, Rocket000, STyx, TwoWings, Wouterhagens, YLSS, 5 anonymous edits ... 150
Figure 66 *Source:* https://en.wikipedia.org/w/index.php?title=File:World_War_I_Fokker_aircraft-bi-plane_in_knowlton_quebec.jpg *Contributors:* User:Pjrsoap ... 151
Figure 67 *Source:* https://en.wikipedia.org/w/index.php?title=File:Trageweise_(Heer_+_Luftwaffe)_(Luftwaffenfarben).svg *License:* Creative Commons Zero *Contributors:* Flor!an ... 152
Figure 68 *Source:* https://en.wikipedia.org/w/index.php?title=File:Eurofighter_Luftwaffe_(26437961262).jpg *License:* Creative Commons Attribution-ShareAlike 2.0 *Contributors:* Rob Schleiffert from Holland ... 153
Figure 69 *Source:* https://en.wikipedia.org/w/index.php?title=File:84+99_German_Army_Sikorsky_CH-53G_Super_Stallion_ILA_Berlin_(cropped).jpg *Contributors:* FOX 52 ... 155
Figure 70 *Source:* https://en.wikipedia.org/w/index.php?title=File:54+08_Luftwaffe_A400M_Maiden_Flight_-(cropped).jpg *Contributors:* FOX 52 ... 155

173

License

Creative Commons Attribution-Share Alike 3.0
//creativecommons.org/licenses/by-sa/3.0/

Index

.300 Winchester Magnum, 101
.338 Lapua Magnum, 101
.45 ACP, 99

A321-200, 154
A340-300, 154
A400M Atlas, 145
Aachen, 28
Able Seaman, 24
Accuracy International AWM, 101
ACE Mobile Force (Land), 87
Admiral (Germany), 25, 118, 119
Adolf Hitler, 3, 41, 85
Aerial refueling, 153
Aerial warfare, 127, 128
Afghanistan, 14, 49, 137
After 1955, 20
AGM-88 HARM, 136
AIM-9 Sidewinder, 136
Airbus, 2, 139
Airbus A310, 145, 154
Airbus A310 MRTT, 128, 138, 154
Airbus A319, 128, 145, 154
Airbus A321, 154
Airbus A330 MRTT, 139, 154
Airbus A340, 128, 145, 154
Airbus A400M, 16, 18, 138, 150
Airbus A400M Atlas, 128, 141, 154
Airbus Helicopters H145M, 128
Aircraft, 111
Aircraftman, 22
Air force, 127
Air Force Command, 140
Air Force Forces Command, 140
Air Force Office, 140
Air Forces of the National Peoples Army, 7, 128, 134
Airlift, 154
Airman Basic, 22
Airman First Class, 23
Airmobile Operations Division (Germany), 88
Air Staff (United States), 140
Air-to-air missile, 133, 136
Air-to-ground missile, 136

Air-to-surface, 133
Air transports of heads of state and government, 154
Air Transport Wing 62, 145, 149
Air Transport Wing 63, 145, 149
Alliance Ground Surveillance, 144
Allied Air Command, 144
Allied Command Transformation, 113
Allied Control Commission, 129
Allied Force Command Heidelberg, 87
Allied Forces Baltic Approaches, 87, 112, 130
Allied-occupied Germany, 28, 54
Allied Rapid Reaction Corps, 88, 136
Allies of World War I, 54
Allies of World War II, 5, 83
Amphibious vehicle, 106
Amt Blank, 6, 73, 84
Andernach, 85
Andreas Krause (admiral), 110
Angela Merkel, 2
Angles, 29
Anti-Submarine Warfare, 122
Anti-tank warfare, 101
Antoine-Henri Jomini, 36
Appen, 146
Ardennes, 42
Arizona, 145, 146
Armistice with Germany (Compiègne), 66
Armored fighting vehicle, 103
Armoured personnel carrier, 103
Armoured recovery vehicle, 105
Armoured vehicle-launched bridge, 105, 106
Army, 81
Army Command, 91
Arnhem, 94
Arthur Wellesley, 1st Duke of Wellington, 35
AS.34 Kormoran, 138
ATF Dingo, 13, 104
Attack aircraft, 128
Attack submarine, 122
Aufklärungsgeschwader 51, 137
Auftragstaktik, 74
Augustdorf, 93
August von Gneisenau, 3, 34

177

Austria, 106
Austria-Hungary, 54, 66
Austrian Empire, 34
Austro-Prussian War, 37
Auxiliary ship, 113, 122

B61 nuclear bomb, 133
Baden-Württemberg-class frigate, 122
Badge of Honour of the Bundeswehr, 25, 82, 111
Bad Reichenhall, 93
Bad Sülze, 145, 150
Balkenkreuz, 152
Baltic Air Policing, 137
Baltic Fleet, 48
Baltic Sea, 8, 29, 31
Baltic states, 9
Balts, 31
Bandvagn 206, 103
Barrett M82, 101
Basic Law for the Federal Republic of Germany, 2, 7
Basic Law of the Federal Republic of Germany, 84
Battle of Aussig, 31
Battle of Austerlitz, 33
Battle of Berlin, 46
Battle of Britain, 42
Battle of Cambrai (1917), 40
Battle of Caporetto, 40
Battle of Dunkirk, 42
Battle of Dybbøl, 37
Battle of France, 42
Battle of Gravelotte, 38
Battle of Grunwald, 31
Battle of Hochkirch, 33
Battle of Iconium (1190), 31
Battle of Jena-Auerstedt, 34
Battle of Jutland, 40
Battle of Kolin, 33
Battle of Königgrätz, 37
Battle of Kunersdorf, 33
Battle of Kursk, 44
Battle of Lechfeld, 30
Battle of Legnano, 31
Battle of Leipzig, 35
Battle of Leuthen, 33
Battle of Lipany, 31
Battle of Lobositz, 33
Battle of Lützen (1632), 32
Battle of Mulhouse, 56
Battle of Rossbach, 33
Battle of Sedan, 38
Battle of Stalingrad, 44
Battle of Tachov, 31
Battle of Tannenberg (1914), 40, 56

Battle of Tetovo, 81
Battle of the Bulge, 45
Battle of the Frontiers, 56
Battle of the Somme, 57
Battle of the Teutoburg Forest, 29
Battle of Tornow, 33
Battle of Verdun, 57
Battle of Vienna, 32
Battle of Waterloo, 35
Battle of Zorndorf, 33
Bavaria, 30, 93, 149
Beautiful rides, 31
Beechcraft T-6 Texan II, 145
Beja Airbase, 131
Belgium, 146
Bendlerblock, 4
Benito Mussolini, 45
Berlin, 1, 46, 91, 129, 134, 148
Berlin-class replenishment ship, 123
Berlin Tegel Airport, 145, 148, 150
Berlin Tempelhof Airport, 142, 144
Berlin Wall, 47
Bernhard von Bülow, 54
Black Cross (Teutonic Order), 3
Blank (cartridge), 19
Blitzkrieg, 41
Blockade of Germany, 55, 63
Boeing CH-47 Chinook, 139
Bombardier Global Express, 128, 145, 154
Bonn, 1
Bootsmann, 24, 119, 120
Bosnia & Herzegovina, 136
Bosnian Serb, 136
Bottsand-class oil recovery ship, 123
Boxer (armoured fighting vehicle), 101, 103
Boxer MRAV, 16, 17
Brakel, Germany, 142, 143
Brandenburg-class frigate, 122
Braunschweig class corvette, 120, 121
Braunschweig-class corvette, 122
Brekendorf, 142, 143
Bremen-class frigate, 122
Bremerhaven, 117
Brigade, 86
Brigadegeneral, 24, 95
Brigades, 10
Brigadier, 24
Brigadier General, 24, 95
British Army, 19
British Expeditionary Force (World War I), 56
British Expeditionary Force (World War II), 42
Brockzetel, 142, 143
Brück, 94
Büchel, 130, 148
Büchel Air Base, 134, 141, 144, 148, 150
Bulgaria, 66

Bundesmarine, 50, 138
Bundestag, 13
Bundeswehr, 1, 47, 49, 73, 82, 109, 111, 128, 129, 137, 158
Bundeswehr Fallschirmj.C3.A4ger .28after 1945.29, 159
Bundeswehr Joint Medical Service, 1, 3, 12
Bundeswehr Joint Operations Command, 157
Bundeswehr Military History Museum, 129
Buzz number, 152

C-160, 138
C-160 Transall, 145
Calw, 94, 157
Cambodia, 14, 49
Camcopter S-100, 114, 121
Camille de Tallard, 32
Canada, 154
Canadair CL-13, 129
Captain at Sea, 25
Captain (land), 96
Captain Lieutenant, 25
Captain (naval), 25
Captain (OF-2), 24
Cargo aircraft, 128
Carl Gustav recoilless rifle, 102
Carl von Clausewitz, 3, 36
Carolingian Empire, 30
Category:History of Germany, 27, 53
Celts, 29
Central Powers, 54
Centre of Excellence for Operations in Confined and Shallow Waters, 113
Ceremonial oath of the Bundeswehr, 4
CFB Goose Bay, 146, 147
Chain of command, 74
Cham, Germany, 93
Chancellor of Germany (Federal Republic of Germany), 2
Charlemagne, 28
Charles V, Holy Roman Emperor, 32
Chief Master Sergeant, 23
Chief petty officer, 24, 120
Chin-up, 22
Cimbri, 29
Claus von Stauffenberg, 3
Close Air Support, 131
Coalition combat operations in Afghanistan in 2006, 49
Cold War, 7, 47, 128
Cologne, 148
Cologne Bonn Airport, 144, 145, 148, 150
Colonel, 24, 95
Colonel General, 95
Cölpin, 142, 144
Combat Action Medal of the Bundeswehr, 25

Combat aircraft, 153
Combined arms, 86
Combined Task Force 150, 110
Command and obedience in the Bundeswehr, 73
Commander, 25
Commander.2C Allied Naval Forces Baltic Approaches, 112
Commons:Category:Air force of Germany, 156
Commons:Category:Bundeswehr, Military of Germany, 26
Commons:Category:Heer (Bundeswehr), 98
Commons:Category:Military history of Germany, 52
Commons:Category:Navy of Germany, 121
Confederation of the Rhine, 28, 33, 53
Congress of Vienna, 35
Conscientious objector, 47
Conscription, 7
Conscription in Germany, 4, 7
Constitution of Germany, 13
Contravention, 78
Convention of Artlenburg, 34
Copyright status of work by the U.S. government, 25
Corporal, 23, 96
Corps, 12
Corvette, 122
Corvette Captain, 119
Corvettes, 113, 122
Counter Admiral, 25, 119
Crusades, 31
Cyber and Information Space Command (Germany), 1, 3, 12, 82
Czech Republic, 11

David Glantz, 162
De:DM51, 101
De:Innere Führung, 73
Denmark, 36
Denmark in World War II, 42
De:Schifffahrtmedizinisches Institut der Marine, 116
De:Standortkommando Berlin, 88
De:Territorialkommando Schleswig-Holstein, 85
De:Territorialkommando Sud, 85
De:Wehrbereichskommando, 85
Diepholz Air Base, 145, 146, 150
Dieter Naskrent, 127
Dissimilar air combat training, 136
Division (military), 12, 86
Djibouti, 49
Döbern, 142, 144
Döbraberg, 142, 144

Dornier Alpha Jet, 132, 133
Dornier Do 228, 114
Dreadnought (book), 162
Dress uniform, 152, 153
Duchy of Masovia, 31
Dutch Corps, 88
Dutch people, 28

Eastern Bloc, 134
Eastern Front (World War I), 54
East Francia, 27, 53
East Germany, 7, 46, 51, 87, 112, 128, 134
East Prussia, 40, 56
Eckernförde, 114, 158, 160
Economic history of Germany, 27, 53
Edelweiss, 19
Egypt, 44
Eindhoven Air Base, 144
Einsatzflottille 1, 114
Einsatzflottille 2, 116
Elbe, 29
Elbe-class replenishment ship, 123
Electorate of Hanover, 34
Electronic countermeasure, 136
Electronic warfare, 128
Electronic-warfare aircraft, 153
Elizabeth of Russia, 33
Engineering and driver training tanks, 105
English, 64
Ensdorf-class minesweeper, 123
Ensign (rank), 23, 25, 119
Erbeskopf, 142, 143
Erding, 149
Erding Air Base, 130, 146, 149, 150
Erich Hartmann, 128, 129, 131
Erich Ludendorff, 40, 59
Erich von Manstein, 42
Erndtebrück, 142, 143, 146
Erwin Rommel, 44
Euro, 50
Eurocopter AS532 Cougar, 145, 154
Eurocopter Cougar, 128
Eurocopter EC135, 114
Eurocopter EC 135, 107
Eurocopter EC145, 16, 145, 154
Eurocopter Tiger, 16, 107
Eurocorps, 88, 94
Eurofighter, 152
Eurofighter Typhoon, 16, 128, 136–138, 140, 141, 144, 145, 150, 153, 154
Europe, 54, 83
European Air Transport Command, 138, 144
European Court of Justice, 21
European Defence Community, 5, 6, 83, 84
European Union, 2, 3, 13, 128

European Union Naval Force Somalia – Operation ATALANTA, 110
EUROSPIKE, 102
EUTM Mali, 15
EUTM Somalia, 15

F-104 Starfighter, 146
F125 class frigate, 17
F125-class frigate, 120, 122
F-4 Phantom II, 137
F-84F Thunderstreak, 146
Fahnenjunker, 20, 23, 96
Fähnrich, 20, 23, 96, 119
Fähnrich zur See, 24, 119
Faßberg Air Base, 146
Fast Attack Craft, 113
Federal agency (Germany), 2
Federal Ministry of Defence (Germany), 2, 73, 84, 85, 137
Federal Police (Germany), 5, 9
Federal Republic of Germany, 82
Federal Research Division, 25
Feldjäger, 75, 99
Feldwebel, 20, 23, 96
Fennek, 17, 101, 104
Fernspählehrkompanie 200, 159
Fighter aircraft, 128
Fighter-bomber, 134
Fighter plane, 137
File:De-Marine-pronunciation.ogg, 111
File:Relief Map of Germany.svg, 91, 142, 150
Fin flash, 130
Finland, 105
First Battle of the Marne, 38, 56
First Battle of the Masurian Lakes, 40
First Defenestration of Prague, 31
First-generation production, 154
First Sergeant, 75
First World War, 38
Flag of Germany, 112
Flecktarn, 130
Flemish people, 28
Flensburg, 116
Flieger (rank), 22
Flight and expulsion of Germans (1944–50), 28, 54
Flight Sergeant, 23
Florida, 145
Flotilla Admiral, 25
Flottillenadmiral, 25, 118, 119
Flugabwehrraketengeschwader 1, 145, 150
Fog of war, 36
Former eastern territories of Germany, 28, 54
Fort Bliss, 131, 145
Forward looking infrared, 136
Fourth Allied Tactical Air Force, 130

180

FPS-117, 143, 144
France, 28, 30, 44, 102
Francia, 27, 53
Franco-German Brigade, 50, 88, 91, 94
Franco-German War, 6
François Pascal Simon, Baron Gérard, 34
Franco-Prussian War, 37
Frankenberg, Saxony, 94
Frankenthal-class minehunter, 123
Frankfurt Parliament, 112
Frankish language, 28
Franklin D. Roosevelt, 41
Franks, 28, 30
Frederick I, Holy Roman Emperor, 31
Frederick the Great, 33
Frederick William III of Prussia, 34
Frederick William I of Prussia, 32
Free Democratic Party of Germany, 3
Fregattenkapitän, 25, 118, 119
Freising, 142, 143
French–German enmity, 6
Friedrich Engels, 48
Friedrich Ruge, 110
Frigate Captain, 119
Frigates, 113, 122
F Super Hornet, 140
Führungsakademie der Bundeswehr, 85
Fürstenfeldbruck, 146
Fuselage, 152

Garde Mobile, 38
Gatow, 134
Gebhard Leberecht von Blücher, 34
Gebirgsjäger, 19, 95, 159
Gebirgsjäger in the modern German forces, 19
Gefreiter, 20, 22, 24, 97, 119, 120
General, 82, 95
General der Panzertruppe, 85
General (Germany), 23, 24, 95
Generalleutnant, 24, 95, 127
Generalmajor, 24, 95, 128
General surgeon, 75
George III, 34
Georgia (country), 49
Gerhard Barkhorn, 129
Gerhard Hirschfeld, 72
Gerhard von Scharnhorst, 3, 6, 34, 48
German Air Force, 1, 3, 82, 85, **127**, 158
German Air Force Regiment, 145, 150, 153
German Armed Forces, 111, 157
German Armed Forces Badge for Military Proficiency, 25, 82, 111
German Armed Forces Badge of Marksmanship, 25, 82, 111
German Armed Forces casualties in Afghanistan, 16

German Armed Forces Service Medal, 25, 82
German arms procurement agency designation, 100
German Army, 1, 2, 13, **81**, 82, 99, 137, 153, 157
German Army Aviation Corps, 87, 158
German Army Forces Command, 87
German Army (German Empire), 38, 83
German Army rank insignia, 75
German Army (Wehrmacht), 41, 83
German auxiliary Alster (A50) (1988), 123
German auxiliary Berlin (A1411), 123
German auxiliary Bonn (A1413), 123
German auxiliary Donau (A516), 123
German auxiliary Elbe (A511), 123
German auxiliary Frankfurt am Main (A1412), 123
German auxiliary Main (A515), 123
German auxiliary Mosel (A512), 123
German auxiliary Oker (A53), 123
German auxiliary Oste (A52), 123
German auxiliary Rhein (A513), 123
German auxiliary Werra (A514), 123
German commando frogmen, 111, 158
German Confederation, 28, 35–37, 53
German corvette Braunschweig (F260), 122
German corvette Erfurt (F262), 122
German corvette Ludwigshafen am Rhein (F264), 122
German corvette Magdeburg (F261), 122
German corvette Oldenburg (F263), 122
German Democratic Republic, 6, 134
German Empire, 28, 35, 38, 53, 54, 83, 151
German Flood Service Medal (2002), 25, 111
German Flood Service Medal (2013), 25, 82, 111
German frigate Augsburg (F213), 122
German frigate Baden-Württemberg (F222), 122
German frigate Bayern (F217), 122
German frigate Brandenburg (F215), 122
German frigate Hamburg (F220), 122
German frigate Hessen (F221), 122
German frigate Lübeck (F214), 122
German frigate Mecklenburg-Vorpommern (F218), 122
German frigate Sachsen (F219), 122
German frigate Schleswig-Holstein (F216), 122
German General Staff, 34, 56
Germanic peoples, 27, 29, 53
Germanic Wars, 29
German interest in the Caribbean, 38
German involvement in the Spanish Civil War, 41
German language, 28, 58, 73–76, 82, 111, 128

German Mediatisation, 34
German minehunter Bad Bevensen (M1063), 123
German minehunter Rottweill (M1061), 123
German minesweeper Pegnitz (M1090), 123
German minesweeper Siegburg (M1098), 123
German Mine Sweeping Administration, 50, 112
German Navy, 1, 3, 10, 12, 51, 75, 82, 85, 99, **109**, 110, 118, 119, 122, 157
German Parachutist Badge, 25
German Peasants War, 32
German Reich, 28, 53
German resistance, 85
German reunification, 8, 28, 47, 54, 83
German Revolution, 61, 66
German Revolution of 1918–19, 54, 66
German special forces, **157**
German submarine U-31 (S181), 122
German submarine U-32 (S182), 122
German submarine U-33 (S183), 122
German submarine U-34 (S184), 122
German submarine U-35 (S185), 122
German submarine U-36 (S186), 122
German tanker Rhön, 123
German tanker Spessart, 123
Germany, 2, 19, 81, 99–107, 109, 111, 118, 119, 127, 128
Germany in the early modern period, 27, 53
Germersheim, 146
Gleina, 142, 144
Global 5000, 154
Glons, 146
Gorch Fock (1958), 124
Gorget patches, 153
Goths, 29
Grand Duchy of Baden, 37
Greece, 28, 43
Grenade, 101
Grenade launcher, 101
Grob G-120, 128
Großer Arber, 142, 144
Großer Zapfenstreich, 3, 4
Ground Master 400, 143
Gruß an Kiel, 109
GSG 9, 9, 160
Günter-Erhard Giesa, 128
Günter Luther, 110
Günther Rall, 128, 129, 131
Gustav Dore, 30
Gustavus Adolphus of Sweden, 32

Habsburg, 32
Hamburg, 85
Handgun, 99
Hans Rottiger, 85

Hans von Seeckt, 41
Hasso von Manteuffel, 3, 6
Hauptbootsmann, 24, 119
Hauptfeldwebel, 20, 75, 96
Hauptfeldwebel (rank), 23
Hauptgefreiter, 20, 119
Hauptmann, 24, 96
Havelte, 93
Heckler & Koch, 2
Heckler & Koch AG36, 101
Heckler & Koch FABARM FP6, 101
Heckler & Koch G3, 100
Heckler & Koch G36, 19, 100
Heckler & Koch GMG, 101
Heckler & Koch HK417, 99, 101
Heckler & Koch HK69A1, 101
Heckler & Koch MG4, 100
Heckler & Koch MG5, 100
Heckler & Koch MP5, 99
Heckler & Koch MP7, 99
Heckler & Koch P2A1, 99
Heckler & Koch P30, 99
Heckler & Koch P7, 99
Heckler & Koch P8, 115
Heckler & Koch USP, 99
Hegel, 36
Heide, 146
Heinrich Zille, 57
Heinz Guderian, 41
Helgoland-class tug, 123
Helicopter, 128, 137, 154
Helicopter Wing 64, 145, 149, 158
Helmuth von Moltke the Elder, 38
Henning von Tresckow, 3
Henry the Fowler, 30
Himmerod Abbey, 6
Himmerod memorandum, 84
Hindu Kush, 13
Historiography of Germany, 27, 53
History of German women, 27, 53
History of Germany, 27, 53
History of Germany (1945–90), 28, 54
History of Germany during World War I, 28, 53, **53**
History of Germany since 1990, 28, 54
Hither Pomerania, 93
HK 4.6×30mm, 99
HK G3, 84
HNLMS Karel Doorman (A833), 113, 121
Hohn Air Base, 145, 149, 150
Hohn, Schleswig-Holstein, 149
Holloman Air Force Base, 145–147
Holstein, 36
Holy Roman Empire, 27, 28, 30, 53
Holzdorf Air Base, 145, 146, 149, 150, 158
Holzdorf (Jessen), 149

Horn of Africa, 15
Howaldtswerke-Deutsche Werft, 2
HR-3000, 143
Hughes HR-3000, 143
Hundred Days Offensive, 61
Hungarian people, 30
Hussite Wars, 31
Husum, 141
Husum Schwesing Airport, 145, 150

IAI Heron TP, 154
IATA, 148
ICAO, 148
IdZ, 17, 93
IFOR, 81
I German Corps, 87
III Corps (Bundeswehr), 85, 87
ILA Berlin Air Show, 155
Immediate Reaction Cell, 9
Imperial German Navy, 40, 50, 111, 112
Independent Social Democratic Party of Germany, 58
Indonesia, 9
I Netherlands Corps, 87
Infantry Fighting Vehicle, 103
Infiltration tactics, 40
Ingo Gerhartz, 127
Ingolstadt Manching Airport, 146
Inspector General of the Bundeswehr, 2, 12, 74
Inspector of the Air Force, 12, 127, 140
Inspector of the Army, 12, 91
Inspector of the Navy, 12, 110, 114
Integrated NATO Air Defense System, 48
Intermediate-Range Nuclear Forces Treaty, 133
International Security Assistance Force, 49, 83
International Standard Book Number, 25, 68, 69, 98, 154, 156
Invasion of Poland, 41
Iraq, 14, 16, 87
Iron Cross, 1, 3, 35, 151
Israel, 102, 154
Israeli Air Force, 139
ISR (Intelligence, surveillance and reconnaissance), 114
Italy, 30, 31, 101, 104

Jagdbombergeschwader 33, 134
Jagdgeschwader 73, 136
Jan Hus, 31
Jan Žižka, 31
Jever Air Base, 145, 150
Johannes Steinhoff, 128, 129, 131
Johann von Kielmansegg, 7
John Lewis Gaddis, 7
John Wheeler-Bennett, 98

Joint Air Power Competence Centre, 144
Joint Chiefs of Staff, 12
Joint Medical Service (Germany), 82, 89
Joint Support Service (Germany), 1, 3, 82, 88
Joint Support Ship, 113
Jörg Schönbohm, 82, 87
Josef Kammhuber, 128, 130
Journal of Military History, 162
July 20 plot, 4
Junker, 54

Kai-Uwe von Hassel, 131
Kalkar, 143
Kalkhorst, 142, 144
Kapitänleutnant, 25, 118, 119
Kapitän zur See, 25, 118, 119
Karabiner 98k, 100
Karl Wilhelm Friedrich Schlegel, 28
Kaufbeuren, 130
Kaufbeuren Air Base, 146
Kawasaki BK 117, 158
Keiler (mine flail), 105
Kiel, 66, 113, 114, 158
Kiev, 61
Kingdom of Bavaria, 37
Kingdom of Bohemia, 31
Kingdom of Galicia and Lodomeria, 38
Kingdom of Germany, 27, 53
Kingdom of Hungary, 32
Kingdom of Prussia, 27, 28, 34, 53
Kingdom of Serbia, 54
Kingdom of Württemberg, 37
Kings German Legion, 34
Kleinaitingen, 145
Kleinstaaterei, 27, 53
Klosterlechfeld, 149
KMW Grizzly, 17, 104
Kommando Luftwaffe, 142
Kommando Spezialkräfte, 9, 49, 87, 91, 94, 99, 157
Kommando Spezialkräfte Marine, 116
Konrad Adenauer, 6, 83
Konrad I of Masovia, 31
Konteradmiral, 25, 118, 119
Korean War, 6
Korvettenkapitän, 25, 118, 119
Kosovo, 14, 137
Kosovo Force, 14
Kosovo War, 81, 127, 136
Krauss-Maffei Wegmann, 2
Kriegsmarine, 41, 50, 111, 112
Kriegsrohstoffabteilung, 63

Laage, 149
Lance Corporal, 23, 97
Lance sergeant, 23

Land Forces of the National Peoples Army, 83
Landsberg am Lech, 149
Landsberg-Lech Air Base, 146, 149, 150
Landsknecht, 3
Lanyard, 76
LAPV Enok, 103
Latin, 29
Lauda-Königshofen, 142, 143
Laupheim Air Base, 145, 150
Lead-in fighter training, 154
Leading Seaman, 24
Lebanon, 15, 113
Lechfeld Air Base, 149, 150
Leguan bridge layer, 106
Leipzig, 91
Leopard 2, 6, 102
Leopard 2A6, 89
Leutnant, 24, 96
Leutnant zur See, 25, 118, 119
Library of Congress, 25, 72
Lieutenant, 95, 119
Lieutenant Colonel, 24, 95
Lieutenant Commander, 25, 119
Lieutenant General, 24, 82, 95, 128, 140
Lieutenant (junior grade), 25
Lieutenant Junior Grade, 119
List of active German Navy ships, 113, **122**
List of German defence ministers, 2
List of German monarchs, 27, 53
List of German Navy ship classes, 111
List of modern equipment of the German Army, **99**
List of states in the Holy Roman Empire, 31
LIV (SO) Serval, 100, 104
Lockheed F-104 Starfighter, 130
Lockheed Martin C-130J Super Hercules, 128
Lockheed Martin F-35 Lightning II, 139
Lockheed P-3 Orion, 114
Lombard League, 31
London and Paris Conferences, 84
Long-range reconnaissance patrol, 159
Lower Saxony, 149
Luftstreitkräfte, 130, 151
Luftwaffe, 41, 128
Luke Air Force Base, 146
Lutheran, 32

M270 Multiple Launch Rocket System, 104
M2 Browning, 100
M3 Amphibious Rig, 106
M43 field cap, 95
M-47 Patton, 85
M47 Patton, 86
Maat (rank), 24, 119, 120
Machine gun, 100
Maginot Line, 42

Main Battle Tank, 102
Major, 96
Major General, 24, 95
Major (Germany), 24, 96
Majority Social Democratic Party of Germany, 58
Mali, 15
MAN KAT1, 106
Marder (IFV), 103
Maria Theresa of Austria, 33
Marienbaum, 142, 143
Marineflieger, 109, 130
Maritime patrol aircraft, 114
Maroon beret, 20
Master Chief Petty Officer, 24, 120
Master Corporal, 23
Master Seaman, 24
Master Sergeant, 23, 96
MATADOR, 102
Matrose (Germany), 24, 119, 120
Mazar-i-Sharif, 137
McDonnell Douglas, 131
McDonnell Douglas F-15E Strike Eagle, 140
McDonnell Douglas F-4 Phantom II, 131, 133
Mecklenburg-Vorpommern, 149
Media:De-Bundeswehr-pronunciation.ogg, 2
Media:De-Luftwaffe-pronunciation.ogg, 128
Media:De-Marine-pronunciation.ogg, 111
Medical evacuation, 16
Mediterranean Sea, 16
Memmingen Air Base, 134
Mercedes-Benz G-Class, 107
Mercedes-Benz Zetros, 106
Meßstetten, 142, 143
MG3, 84
Mg42, 100
MGM-1 Matador, 130
Middle East, 16
Midshipman, 24, 119
MiG 29, 7
MiG-29, 134, 135
Migration Period, 27, 53
Mikhail Gorbachev, 48
Mikoyan-Gurevich MiG-21, 134
Mikoyan-Gurevich MiG-23, 134
Mikoyan MiG-29, 136
MILAN, 102
Military, 85
Military Assistance Advisory Group, 7
Military beret, 153
Military court, 79
Military engineering vehicle, 105
Military history of Germany, 27, **27**, 53
Military intervention against ISIL, 127
Military music, 21
Military order (society), 31

Military tattoo, 3
Military transport aircraft, 154
MIM-104 Patriot, 133, 140, 141, 145
MIM-14 Nike-Hercules, 133
Minehunter, 113, 122
Minentaucher, 160
Minesweeper, 123
Minesweeper (ship), 113, 122
Minister of Defence (Germany), 74
Minurso, 16
MINUSMA, 15
Miracle of the House of Brandenburg, 33
Missile Wing 1, 133
Missile Wing 2, 133
Monarchy of Germany, 54
Mortar (weapon), 105
Mountain Troops, 95
Mowag Duro, 104
Mowag Eagle, 103
MQ-4C Triton, 154
MRAP, 103
Müllheim, 94
MultiCam, 19
Multinational Corps Northeast, 88
Multinational Corps North East, 88, 94
Multiple rocket launcher, 104
Multirole combat aircraft, 153
Mungo ESK, 101, 104
Münster, 94
Munster, Lower Saxony, 93

Nächstbereichschutzsystem MANTIS, 141, 145
Napoleonic era, 33
Napoleon III, 37
Napoleon III of France, 38
Napoleon I of France, 33
Napoleons Invasion of Russia, 34
NATINAD, 8
Nationale Volksarmee, 7, 8
National Peoples Army, 48, 87, 112, 128
Nation state, 28
Nation-state, 38
NATO, 5, 6, 10, 16, 46, 83, 85, 95, 111, 112, 129, 133, 136, 143, 144, 146, 154
NATO Air Base Geilenkirchen, 144
NATO Integrated Air Defense System, 143
Naval Academy Mürwik, 116
Naval Air Station Pensacola, 145
Naval aviation, 114
Naval boarding, 160
Naval Force Protection Battalion, 114, 160
Naval Force Protection Battalion (Germany), 121
Naval Historical Team, 112
Naval Special Forces Command, 157

Navy, 109, 111
Navy Command (Germany), 109, 111, 114
Nazi Germany, 28, 53, 73, 100
Nazi Party, 83
Netherlands, 103, 104
Netherlands) Corps, 94
Netherlands Marine Corps, 121
Neubrandenburg, 93
Neubrandenburg Airport, 146
Neuburg Air Base, 145, 149, 150
Neuburg an der Donau, 149
Neustadt in Holstein, 117
New Mexico, 145–147
New states of Germany, 28, 54
NH90, 16, 17
NHIndustries NH90, 90, 107
NHI NH90, 114
Non-aggression pact, 44
Non-Commissioned Officer, 146
Non-commissioned officers, 76
Nordholz, 158
Nordholz Naval Airbase, 116
Nordic Bronze Age, 29
Normandy landings, 45
North African Campaign, 43
North American F-86, 130
Northern Army Group, 87
Northern Mali conflict, 127
North German Confederation, 28, 37, 53
North German Federal Navy, 50, 111, 112
North Kosovo crisis, 81
North Rhine-Westphalia, 148, 149
Northrop T-38 Talon, 128, 145
North Sea, 8
Nörvenich, 149
Nörvenich Air Base, 130, 134, 144, 149, 150
Norway, 44
Norwegian Campaign, 42
Nuclear sharing, 133
Nuclear weapon, 133
Nuremberg Trials, 46

Obedience (human behavior), 73
Oberbootsmann, 24, 119
Oberfähnrich, 23, 96
Oberfähnrich zur See, 24, 119
Oberfeldwebel, 20, 23, 96
Obergefreiter, 23, 24, 97, 119, 120
Oberleutnant, 24, 96
Oberleutnant zur See, 25, 118, 119
Obermaat, 24, 119
Oberst, 24, 95
Oberstabsbootsmann, 24, 119
Oberstabsfeldwebel, 23, 96
Oberstabsgefreiter, 23, 24, 97, 119
Oberstleutnant, 24, 95

OCLC, 68
Officer candidate, 118
Oldenburg, 93
Old Prussians, 31
Operation Active Endeavour, 110, 113
Operation Atalanta, 15
Operation Barbarossa, 44
Operation Counter Daesh, 16
Operation Deliberate Force, 127, 136
Operation Enduring Freedom, 49, 113
Operation Enduring Freedom – Horn of Africa, 110
Operation Essential Harvest, 81
Operation Libelle, 81
Operation Sea Lion, 42
Operation Sharp Guard, 110
Operation Sophia, 16
Operation Weserübung, 42
Organisation for Joint Armament Cooperation, 154
Organization, 111
Oste-class fleet service ship, 123
Ostsiedlung, 27, 53
Otto I, Holy Roman Emperor, 30
Ottoman Empire, 32, 66
Otto von Bismarck, 35, 36

Palatinate (region), 32
Panavia Tornado, 10, 128, 131–133, 137, 141, 144, 145, 147, 150, 152–154
Panzer division, 84
Panzerfaust 3, 101
Panzerhaubitze 2000, 89, 105
Panzerlehrbrigade 9, 91, 93
Papal bull, 31
Paratrooper Battalion 261 (Germany), 92
Parow, Germany, 116
Paul von Hindenburg, 40
Peacekeeping, 21
Peace of Westphalia, 32
Peaked cap, 153
Permanent Joint Headquarters, 88
Pershing 1, 133
Pershing 1a, 133
Peshmerga, 100
Peter III of Russia, 33
Peter Struck, 137
Petty Officer 1st Class, 24, 120
Petty Officer 2nd Class, 24, 120
Petty Officer 3rd Class, 24, 120
Pfullendorf, 159
Philipp Scheidemann, 66
Phoenix Goodyear Airport, 145
Phoney War, 42
Pirmasens, 94
Planet-class research ship, 124

Planet (research ship), 124
Plön, 116
Poland, 28
Police dog, 159
Police Tactical Unit, 160
Polish Air Force, 136
Pope, 30
Pope Martin V, 31
Portal:Germany, 28, 54
Portugal, 131
Potsdam, 1, 87, 88, 157
Praeger Publishers, 25
Prangendorf, 145
Preußische Marine, 112
Prince Eugene of Savoy, 32
Private 1st Class, 97
Private (rank), 22, 97
Prokop the Great, 31
Provincial Reconstruction Team, 49
Prussia, 83
Prussian Army, 32
Prussian Crusade, 31
Prussian Navy, 50, 111
Prussia (region), 31
Puma (IFV), 16, 103
Putgarten, 142, 144
Pyrrhic victory, 33

Quartermaster Sergeant, 23

RAF, 136
RAF Ahlhorn, 130
Rainer Brinkmann (admiral), 110
Ramstein Air Base, 4, 134, 144
Rank insignia of the German armed forces, 153
Ranks and insignia of NATO, 76
Rapid Forces Division, 91, 94
Rear Admiral, 25, 119
Reconnaissance, 137
Regen, 144
Regiment, 93
Reichsflotte, 50, 112
Reichsmarine, 50, 111, 112
Reichstag (building), 4
Reichstag (German Empire), 54
Reichswehr, 3, 40, 83
Remaining units, 152
Remington Model 870, 101
Rendsburg, 130
Replenishment oiler, 123
Republic F-84 Thunderstreak, 130
Resolute Support Mission, 14
Reunification of Germany, 7, 128
Reuters, 161
Revolutions of 1848, 112

Revolutions of 1848 in the German states, 28, 53
Rheinmetall, 2
Rheinmetall MG3, 100
Rheinmetall YAK, 104
Rhineland-Palatinate, 148
Rhön-class tanker, 123
Richard von Weizsäcker, 12
Rifle, 99
RMMV HX range of tactical trucks, 106
RMMV TG MIL range of trucks, 106
Robert M. Citino, 51
Roland (missile), 133
Roll-off, 113
Romania, 11
Romanticism, 36
Rostock, 109, 114
Rostock-Laage Airport, 136, 145, 146, 149, 150
Royal Air Force, 42
Royal Canadian Air Force, 146
Royal Danish Navy, 113
Royal Navy, 54
Royal Netherlands Air Force, 139
Royal Netherlands Army, 10, 93, 94, 145
Royal Prussian Army of the Napoleonic Wars, 34
Rugii, 29
Runway, 148
Russia, 44
Russian invasion of East Prussia (1914), 54

Saarlouis, 94
Sachsen-class frigate, 122
Safety record, 131
Sanitz, 145, 150
Sarajevo, 136
Saxons, 29, 30
Saxony-Anhalt, 149
Scandinavia, 29
Schleswig, 36
Schleswig Air Base, 141, 145, 149, 150
Schleswig-Holstein, 130, 149
Schleswig, Schleswig-Holstein, 149
Schlieffen plan, 38, 55
Schönewalde, 142, 143
Schütze, 22
Schützenpanzer SPz 11-2 Kurz, 84
Schutzstaffel, 83
Schweinemord, 55
Sea lines of communication, 111
Seaman, 24, 120
Seaman Apprentice, 24, 120
Seaman Recruit, 24, 120
Search and rescue, 114
Second Allied Tactical Air Force, 130

Second Battle of Langensalza, 37
Second International, 54
Second Schleswig War, 37
Seekadett, 24, 119
Self-propelled artillery, 105
Senegal, 15
Senior Airman, 23
Senior Captain, 24
Senior Chief Petty Officer, 24, 120
Senior Master Sergeant, 23
Sergeant, 23, 76, 96
Sergeant 1st Class, 96
Sergeant First Class, 23
Sergeant Major, 23, 96
Service, 99
Seventeenth Air Force, 133
Seven Years War, 33, 34
Sheppard Air Force Base, 145
Ship-of-the-line Captain, 119
Shotgun, 101
Side cap, 153
Siege of Marienburg (1410), 31
Siege of Metz (1870), 38
Siege of Paris (1870-1871), 38
Siege of Prague, 33
SIGINT, 154
Sigismund, Holy Roman Emperor, 31
Sigonella Air Base, 144
Sikorsky CH-53, 128, 145
Sikorsky CH-53K King Stallion, 139
Sikorsky CH-53 Sea Stallion, 49, 139, 150, 154
Silesia, 33
Silesian Wars, 33
Singapore, 102
Sixth Coalition, 35
SLT 50 Elefant, 106
Sniper rifle, 100
Social Democratic Party of Germany, 54, 66
Socialist Federal Republic of Yugoslavia, 49
Soldat (rank), 97
Somalia, 14, 15, 49
South Sudan, 14
Soviet Union, 5, 129
Spanish Civil War, 41
Spartacus Educational, 72
Special Operations Division (Bundeswehr), 157
Special Operations Division (Germany), 88
Special Operations Forces, 154
Spirit of 1914, 54
Spring Offensive, 38, 40
Stab-in-the-back legend, 67
Stabsbootsmann, 24, 119
Stabsfeldwebel, 23, 96
Stabsgefreiter, 23, 24, 97, 119
Stabshauptmann, 24, 96

Stabskapitänleutnant, 25, 118, 119
Stabsunteroffizier, 23, 96
Stadtallendorf, 94
Staff Sergeant, 23, 96
Stahlhelm, 83
Standard German, 2, 128
State of Defence (Germany), 2, 74
State of the Teutonic Order, 31
States of Germany, 2, 148
Stormtrooper, 40
Straelen, 94
Stralsund, 116
Strasbourg, 94
Strausberg, 91, 134
Streitkräftebasis, 12, 157
Structure of the German Army, 92
Sublieutenant, 25, 119
Submachine gun, 99
Submarines, 113, 122
Subordinate, 73
Sudan, 14, 49
Sukhoi Su-17, 134
Superior (hierarchy), 73
Suppression of Enemy Air Defenses, 153
Surface Vessels, 111
Swabia, 30
Sweden, 102, 103
Swedish iron mining during World War II, 42
Switzerland, 103, 104
Szczecin, 94

T-6 Texan II, 128
Taktisches Luftwaffengeschwader 31, 130, 144, 149
Taktisches Luftwaffengeschwader 33, 144, 148
Taktisches Luftwaffengeschwader 51, 141, 145, 149
Taktisches Luftwaffengeschwader 71 Richthofen, 130, 145, 149
Taktisches Luftwaffengeschwader 73, 145, 149
Taktisches Luftwaffengeschwader 74, 145, 149
Tampella, 105
Tanja Kreil, 21
Tank transporter, 106
Technical Sergeant, 23
Template:History of Germany, 28, 54
Template talk:History of Germany, 28, 54
Tent peg, 131
Territorial evolution of Germany, 2, 27, 53
Terrorism, 113
Teutonic knights, 3, 31
Teutons, 29
Texas, 145
The Enlightenment, 33
Theodor Blank, 6, 84
The start of the Berlin Airlift, 47

The Sun (United Kingdom), 136
Third Crusade, 31
Third Reich, 129
Thirty Years War, 32
Thomas de Maizière, 141, 151
Thorsten Kähler, 110
ThyssenKrupp, 2
Timeline of German history, 27, 53
Todendorf, 145, 150
Tonne, 113
Tornado ECR, 153
Tornado IDS, 153, 154
Total war, 64
TPz Fuchs, 101, 103
Trainer (aircraft), 128, 154
Transall, 137
Transall C-160, 128, 133, 150, 154
Transport plane, 137
Treaties of Tilsit, 34
Treaty of Hubertusburg, 33
Treaty of Verdun, 30
Treaty of Versailles, 40
Treaty on Conventional Armed Forces in Europe, 8
Treaty on the Final Settlement with Respect to Germany, 8, 49
Trench warfare, 38
Turkic peoples, 31
Turnip Winter, 54
Type 212, 120
Type 212 submarine, 17, 122

Uedem, 142, 143
UH-1 Iroquois, 107
Ukraine, 29
Ulrich de Maiziere, 7
Ulrich de Maizière, 82
Ulrike Flender, 22
Ummendorf, Baden-Württemberg, 146
UNAMID, 14
Unification of Germany, 28, 53, 83
UNIFIL, 15, 110
Unimog U5000 437.430, 106
United Arab Emirates, 16
United Kingdom, 101
United Nations Interim Force in Lebanon, 113
United Nations Operation in Somalia II, 81
United States, 2, 66, 100, 101, 104, 133, 154
United States Air Force, 140, 147
Unmanned aerial vehicle, 16, 121, 141, 154
UNMISS, 14
Unteroffizier, 20, 23, 96
Upper Palatinate, 93
Ursula von der Leyen, 2, 11, 138
US Army, 19
USP Tactical, 99

UZI, 99

Vandals, 29
Variable-sweep wing, 153
Variants, 154
V Corps (United States), 88
Veitshöchheim, 93
Verena von Weymarn, 21
Vertical stabilizer, 152
VFW-Fokker, 166
Vice Admiral, 25, 119
Vichy France, 42
Vienna, 32
Visselhövede, 142, 143
Vizeadmiral, 25, 118, 119
Vladimir Komarov, 136
VLF transmitter DHO38, 120
Volcae, 29
Volksmarine, 51, 111, 112
Volkswagen Transporter, 107

Wachbataillon, 4
Waffenfarbe, 95
Waffen-SS, 83
Wagenburg, 31
Walter Rathenau, 63
Walther arms, 2
Wangerooge-class tug, 123
War crime, 46
War crimes of the Wehrmacht, 42
War in Afghanistan (2001–14), 13
War in Afghanistan (2001–present), 81, 127
Warnemünde, 114
War of Austrian Succession, 33
War of the Spanish Succession, 32
Warplane, 137
Warsaw, 40
Warsaw Pact, 46, 83, 84, 129
Washington Naval Treaty, 40
Wehrmacht, 3, 5, 41, 83–85, 129
Weimar Republic, 3, 28, 41, 53, 54, 61, 67
Werner Panitzki, 131
Weser, 29
West Berlin, 47
Western Europe, 28
Western Front (World War I), 38, 54
Western Sahara, 16
West Germany, 3, 46, 99–103, 105, 112, 128
Westland Lynx, 114, 115, 138, 158
Westland Sea King, 114, 158
Wiederbewaffnung, 84
Wiesel AWC, 103
Wikipedia:Citation needed, 7, 28, 50, 87, 88
Wikipedia:Media help, 111
Wikt:prioritization, 77
Wilhelm Deist, 69

Wilhelm II, German Emperor, 35, 62
Wilhelmshaven, 116
William I, German Emperor, 38
Wing (air force unit), 136
Winston Churchill, 41
Wittmund, 149
Wittmundhafen Air Base, 145, 149, 150
Wolfgang Schneiderhan (general), 23
Wolf Graf von Baudissin, 7
World War I, 6, 54, 83
World War II, 5, 6, 83, 128, 129, 136
Wunstorf, 149
Wunstorf Air Base, 141, 145, 146, 149, 150

Yugoslavia, 14, 43

Zollverein, 28, 53

www.ingramcontent.com/pod-product-compliance
Lightning Source LLC
Chambersburg PA
CBHW020329240426
43665CB00044B/1096